Northern Tokyo
Pages 48–59

NORTHERN
TOKYO

CENTRAL TOKYO

Central Tokyo
Pages 38–47

EYEWITNESS TRAVEL

TOKYO

EYEWITNESS TRAVEL

TOKYO

DK

LONDON, NEW YORK,
MELBOURNE, MUNICH AND DELHI
www.dk.com

Managing Editor Aruna Ghose
Editorial Manager Joseph Mathai
Design Manager Priyanka Thakur
Project Editor Arundhti Bhanot
Project Designer Rajnish Kashyap
Designer Anchal Kaushal
Senior Cartographic Manager Uma Bhattacharya
Cartographer Alok Pathak
Senior DTP Designer Vinod Harish
Senior Picture Researcher Taiyaba Khatoon
Picture Researcher Sumita Khatwani

Main Contributors
Jon Burbank, Emi Kazuko,
Stephen Mansfield, Robbie Swinnerton

Photographer
Martin Hladik

Illustrators
Richard Bonson, Gary Cross, Richard Draper, Paul Guest,
Claire Littlejohn, Maltings Partnership, Mel Pickering, John Woodcock

Printed and bound in Malaysia

First American Edition, 2008
14 15 16 17 10 9 8 7 6 5 4 3 2 1

Published in the United States by DK Publishing,
345 Hudson Street, New York, New York 10014

Reprinted with revisions 2010, 2013, 2015

Copyright © 2008, 2015 Dorling Kindersley Limited, London
A Penguin Random House Company

Published in Great Britain by Dorling Kindersley Limited.

A catalog record for this book is available from the Library of Congress.

ISSN 1542-1554
ISBN: 978-1-46542-572-0

Floors are referred to throughout in accordance with
American usage; ie the "first floor" is at ground level.

MIX
Paper from
responsible sources
FSC™ C018179

**The information in this
DK Eyewitness Travel Guide is checked regularly.**
Every effort has been made to ensure that this book is as up-to-date as possible
at the time of going to press. Some details, however, such as telephone numbers,
opening hours, prices, gallery hanging arrangements, and travel information are
liable to change. The publishers cannot accept responsibility for any consequences
arising from the use of this book, nor for any material on third party websites, and
cannot guarantee that any website address in this book will be a suitable source of
travel information. We value the views and suggestions of our readers very highly.
Please write to: Publisher, DK Eyewitness Travel Guides, Dorling Kindersley,
80 Strand, London WC2R 0RL, UK, or email: travelguides@dk.com.

Front cover main image: Signage in the entertainment district Kabukicho

Bugaku musicians and dancers at the Meiji Shrine Spring Festival

Contents

Great Buddha statue at Kamakura

Introducing Tokyo

Tokyo Area by Area

Post-modernist masterpiece, Glass Hall,
Tokyo International Forum

The expansive Yokohama Bay Bridge

A typical selection of Japanese food in a *bento* box

1825 print by Hokusai depicting the stages of wood-block printing

Imperial figure at Yomeimon Gate, Tosho-gu shrine, Nikko

Tosho-gu shrine, Nikko

HOW TO USE THIS GUIDE

This guide helps you to get the most from your visit to Tokyo. It provides detailed practical information and expert recommendations. *Introducing Tokyo* maps the city and the region, sets it in its historical context, and guides you through the succession of significant cultural events. *Tokyo Area by Area* is the main sightseeing section, giving detailed information on all the major sights, with photographs, illustrations, and detailed maps. *Farther Afield* looks at major sights of interest outside the city center, and *Beyond Tokyo* explores other places to visit within easy reach of the city. Carefully researched suggestions for restaurants, hotels, and shopping are found in the *Travelers' Needs* section of the book, while the *Survival Guide* contains useful advice on everything from changing money to traveling on the extensive Tokyo subway network.

Tokyo

The center of Tokyo has been divided into three sightseeing areas, each with its own chapter, color-coded for easy reference. Every chapter opens with an introduction to the part of Tokyo it covers, as well as an *Area Map*. This is followed by a Street-by-Street map illustrating the heart of the area.

Sights at a Glance lists the area's key sights by category, such as Notable Districts, Historic Buildings, Parks and Gardens, and Markets.

1 Area Map
The sights are numbered and located on a map. City center sights are also marked on the Street Finder maps.

A locator map shows where you are in relation to other areas in the city center.

Each area has color-coded thumb tabs.

2 Street-by-Street map
This map gives a bird's-eye view of interesting and important parts of each sightseeing area.

A suggested route takes in some of the most interesting streets in the area.

The Visitors' Checklist provides detailed practical information.

Stars indicate the sights that no reader should miss.

3 Tokyo's main sights
These are given two or more full pages. All top sights in Tokyo are described individually.

Tokyo Area Map

The colored areas shown on this map *(see inside front cover)* are the five main sightseeing areas used in this guide. Each is covered in a full chapter in *Tokyo Area by Area (see pp38–105)*. They are highlighted on other maps throughout the book. In *Tokyo at a Glance*, for example, they help you locate the top sights. They are also used to help you find the position of the three walks *(see pp80–85)*.

Tokyo Area by Area
The map below shows the three central areas of Tokyo that contain most of the sights in this guide. The sights surrounding central Tokyo are covered in Farther Afield, while the Beyond Tokyo chapter describes places worth visiting that lie outside the capital. Each of the main sightseeing areas has been color coded for easy reference.

4 Farther Afield
This section covers those sights of interest to visitors that lie just outside the city of Tokyo and are easily accessible from the city center.

A key outlines the symbols used to read the map.

5 Beyond Tokyo
Places worth visiting that are within a day's travel of Tokyo are described here. The general introduction is followed by a map that gives an illustrated overview of the region, with major roads marked and useful tips on getting around by bus and train.

A map of the city shows the location of Farther Afield sights in relation to the city center.

The introduction outlines the areas covered in this section and their historical context.

Special features, such as this one on Zen Buddhist Temples, are highlighted with maps or illustrations.

6 Detailed Information
All the important sights are listed in order, following the numbering on the *Area Map*. Practical information, including map references, opening hours, and telephone numbers, is also provided.

INTRODUCING TOKYO

GREAT DAYS IN TOKYO

In little more than 400 years Tokyo has grown from being an impoverished fishing village to arguably the world's largest metropolis. These itineraries sample the traditional sights of Edo *(see p27)*, such as the Imperial Palace and its moats, and the historically important Sumida River, as well as taking in the city's famed futuristic architecture. They are designed to give a broad flavor of Tokyo and illustrate how this vibrant city preserves its past while striding boldly into the future. Prices mentioned include cost of travel, food, and admission fees.

Akihabara, or "Electric Town," lined with high-tech stores

Architecture and Electronics

Family of 4 allow at least ¥10,000

- **A museum of the future**
- **Majestic Rainbow Bridge**
- **Lunch in Akihabara**
- **Tokyo International Forum, an architectural marvel**

Morning

Start at the **Miraikan** *(see p84)*. This superbly designed museum in Odaiba *(see p77)* is dedicated to science and the latest in cutting-edge Japanese technology. Follow the elevated railway across Dream Bridge to **Tokyo Big Sight** *(see p84)*, an exhibition and convention center. A gravity-defying structure, the center building consists of four inverted pyramids standing on a deceptively small base. Next, take the Yurikamome Line to Daiba Station. Stop at one of the outdoor cafés at **Decks Tokyo Beach** *(see p85)*, where the walkways look down onto the sandy strip of Odaiba Marine Park and the picturesque Rainbow Bridge.

Afternoon

Take the Yurikamome Line to Shimbashi Station, changing to the JR Yamanote Line for **Akihabara** *(see p47)*, the electronics district. Enjoy a tempura lunch at **Daikokuya** *(see p131)*. Explore the area's electronic emporiums and mangaesque buildings before visiting the **Tokyo Anime Center** *(see p47)*, a colorful, interactive space dedicated to anime culture. Return to the station and take the Yamanote Line to Yurakucho, site of the **Tokyo International Forum** *(see p45)*, one of the city's most striking examples of post-modernist architecture.

A Family Day

Family of 4 allow at least ¥18,000

- **Fun at the Children's Castle**
- **Toys at Kiddyland**
- **Thrills at Tokyo Dome**
- **Sunset at a Shinjuku skyscraper**

Morning

Begin this day, centered around kids and young-at-heart adults, at the **National Children's Castle** *(see p70)*. Each floor has a different theme, from chutes and slides for the very young to music rooms where kids can try out musical instruments. Do not miss the rooftop play garden, with its go-karts and jungle gyms. After, take the JR Yamanote Line from Shibuya to Harajuku Station and walk along Omotesando-dori to **Maisen** *(see p133)*, for a great lunch of *tonkatsu* (deep-fried pork cutlets) before checking out **Crayon House** *(see p141)*, an excellent children's bookstore.

Afternoon

The next stop is **Kiddyland** *(see p145)*, a multistory toy shop. Take the train or subway to Suidobashi Station for the soaring **Tokyo Dome** *(see p149)*. Here you can watch exciting baseball games (Japan's de facto national sport). Tickets always sell out, so book in advance.

Evening

Take the Toei Oedo Line to Shinjuku Station and walk to the west exit of the **Tokyo Metropolitan Government Building** *(see pp16–17)*. Its

Post-modernist masterpiece, Glass Hall, Tokyo International Forum

◄ Wood-block print from the series *Thirty-Six Views of Mount Fuji* by Katsushika Hokusai (1790–1849)

high-speed elevator goes up to the 45th-floor observation gallery for the city's best sunset and night views.

An Outdoors Day

Two adults allow at least ¥10,000
- **A relaxing river cruise**
- **Stroll around the historic Imperial Palace Garden**
- **A stroll in Shinjuku-Gyoen Garden**
- **Shopping and a *shabu-shabu* dinner**

Imperial Palace Garden, a pleasant retreat in the heart of the city

Morning
Board the Suijo Bus (river cruise) *(see p170)* at Asakusa's Azuma Bridge. The Sumida River provides the setting for one of the most interesting concentrations of bridges in Japan. On alighting, walk straight into the grounds of the **Hama Detached Palace Garden** *(see pp42–3)*. This stunning, spacious, landscaped garden dating from the 1650s includes an elegant tea pavilion on the edge of its tidal salt pond. Next, walk through the Ginza district or take the metro to **Hibiya Park** *(see p45)*, a spacious Western-style park, full of shady arbors. Stroll along the outer moat of the Imperial Palace to the Marunouchi Building *(see p44)* and lunch at Kua'Aina, a popular Hawaiian burger restaurant located right in

front of **Tokyo Station** *(see p44)* and its red brick, Queen Anne-style facade.

Afternoon
Return to the palace moat and Otemon gate, the main entrance to the **Imperial Palace Garden** *(see p45)*. The green of manicured lawns contrasts with gigantic stones and a ruined keep that give a vivid sense of the grandeur of the original castle grounds. After, head for JR Yurakucho Station to **Shinjuku-Gyoen Garden** *(see p179)*, a cherry blossom-viewing spot. The former estate of a feudal lord, this is the closest you can get to a great outdoors experience in Tokyo. Stroll over to **Takashimaya Times Square** and **Tokyu Hands** *(see p140)* for window shopping. For dinner, sample the superb *shabu-shabu* at **Nabe-zo** *(see p133)*.

Art Browsing

Two adults allow at least ¥10,000
- **Treasures at the Tokyo National Museum**
- **A fine art museum**
- **A crafts museum**

Morning
Begin this day of museums, galleries, and cultural sights with the world's largest collection of Japanese art and antiquity at the **Tokyo National Museum** *(see pp52–5)*. The cafés around nearby Shinobazu Pond, with the Benten shrine sitting on an islet surrounded by lotuses, are a good place for a coffee break. Take the Ginza Line to Omotesando for the next cultural treat, the **Nezu Museum of Fine Arts** *(see p70)*. Finally, lunch on authentic sushi at **Sushi Gotoku** *(see p134)*.

Afternoon
It is just two stops from Shibuya on the Keio-Inokashira Line to Komaba-Todaemae and the **Japan Folk Crafts Museum** *(see p79)*, housed in a wonderful 1936 residence. Return to Shibuya Station and the **Bunkamura** *(see p68)* cross-cultural center, which houses regular exhibitions. After spending an hour or two here, you will be well positioned for a night out in Shibuya.

Exhibition of flag models at the Japan Folk Crafts Museum

2 Days in Tokyo

- Walk in the footsteps of shoguns and emperors in the grounds of the Imperial Palace
- Mingle with crowds of pilgrims at Senso-ji Temple
- Be amazed by the panoramic views from atop the Tokyo SkyTree

Day 1

Morning Join a free guided tour of the grounds of the **Imperial Palace** (p45); fragments of the old Edo Castle can still be seen here. Across the moat, discover the collection of local works at the **National Museum of Modern Art** (p46) and the nearby **Crafts Gallery** (p46), showcasing Japanese crafts.

Afternoon In the **Marunouchi** district (p44), the majestic **Tokyo Station** (p44) combines a handsome early 20th-century red brick building with contemporary architecture. The designer boutiques and department stores of **Ginza** (pp40–41) are only a short stroll away, as is the grand **Kabuki-za Theater** (p42). Next, take the subway to buzzing **Shinjuku** (pp62–5) and visit the tiny bars of the **Golden Gai** (p63).

Day 2

Morning Start bright and early with a visit to the fish market in **Tsukiji** (p42), then take the Yurikamome monorail line one stop across Tokyo Bay to Shijomae station. From here, take the subway to Tsukijishijo, enjoying

The Kabuki-za Theater, Tokyo's main venue for traditional Kabuki performances

The iconic Tokyo SkyTree, the tallest building in Japan

the **Hama Detached Palace Garden** (pp42–3), with its teahouse, duck pond, and wisteria trellises. From beside the garden, board the **water bus** (p170) and cruise down the Sumida River to **Asakusa** (p49).

Afternoon Approach **Senso-ji** (pp58–9), Tokyo's most venerable Buddhist temple, via Nakamise-dori, an arcade of craft and souvenir shops. Cross the river for the view from the top of the **Tokyo SkyTree** (p56).

3 Days in Tokyo

- Savor the spiritual Shinto atmosphere of Meiji Shrine
- Browse the shops along the tree-lined Omotesando boulevard
- Marvel at the view atop the Tokyo Tower observation deck

Day 1

Morning Crunch down the gravel pathway to **Meiji Shrine** (p66), the city's principal Shinto shrine. View the stadium created for the 1964 Tokyo Olympics in **Yoyogi Park** (p66), then browse teen fashion and culture on the shopping street **Takeshita-dori** (p67), in the vibrant **Harajuku** district (p67).

Afternoon Window-shop along **Omotesando** (p67), where you'll find the **Oriental Bazaar** (p67), perfect for souvenir shops and

striking contemporary architecture, including **Prada Aoyama** (p70). The **Nezu Museum** (p70) is a lovely introduction to the arts of the region, with its serene garden and teahouse. Finish the day bathed by the neon lights of **Shibuya** (pp68–9), accessed by subway or a short taxi ride.

Day 2

Morning Join the fishermen and traders offering prayers at the **Namiyoke Inari Jinja** (p42), on the outskirts of Tsukiji. Sip green tea at the Nakajima Teahouse, within the **Hama Detached Palace Garden** (pp42–3), then head to **Shiba Park** (p43). Admire the huge old wooden gates fronting **Zojo-ji Temple** (p43) and the iconic **Tokyo Tower** (p43) in the background.

Afternoon Ride the subway from Daimon to Asakusa. Explore this atmospheric area, which includes the venerable **Senso-ji Temple** (pp58–9) and the fun **Drum Museum** (p56). Discover shops selling realistic-looking plastic food on **Kappabashi-dori** (p56), then hop across the Sumida River for a view of the city from atop the **Tokyo SkyTree** (p56).

Day 3

Morning Pass through the huge stone gate to reach the **East Garden of the Imperial Palace** (p45), where you'll find some remains of Edo Castle. North of here is **Kitanomaru Park** (p46), home to the **National Museum of Modern Art**, the **Crafts Gallery**, and the **Nippon Budokan** performance hall. **Yasukuni Shrine** (p46), honoring Japan's World War II dead, is just north of the park.

Afternoon Take the subway to the **Nihonbashi District** (p44) and pop into the grand department store **Mitsukoshi** (p44). Next, cross the elegant **Nihonbashi Bridge** (p44) and continue walking toward **Ginza** (pp40–41), dropping by the **Sony showroom** (p40) to play with the latest electronic gadgets.

5 Days in Tokyo

- Browse galleries by day and bar-hop by night in lively Roppongi
- View national treasures and exquisite art at the Tokyo National Museum
- Enjoy a relaxing soak at the colorful Oedo Onsen Monogatari bathhouse

The distinctive exterior of the National Art Center, Japan's largest exhibition space

Day 1

Morning Pass under the wooden *torii* (gate) to reach **Meiji Shrine** *(p66)*. Later, in the backstreets of Harajuku, look for the **Ukiyo-e Ota Memorial Museum of Art** *(p67)*, with its splendid collection of prints. Walk down chic **Omotesando** *(p67)*, famous for its shopping.

Afternoon It's a short subway ride to the lively district of **Roppongi** *(pp70–71)*. As well as shops and restaurants, there are several art spaces here, including the **Mori Art Museum** *(p71)* in Roppongi Hills, the striking **National Art Center** *(p71)*, and the **Suntory Museum of Art** *(p71)* in Tokyo Midtown.

Day 2

Morning Visit the world's largest collection of Japanese art at the **Tokyo National Museum** *(pp52–5)*. After, stroll around **Ueno Park** *(pp50–51)*, home to the Shinobazu Pond, the Tosho-gu Shrine, and the **Shitamachi Museum** *(p56)*. Don't miss the bustling **Ameyoko Market** *(p56)*, found by the raised train lines between Ueno and Okachimachi stations.

The vermilion Tsukenkyo Bridge in Koishikawa Korakuen Garden

Afternoon Delight in the powerful incense burned in front of **Senso-ji Temple** *(pp58–9)* before heading to the colorful district of Asakusa. Cruise down the Sumida River to the **Hama Detached Palace Garden** *(pp42–3)*, then walk to the skyscraper development of **Shiodome** *(p43)*, where ADMT, the Advertising Museum of Tokyo, is well worth a look.

Day 3

Morning After taking a free guided tour of the **Imperial Palace** grounds *(p45)*, head across the northern moat to visit the **National Museum of Modern Art** *(p46)* and the **Crafts Gallery** *(p46)*. Due east of the palace is the **Marunouchi District** *(p44)*, home to the contemporary architecture of the **Tokyo International Forum** *(p45)* and the restored 1914 section of **Tokyo Station** *(p44)*.

Afternoon Take a stroll through the neatly clipped **Koishikawa Korakuen Garden** *(p47)*. A few subway stops to the west, the skyscrapers of **Shinjuku** *(pp62–5)* beckon, including the **Tokyo Metropolitan Government Offices** *(p64)*, seat of the local government; there's a free observation deck on the 45th floor. Experience the neon-lit buzz of **Kabukicho** *(p62)* and the cozy warren of drinking dens in the **Golden Gai** *(p63)*.

Day 4

Morning Catch **Toyosu** *(p42)* fish market before 9am, then travel one stop on the subway to Tskudashima, from where a connecting line goes to **Ryogoku** *(p76)*, three stops away. Whether or not there is a *basho* (tournament) happening at the **National Sumo Stadium** *(p76)*, it's still worth coming to this district for the colossal **Edo-Tokyo Museum** *(p76)*. Next, visit **Fukagawa** *(pp76–7)*, where there's the **Kiyosumi Teien** garden *(p77)* and the **Fukagawa Edo Museum** *(p76)*.

Afternoon Back on the west side of the Sumida River, the **Akihabara Electronics District** *(p47)* is associated with anime, manga, and other aspects of Japanese pop culture. Visit the **Tokyo Anime Centre** *(p47)*, then take the short walk to the **Kanda Myojin Shrine** *(p47)*. Round the day off with shopping and dinner in **Ginza** *(pp40–41)*.

Day 5

Morning Explore **Yanaka** *(pp82–3)*, one of the best-preserved quarters of early 20th-century Tokyo, with its shrines, temples, and traditional shops. Ride the monorail over the Rainbow Bridge to **Odaiba** *(p77 and pp84–5)*, location of many futuristic buildings, such as the Kenzo Tange-designed **Fuji TV Building** *(p16)*.

Afternoon Learn all about Japanese robot technology at the **National Museum of Emerging Science and Innovation** *(p77)*. Afterwards, relax in the extraordinary bathhouse at **Oedo Onsen Monogatari** *(p77)*.

Putting Tokyo on the Map

Tokyo, Japan's official capital city since 1868, lies on the Japanese archipelago's largest island, Honshu. This island chain is situated to the east of mainland Asia, in the northwest of the Pacific Ocean. Tokyo is located at the southern end of the Kanto Plain, on Tokyo Bay, and is bordered by Chiba, Yamanashi, Kanagawa, and Saitama prefectures.

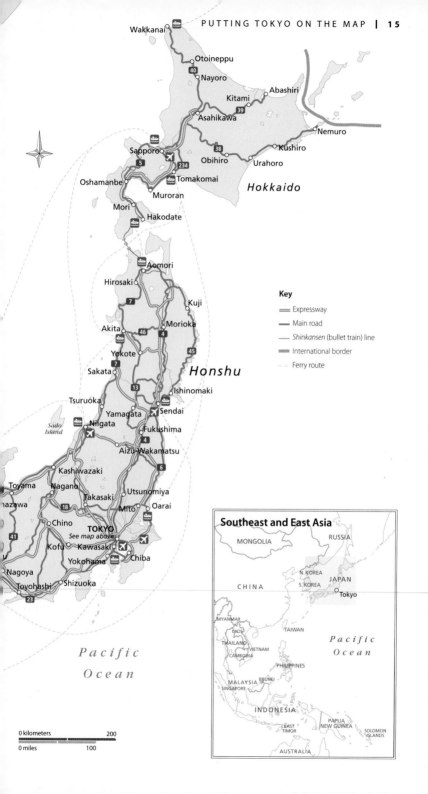

Key

Expressway
Main road
Shinkansen (bullet train) line
International border
Ferry route

Southeast and East Asia

MONGOLIA

RUSSIA

CHINA

N. KOREA

S. KOREA

JAPAN

○ Tokyo

MYANMAR

LAOS

TAIWAN

THAILAND

VIETNAM

CAMBODIA

Pacific Ocean

PHILIPPINES

MALAYSIA

BRUNEI

SINGAPORE

INDONESIA

EAST TIMOR

PAPUA NEW GUINEA

SOLOMON ISLANDS

AUSTRALIA

Pacific Ocean

0 kilometers 200
0 miles 100

Architecture in Tokyo

Tokyoites have been obliged to rebuild their city so many times that what meets the eye is a mishmash of architectural styles. First impressions suggest chaos, but there is a dynamism, perhaps even a hidden order, to Tokyo's macramé of older wood and mortar buildings and its hi-tech modernity. From the splendid futuristic creations of Odaiba *(see p77)* to the triangulated rooftops and glass sheets of Tadao Ando's 21_21 Design Sight in Roppongi *(see pp70–71)*, visitors sense perpetual renewal. In the midst of innovation are traditional structures, but Tokyo's heart, one suspects, is firmly in the future.

Prada Aoyama, the dazzling creation of Jacques Herzog and Pierre de Meuron, has tinted, diamond-shaped outer panels which reveal a stylish interior.

Shinjuku Skyscraper District

Shinjuku district in Tokyo epitomizes the modern Japanese urban labyrinth. Most skyscrapers are clustered to the west of Shinjuku Station. Built of materials such as aluminum, steel, and concrete, the buildings use flexible-frame technologies to withstand powerful earthquakes.

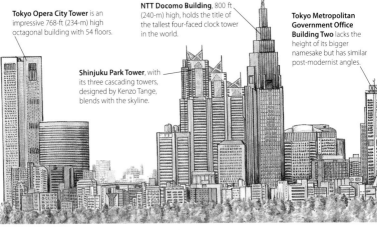

Tokyo Opera City Tower is an impressive 768-ft (234-m) high octagonal building with 54 floors.

NTT Docomo Building, 800 ft (240-m) high, holds the title of the tallest four-faced clock tower in the world.

Tokyo Metropolitan Government Office Building Two lacks the height of its bigger namesake but has similar post-modernist angles.

Shinjuku Park Tower, with its three cascading towers, designed by Kenzo Tange, blends with the skyline.

Asahi Super Dry Hall, an amusing cartoon-like building, was built by French architect Philippe Starck in 1989 for the Asahi beer company.

St Mary's Cathedral, an early Kenzo Tange masterpiece, is covered in sparkling sheets of stainless steel, designed to symbolize the light of Christ.

Fuji-TV Building, another Kenzo Tange creation and a signature building of Odaiba, is a design marvel of girders, sky corridors, and a titanium-clad sphere.

Traditional Architecture

Traditional Japanese architecture is based on the use of wood, combined with interiors consisting of paper screens, paper and wood doors, and *tatami* mat flooring *(see p110)*. In Tokyo's older temples and shrines, architectural aesthetics survive in the polished wood floors, ceramic roof tiles, movable partitions, and the sliding panels and opaque screens that create an interaction between the exterior and interior. Gokoku-ji temple *(see p75)*, which dates from 1681, remains gloriously intact, as does the even older Sanmon gate at Zojo-ji temple *(see p43)*. Though a post-war reconstruction, the Meiji shrine *(see p66)*, located at the centre of a sacred forest, keeps faith with the pure, austere lines and aesthetics of traditional Shinto architecture.

Famous Sanmon gate, Zojo-ji temple

Tokyo Metropolitan Government Office, with its stunning walls of granite and digital-like windows, towers above the Citizen's Plaza. Its 45th-floor observatory is a great sightseeing spot.

The Olympic Pavilion's sweeping curved roof of tensile steel helped Kenzo Tange to win architecture's most coveted award, the prestigious 1967 Pritzker Prize.

Sumitomo Building has an impressive atrium running the entire height of the building.

Sompo Japan Building

Tokyo International Forum, one of Tokyo's architectural marvels designed by New York-based architect Raphael Viñoly, has a soaring 197-ft (60-m) high glass atrium, crisscrossed by walkways and curving walls resembling a crystal ship.

Aoyama Technical College, a sci-fi montage of posts, lightning rods, poles, and capsules by contemporary architect Makoto Watanabe, is an example of just how far Tokyo can go into the architectural beyond.

Japanese Traditional Theater

Four major types of traditional theater are still performed regularly in Japan – Noh, Kyogen, Kabuki, and Bunraku *(see pp150–51)*. Originating in Shinto rites, Noh was first performed by Kan'ami Kiyotsugu (1333–84) and developed by his son Zeami. Adopted by the *daimyo* (feudal lords), Noh became more ritualistic and ceremonial. Gradually its farcical elements were confined to a separate form, Kyogen. By the 17th century, people wanted a more comprehensible and entertaining form of drama, and Kabuki evolved from Noh, starting in Kyoto. A form of puppet theater, Bunraku, was aimed at the general populace.

A Noh play is being performed for the imperial household in this 1863 wood-block print by Taiso Yoshitoshi.

The backdrop is a single pine tree, epitomizing the simplicity of Noh staging.

Slow rhythmic movements, subtle expressions, and sonorous music characterize a Noh performance.

Noh

An austere, restrained, and powerful theatrical form, Noh is performed on a bare, three-sided cypress-wood stage roofed like a shrine, with an entrance ramp to one side. One or two masked characters appear at a time. Their slow, choreographed actions (kata) are performed to music.

Musicians playing traditional drums and flutes sit at the back of the stage and accompany the actors.

Noh actors may be men or women but the majority are men.

Kyogen evolved from comic interludes devised as relief from the demanding nature of Noh. A down-to-earth, colloquial form, its characters highlight human foibles and frailties. Masks are rarely used, and costumes are plain. The actors wear distinctive yellow *tabi* socks.

Noh masks are worn by the leading characters; the greatest masks are classified as National Treasures. The mask on the right represents a samurai, and on the far right, a demon.

Noh costumes are usually richly decorated and heavy. Many layers are worn to make the actors seem larger and more imposing.

Kabuki actors were popular subjects for Edo-era wood-block prints. The tradition can still be seen in this modern poster advertising a Kabuki play.

Bunraku

Bunraku puppets are about 1.2 m (4 ft) tall with carved wooden heads, movable hands, and elaborate costumes. The main puppeteer wears traditional formal dress; his two assistants, one on each side, are clothed in black. *Shamisen (see p151)* music accompanies the action, and a narrator both tells the story and speaks all the parts. Many Kabuki plays were originally written for puppets; Bunraku has in turn borrowed a number of Kabuki dramas.

Bunraku puppet with his manipulator

Stage right is where less important characters are usually located.

Costumes and wigs are highly elaborate, indicating the status and personality of each character.

The pine trees on Kabuki stage backdrops are a reference to its evolution from Noh.

Kabuki

Kabuki is flamboyant and colorful with a large stage and cast. The major actors are stars, often from famous acting dynasties. Elaborate make-up replaced Noh masks, and a curtain allowed set changes. The musicians and chorus sit behind screens on either side or on stage.

Stage sets often incorporate special effects including trapdoors, revolving sections, and overhead cables for flying.

Stage left is usually occupied by characters of high rank or importance.

The hanamichi (flower path) is a raised walkway running from the stage right through the audience and is used for dramatic entrances and exits.

Aragoto, or "rough-style" acting, is used in certain plays by male characters who move in exaggerated, choreographed ways and wear stylized makeup. Eye and facial movements are crucial to an actor's success.

Although Kabuki was founded by a woman, Izumo no Okuni, female actors were soon banned as immoral. All actors are now male, and female roles are played by highly skilled *onnagata*.

Sumo and the Martial Arts

Now more of a professional sport than a martial art, sumo traces its origins back 2,000 years to Shinto harvest rites, and retains strong links with Shinto in many of its rituals. There are six sumo tournaments in Japan every year *(see p148)*, broadcast live on TV and followed enthusiastically. Training is a way of life for sumo wrestlers, and if a tournament is not on, it may be possible to watch practice sessions. Martial arts are known as *budo*, or the "martial way." They aim to cultivate balance, control, speed, and accuracy in a spiritual, mental, and physical sense. Kendo and *kyudo*, the least changed since the days of the samurai, are seen as the purest of the martial arts.

Sumo wrestlers were a highly popular subject for Edo-period wood-block prints.

Throwing salt to purify the ring and the fight to come is part of a complex pre-match ritual that the wrestlers undertake. They also stamp, clap, and raise their hands before crouching down in front of their opponent ready to start.

The gyoji (referee) wears traditional court costume and uses a fan to signal when to begin.

Sumo Wrestling

Despite their size – there are no weight restrictions – sumo wrestlers (rikishi) *move quickly and with agility, and so matches are often short (10 seconds or so). The loser is the first to touch the ground with any part of his body, except the soles of his feet, or to step out of, or be pushed from, the ring. The referee declares the winner.*

Grand champions *(yokozuna)* perform pre-match rituals wearing a richly decorated ceremonial apron and a white hemp-rope belt hung with folded paper (as seen at Shinto shrines). This champion is performing *shiko*, lifting his leg and stamping his foot to banish evil spirits and intimidate his opponent.

A referee pours an offering of sake onto the ring as part of the dedication ceremony before a tournament. The ring is a platform of clay edged by a square of sunken rice-straw bales, with an inner ring (where the match is fought) also marked by sunken bales.

Banners announce a sumo tournament – here at the National Sumo Stadium in Tokyo *(see p149)*. Each tournament lasts 15 days. The lower-ranking wrestlers fight early in the day, while higher-ranking ones appear from mid-afternoon onward.

The wrestlers' hair is oiled and fastened into a topknot *(mage)*.

Only 48 winning techniques are commonly used, but many more have been identified.

A loincloth *(mawashi)* is worn for bouts, along with a thin belt *(sagari)* hung with threads similar to those seen at Shinto shrines.

The ring stands under a suspended roof resembling that of a Shinto shrine. A different-colored tassel hangs from each corner of the roof, representing the four seasons.

Martial Arts

Originally developed as traditional arts of war by the samurai, the martial arts have evolved into forms of austere discipline (shugyo) *aimed at spiritual improvement; some are also competitive sports. The modern forms of kendo and kyudo trace their origins to methods practiced in Japanese antiquity.*

Kendo means the "way of the sword." Originating from samurai fencing, kendo now uses bamboo swords. Contestants wear extensive padding and protection. In a match, points are gained for hitting the head, torso, forearm, or throat.

Kyudo, or the "way of the bow," has close associations with Zen Buddhism. Although accuracy in hitting a target is important, the emphasis is also on concentration of mind and body.

Judo developed from jujitsu. A system of self-defense, it is well established as a sport in which throwing and grappling techniques are used to subdue an opponent.

Karate ("empty hand") reached Japan in 1922 from Okinawa. A form of self-defense as well as spiritual and physical training, it has become a sport, consisting of explosive yet controlled kicks, punches, or strikes, and blocking moves.

Aikido – the "way of harmonious spirit" – uses an opponent's strength and speed against them. Training unites spiritual awareness and physical flexibility.

THE HISTORY OF JAPAN

From the origins of the Japanese race to its military behavior in World War II, Japan's history is still subject to conjecture. What is indisputable is that the people of this archipelago were able to avail themselves of the fruits of continental civilization even as their isolation protected them from attack. As a result, Japan has one of the most distinct of all the many Chinese-influenced cultures in Asia.

During glacial epochs when the sea level was low, Japan's first inhabitants may have reached the archipelago overland from Sakhalin and Siberia, China and Korea, or the Okinawa islands. Crude stone tools found at sites across Honshu, Japan's main island, may date back 40,000 years.

Recent discoveries posit the emergence of the hunting and gathering society known as Jomon around 14,500 BC. Jomon pottery is among the world's oldest and includes vessels and figurines, particularly of women. Mounds of shells and other evidence indicate that the diet included fish, shellfish, deer, wild pigs, and wild plants and seeds. In the Kanto Plain (near Tokyo), the Jomon culture in its later stages included village-like groupings.

Rice agriculture and bronze, iron, and other crafts are believed to have reached Japan via Korea during the Yayoi period. The Yayoi people spread from the southern island of Kyushu to Honshu over time, pushing the earlier inhabitants north. Chinese histories record a visit by an envoy of Himiko, queen of Yamatai, to the Chinese kingdom of Wei in 239, but Yamatai's location is open to debate. Aristocratic orders emerged, including that of the emperor, said to be descended from the sun goddess Amaterasu. Figures of high rank were buried in massive *kofun* (tumuli), along with clay sculptures, armor, mirrors, and jewelry.

By the late 6th century, tribes that had migrated to the fertile lands of the Yamato Plain in Western Honshu were engaged in a power struggle over the introduction of Buddhism. Prince Shotoku, appointed regent by Empress Suiko in 593, helped seal victory for the pro-Buddhist camp.

In 701, the Taiho code, a penal and administrative system based on the Chinese model, was in place. Founded in 710 on the Yamato Plain, the city of Nara became the grand diocese of Buddhism and one of Asia's most splendid cities in its 74-year spell as Japan's first capital. With the completion of the *Man'yoshu*, the earliest known Japanese poetry, in 759, the culture began to establish a clear voice of its own.

Periods at a Glance

Jomon	14,500–300 BC
Yayoi	300 BC–AD 300
Kofun/Asuka	300–710
Hakuho	645–710
Nara	710–794
Heian	794–1185
Kamakura	1185–1333
Muromachi	1333–1568
Momoyama	1568–1600
Tokugawa (Edo)	1600–1868
Meiji	1868–1912
Taisho	1912–1926
Showa	1926–1989
Heisei	1989–present

300 BC–AD 300 Continental methods of farming, metalworking, pottery, and other skills reach southwestern Japan via Korea, and spread through the islands

710 Heijo-kyo (Nara) made capital

701 Taiho code put in place, the basis of the first Japanese legal system

AD 1 — 200 — 400 — 600

Yayoi earthenware

239 Himiko, queen of Yamatai, sends an envoy to the kingdom of Wei in China

587 Power struggle over introduction of Buddhism from China

712 *Kojiki*, Japan's oldest historical account, complete

◀ Detail from a 16th-century screen painting, showing customs month-by-month in the Momoyama period

Court Life and the Tale of Genji

Court life in the Heian period focused on romance, aesthetic pursuits, and fastidious observation of precedent and ritual, as documented in the *Pillow Book* of court lady Sei Shonagon in the late 10th century. The *Tale of Genji*, written in the early 11th century by Sei Shonagon's rival, Murasaki Shikibu, a court lady of the Fujiwara clan, is possibly the world's oldest novel. It depicts the loves and sorrows of a fictitious prince, Genji, and, after he dies, the amorous pursuits of a man whom Genji thought was his son. The story has been illustrated in countless scrolls.

Tale of Genji scroll

Heian Period

The Fujiwara family and Emperor Kammu built a new capital in Western Honshu known as Heian-kyo, now Kyoto, in 794. The new system, also based on Chinese models, held that the land and people were the property of the emperor. Tax-exempt status was granted to Buddhist institutions, large landholders, and settlers who would expand the state's frontiers. Meanwhile, the Fujiwara clan gained influence by acting as regents, and intermarriage with the imperial family. A pattern emerged in which emperors would abdicate, name a younger successor, enter a monastery, then exercise power from behind the scenes.

Buddhism's immense influence continued as proponents such as the Japanese Buddhist monk Saicho adapted it, launching hundreds of separate movements and sects. Powerful temples grew militant in faceoffs with other temples and the government, creating armies of warrior-monks. Ironically, Buddhism's abhorrence of killing fed the nobility's contempt for the farmer-warriors – the early samurai – on the frontier, who battled the indigenous people and each other. After 1100, the court could no longer control infighting, and tensions rose between two clans of farmer-warriors from the northeast – the Taira and the Minamoto. By 1160, the ruthless Taira Kiyomori was the most powerful man in Japan. But the Minamoto, led by the brothers Yoshitsune and Yoritomo, fought back to defeat the Taira and establish the first military shogunate at Kamakura *(see pp92–5)* in 1185.

Heian-period fan

Kamakura Shogunate

Deliberately basing his government far from the imperial court in the village of Kamakura, Minamoto no Yoritomo carefully crafted a system that benefited his *bushi* (warrior) peers and brought 150 years of relative peace and stability. Yoritomo's direct heirs were shoguns only in name, however, as they were dominated by hereditary regents from the military Hojo family of Kamakura. The Hojo assumed the prerogatives of power while granting the imperial institution and nobility the privilege of signing off on policy.

The *Tale of the Heike*, a chronicle of the war between the Taira and Minamoto clans, was

Toji temple

794 Heian-kyo (Kyoto) becomes capital, which it remains until 1868

823 Kukai, leading proponent of Shingon Buddhism, appointed head of Toji temple

985 Genshin writes tract promoting Pure-Land Buddhism

1087 Emperor Shirakawa abdicates and becomes first cloistered emperor

| 800 | 900 | 1000 | 1100 |

801 Warriors sent to Northern Honshu to battle Ezo tribes

866 First Fujiwara regent assumes post

940 First uprising by a warrior member of the Taira clan

c.1000 Court lady Murasaki Shikibu writes *Tale of Genji*

Portuguese in Kyushu – the "Southern Barbarians" who introduced firearms and Christianity to Japan

first recited to *biwa* (lute) accompaniment at this time. Temples and works of art were created in Kamakura, reflecting Yoritomo's warrior ideals of stoicism, self discipline, frugality, and loyalty. Zen Buddhism as imported from China was popular with the samurai, while the Pure-Land, True-Pure-Land, and Nichiren Buddhist sects promoted salvation to the common people.

Mongol invasions were repelled twice in the 13th century, but weakened the resources and command of Kamakura. The end came in 1333, when the Ashikaga clan, led by Takauji, toppled the Kamakura shogunate. However, the power systems instigated by Yoritomo and the Hojo influenced Japanese life for five more centuries.

Muromachi Shogunate

With military power back with the imperial court in Kyoto, arts such as Noh drama and the tea ceremony flowered under the patronage of Shogun Ashikaga Yoshimasa. However, a succession dispute split the court into southern and northern factions.

Muromachi-period sword guard

With leaders engaged in power struggles, chaos and famine were common. The nadir was reached during the Onin War (1467–77), when arson and looting destroyed much of Kyoto.

The Muromachi period, named for the Kyoto district where the Ashikagas built their palace, was a time of craven ambition that unleashed every class in society to vie for advantage. Warfare, once the exclusive business of samurai, now involved armies of footsoldiers (*ashigaru*) recruited from the peasantry, who could hope for promotion based on success in the battlefield.

In 1542, a trio of Portuguese from a shipwrecked junk emerged in Tanegashima, an island off Kyushu, and introduced firearms to Japan. Francis Xavier, a founding member of the Society of Jesus, established a Jesuit mission on Kyushu in 1549. The contact with Europeans further destabilized the political situation and set the stage for the first of the great unifiers, Oda Nobunaga, who entered Kyoto in 1568.

1180–85 Minamoto clan defeats the Taira and establishes Kamakura shogunate

Great Buddha statue at Kamakura

c.1400 Noh theatrical form flourishes under Shogun Ashikaga

1467 Devastating Onin War begins. Vast sections of Kyoto are burned over the next decade

| 1200 | 1300 | 1400 | 1500 |

1160 Ascendant Taira clan under Taira Kiyomori suppresses its rivals, the Minamoto, and dominates court life

1281 Second Mongol invasion

1274 First Mongol invasion

1242 Emperor Shijo dies without naming an heir, setting off succession dispute

1560–80 Oda Nobunaga victorious in battles for hegemony of Japan

1428 Peasant uprising in Kyoto

1401 Formal relations with China reestablished

Screen depicting the Battle of Nagashino in 1575, won by Oda Nobunaga's 3,000 musketeers

Momoyama Period

After Japan had been racked by over a century of debilitating, inconclusive warfare, Oda Nobunaga, who rose through military ranks in the provinces, set out to unify the nation under his rule. From 1568–76 Nobunaga defeated rival warlord Asai Nagamasa; burned down Kyoto's main temple complex, where militant monks had long challenged the court and their Buddhist rivals; drove Ashikaga Yoshiaki into exile; and deployed 3,000 musketeers to massacre the Takeda forces at the Battle of Nagashino. In 1580, in his last great military exploit, Nobunaga obtained the surrender of

Momoyama-period detail at Nishi Hongan-ji, Kyoto

Ishiyama Hongan-ji, a nearly impregnable temple fortress in today's Osaka in Western Honshu. The temple had been the power base of the Buddhist True-Pure-Land sect. By 1582, when he was forced to commit suicide by a treasonous vassal, Nobunaga was in control of 30 of Japan's 68 provinces. Nobunaga's deputy, a warrior of humble birth named Toyotomi Hideyoshi, continued the work of unification, launching epic campaigns that brought Shikoku (1585), Kyushu (1587), the Kanto region (1590), and Northern Honshu (1591) under his control. He followed up by destroying many of the castles and forts belonging to potential rivals, confiscating weapons belonging to peasants, and devising a system in which peasants held their own small plots and paid a fixed tax directly to the central government.

In his later years, Hideyoshi ordered two unsuccessful invasions of Korea and persecuted the Portuguese missionaries and their Japanese converts. Like Oda Nobunaga, however, Hideyoshi never claimed the title of shogun but became obsessed with ensuring the perpetuation of his line after his death. Two years after his death in 1598, however, dissension among his retainers led to the Battle of Sekigahara, in which Tokugawa Ieyasu emerged victorious.

The Tokugawa Shogunate

Named shogun by the emperor in 1603, Ieyasu split the population into rigidly

Osaka Castle

1615 Siege of Osaka Castle

1635 All foreign commerce confined to the artificial island of Dejima in Nagasaki Bay. From 1641, only Dutch and Chinese allowed access

1689 Haiku poet Basho departs on his journey to the north

1707 La eruption of Mour Fuji

1600   **1625**   **1650**   **1675**   **1700**

Statue of Basho

1590 Hideyoshi controls all Japan

1597 Violent persecution of Christians in Nagasaki

1614 Christianity banned

1600 Tokugawa Ieyasu wins battle of Sekigahara, achieves hegemony over Japan

1657 Meireki fire in Edo kills over 100,000

1703 Suicide of the 47 ron

defined hereditary classes. To end turf wars, samurai were forbidden to own land and could reside only within certain quarters of castle towns. Farmers were allotted small plots, which they had to cultivate. Artisans formed the next class, merchants the bottom. Movement between regions was regulated, and families or whole villages could be punished for crimes by their kin or neighbors.

Fireman official's garment in Edo

The *daimyo* or lords who governed regions, now subject to Tokugawa authority, were shuffled to different regions if their service was not approved. After 1635, the *daimyo* and their samurai retinue were forced to reside every other year in the city of Edo (Tokyo), the new seat of the shogunate.

Isolation and the Rise of Edo

William Adams, an Englishman who reached Japan on a Dutch ship in 1600, served Ieyasu in various capacities over the next two decades (as portrayed in James Clavell's 1976 book *Shogun*). During this time, the English, Dutch, Portuguese, Spanish, and New World governments made overtures to the shogunate on trade. However, the increasingly xenophobic Tokugawa regime restricted all foreign shipping to Nagasaki on the island of Kyushu from 1635; only Chinese, Dutch, Korean, and Southeast Asian traders were allowed from 1641. This heralded 200 years of isolation from the rest of the world.

While Kyoto remained the official capital through the Tokugawa period, Edo eclipsed it in size and was probably the largest city in the world by around 1700. Edo also hosted an explosion of arts such as Kabuki and Bunraku theater *(see pp18–19)* and the *ukiyo-e* works *(see p57)* of Utamaro, Sharaku, Hokusai, and Hiroshige. Patrons included the merchant class and samurai.

In 1853 Commodore Matthew Perry steamed into Edo Bay with four US vessels to challenge Japan's refusal to enter into international relations. Weakened by unrest from within its own and other ranks, the shogunate could only accede to Perry's demands. Samurai from the Satsuma, Choshu, and Tosa domains in Kyushu, Western Honshu, and Shikoku became the driving force behind a successful restoration of imperial power and a reorganization of the government carried out in 1868.

Early map of Edo, which outgrew Kyoto under the Tokugawa shogunate

1748 Kabuki drama *Chushingura* debuts, based on the suicide by 47 *ronin*

A Hokusai view of Mount Fuji

1831 Hokusai's *Thirty-Six Views of Mount Fuji* published

| 1725 | 1750 | 1775 | 1800 | 1825 |

1723 Love suicides (*joshi*), spurred by rigid customs and hierachy during the Edo period, reach a peak

1782 Tenmei Famine claims as many as 900,000 lives

1853 Commodore Matthew Perry anchors in Edo Bay; Kanagawa Treaty between US and Japan signed

Wood-block print of Sino-Japanese War of 1894–5

Meiji Restoration

The Meiji Emperor (1852–1912) was 16 when the restoration of imperial rule was declared on January 3, 1868. Tokyo was swiftly made the new capital.

A new centralized system pressed for changes to render Japan capable of competing with the West. Military conscription and the elimination of the hereditary samurai class were undertaken to create a modern fighting force, provoking furious resistance from samurai in 1874–6. *Daimyo* domains were gradually transformed into prefectures, although *daimyo* and court nobles lingered in the form of a new class called *kazoku*. Universal literacy became a goal. By 1884, tax and banking reforms, and an industrial strategy aimed at exports were underway. The Meiji Constitution of 1889, promulgated by the emperor, allowed the military direct access to the throne while creating a house of peers and a lower house.

Following disputes over control of the Korean peninsula, the Sino-Japanese War of 1894–5 ended with Japan's victory over China,

but showed that greater military strength would be needed for the nation to contend as an imperial power equal with the West.

By the turn of the century, the transformation to an industrial economy, with textiles the chief export, was well underway. The Russo-Japanese war of 1904–5 ended with Japan aggrandizing its claims to Korea, which was annexed in 1910, and southern Manchuria in China.

During the final decade of the Meiji Emperor's reign, the home ministry stressed reverence for the emperor, the family, the Shinto religion, and military and national heroes. Suppression of groups seen as enemies of the state became the government's prerogative.

War with China and World War II

The attempt to transform Japan from a feudal to a modern industrial state caused severe dislocation. By 1929, when the stock market collapsed, resentment against those who had prospered from exports intensified. Young officers, chafing to restore national pride, began assassinating rich moderates, while militarists and oligarchs in the government believed that seizing land from China and Russia would secure raw materials and improve national security. At the same time, a pan-Asianist movement, which saw Japan on a mission to lead Asia out of servility, took the Chinese resistance to Japanese domination as an insult. By 1937, the country was

The Meiji Emperor (1852–1912), first emperor of modern Japan

1868 Meiji Restoration; Edo is renamed Tokyo and made capital

1889 Imperial constitution promulgated

1895 China cedes territory to Japan, ending war. Russia, France, and Germany force Japan to relinquish the territory

1910 Korea becomes Japanese colony

1932 Young naval officers assassinate prime minister and attempt coup

1865	1880	1895	1910	1925

Diet Building

1869 Colonization of Hokkaido begins

1890 Imperial Diet convenes for first time

1904 Russo-Japanese war begins

1905 Treaty of Portsmouth ends war. Korea becomes a Japanese protectorate

1933 Japan withdraws from League of Nations

1894 Sino-Japanese war begins

1923 Great Kanto Earthquake

Aftermath of the bombing of Tokyo in 1945

embroiled in a war with China that further estranged it from the rest of the world.

When the US cut off Japanese access to oil, Tokyo made the desperate decision to seize Pacific territory in a sneak attack on Pearl Harbor, Hawaii, in December 1941. A few months later, Japan took Southeast Asia.

By 1944, American bombers were decimating Japanese cities, but the Japanese army was determined not to surrender, opting instead for a suicidal defensive strategy. In August 1945, the US dropped atomic bombs on Hiroshima and Nagasaki, and the Soviet Union entered the war in the Pacific. Emperor Hirohito ordered the cabinet to sue for peace.

Akihito, who was made emperor in 1989

Japan Since 1945

After World War II, the Allied Occupation Force began arriving as millions of homeless Japanese returned to bombed-out cities. The emperor renounced his divine status; land reform was implemented; and war-crimes trials were soon underway.

By 1952, the occupation had ended and the Korean war had turned into a boon for the Japanese economy. Industrial production surged as the average household wanted to own a TV, washing machine, and refrigerator.

In 1960, protests against the ratification of the US-Japan Security Treaty rocked Japan. The prime minister resigned. His successors focused on economic growth. By the time of the 1964 Tokyo Olympics, annual growth was around 10 per cent and rising. Prosperity based on exports such as cars, electronics, and technological products made Japan one of the world's richest nations.

The effects of the recession of the 1990s – unemployment, plummeting land values, and deflation – were further conflated by the breakdown of the family and rising crime. These days fashions, styles, and tastes are magnifying Japan's presence in the world, and Japanese popular culture ranks second in global terms only to that of the United States. As ever, Tokyo is the engine driving much of this change.

On March 11, 2011, a devastating earthquake and subsequent tsunami caused massive destruction in parts of northeastern Japan. Despite suffering major damage and loss of life, Japan is recovering.

Tokyo skyline as seen from the Sumida River

1937 Sino-Japanese war of 1937–45 begins; 140,000 Chinese massacred in Nanjing

1997 Economic recession in Southeast Asia, spreading to Japan

1945 Atomic bombs dropped on Hiroshima and Nagasaki; Japan surrenders

1995 Great Hanshin Earthquake in Kobe; fanatical cult releases sarin gas on Tokyo subway

2014 Yōichi Masuzoe elected Tokyo Governor

1940   1955   1970   1985   2000   2015

Prayers of a soldier

1964 Tokyo Olympics; first "bullet train"; government begins to promote computer industry

2008 Economy surges; Tokyo undergoes construction boom

1989 Emperor Hirohito (Showa) dies; Akihito is new emperor

Shinkansen ("bullet train")

1941 Japan enters World War II

TOKYO THROUGH THE YEAR

The seasons are closely observed in Japan. Many ritual observances are founded on traditional rural *matsuri* (festivals). There is nothing solemn about these events, however, because hard-working, hard-playing Tokyoites enjoy nothing more than a good festival. The festivals, sports events, trade shows, flower exhibitions, and blossom-viewing all add up to a full cultural calendar.

In addition to seasonal *matsuri* and assorted events, each suburb in the city also organizes its own festivals, more so during the summer months, when dancers in kimonos and Japanese drum groups perform, and clear skies explode with spectacular fireworks. In contrast, the winter months are devoted to travel, especially around the New Year period, and religious ceremonies.

Spring

Spring in Japan is when the new economic year begins, students graduate, and projects are launched. While March and April can be rainy, May is usually sublime. The Japanese tend to value spring for its transience and the cherry, more than any other flower, embodies the impermanence of life. However, there is nothing mournful about the vibrant cherry blossom-viewing parties held at parks throughout the city.

March

Hina Matsuri (*Girls' Day and Doll Festival, Mar 3*). Dolls dressed in traditional Heian-period imperial costumes are displayed in homes and public places.

Golden Dragon Dance (*Mar 18*). This colorful event takes place thrice a day at Senso-ji temple in Asakusa.

April

Hanami (*Cherry blossom-viewing, late Mar to Apr*). A glorious spring rite celebrated wherever there are cherry trees, but most famously in Chidorigafuchi, Ueno Park, and Sumida Park.

Meiji Shrine Spring Festival (*Apr 2–May 3*). An extensive compendium of traditional cultural events attended by devotees, including colorful

court dances, *yabusame* (horseback archery), and music performances.

Hana Matsuri (*Buddha's Birthday, Apr 8*). Devotees pour sweet tea over a small image of the Buddha to honor his birth. Services are held at some temples.

Azalea Festival (*Apr 10–May 5*). Held at various venues, the best known being Nezu Shrine, where countless bushes grow along an embankment.

Tokyo International Anime Fair (*late Mar or early Apr*). One of the world's largest anime events for fans of animation and manga. It is held at Tokyo Big Sight.

Bugaku dancer, Meiji Shrine Festival

May

Kodomo no hi (*Children's Day, May 5*). Focusing largely on boys, families fly colorful *koi nobori* (carp streamers), symbolizing strength and determination.

Summer Sumo Tournament (*mid–May*). This 15-day event is held in the Kokugikan hall in Ryogoku.

Kanda Matsuri (*Sat & Sun before May 15, alternate odd-numbered years*). One of the city's three big festivals. Floats and *mikoshi* (portable shrines) parade through the streets around Kanda Myojin Shrine.

Sanja Matsuri (*3rd Fri–Sun in May*). A wild and heady mix of dance, music, ritual, and the jostling of heavy portable shrines, near Asakusa Jinja.

Design Festa (*mid–late May*). Asia's biggest art event. Thousands of people set up displays at this two-day fair at Tokyo Big Sight.

Visitors at the resplendent Azalea Festival

Average daily hours of sunshine

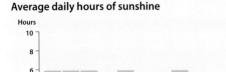

Hours													Hours
10													10
8													8
6													6
4													4
2													2
0	Jan	Feb	Mar	Apr	May	Jun	Jul	Aug	Sep	Oct	Nov	Dec	0

Sunshine Chart
The amount of sunshine per month in Tokyo does not vary greatly, even in the winter months. Winters can see temperatures drop to freezing but the clear skies are rarely disturbed by rain or snow.

Spectacular fireworks display on the Sumida River

Summer

When restaurants serve shaved ice, cold noodles, and glasses of chilled barley tea you know the humid summer days are upon the city. The clammy June rains can seem relentless. In August, as people return to their hometowns to celebrate O-Bon, the city is pleasantly quiet. Spectacular firework festivals along the banks of the Sumida and Edo rivers during the O-Bon festival add a splash of vivid color to the season.

June
Iris Viewing *(early to mid-Jun)*. The iris garden in the grounds of Meiji-jingu shrine and at the Horikiri Iris Garden, Katsushika ward, offer the best viewing.

Sanno-Sai *(mid-Jun)*. In a festival that dates back to the founding of Edo, locals in historical costumes take out processions of *mikoshi*, accompanied by music and dancing at Hie Shrine.

JULY
Asagao Ichi *(Morning Glory Fair, Jul 6–8)*. Dozens of merchants set up stalls outside Iriya Kishibojin temple to sell flowers associated with the horticultural tastes of the Edo era.
Tanabata Matsuri *(Star Festival, Jul 7)*. Based on a Chinese legend; this is said to be the only day when two stars can meet as lovers across the Milky Way. Branches of bamboo are decorated with paper streamers inscribed with scribbled wishes, sometimes in the form of poetry.

Sumidagawa Hanabi Takai *(last Sat in Jul)*. A fireworks display on the Sumida river near Asakusa. The river turns into a sheet of red, green, and violet as lantern-lit boats take to the water.

AUGUST
O-Bon *(Festival of the Dead, mid-Aug)*. Family members return home at a time when, according to a Buddhist belief, the spirits also return to earth. Ancestral graves are visited and tended, and there are joyful Bon-Odori dances and festivals.
Koenji Awa Odori *(late Aug)*. Thousands of participants gather along Koenji's main street to join in the amusing Fool's Dance.
Samba Festival *(last Sat in Aug)*. Dancers from Rio join local samba devotees along Asakusa's Kaminarimon-dori, for an event that draws over half a million spectators.

Vibrantly costumed dancer at the Samba Festival

Average monthly rainfall

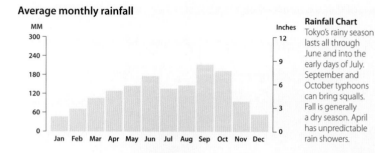

Rainfall Chart
Tokyo's rainy season lasts all through June and into the early days of July. September and October typhoons can bring squalls. Fall is generally a dry season. April has unpredictable rain showers.

Fall

Although the summer heat continues into September, fall is a gentle season, with many fine, clear days and little rainfall. The ginkgo leaf is the symbol of Tokyo and avenues of the yellow-leaved trees can be seen throughout the city. Chrysanthemum festivals are held in temples and gardens. Open-air food stands called *yatai*, and convenience stores start to prepare *oden* (mixed hotpot) toward the end of the season signaling cooler days to come.

Women in traditional costumes at the Jidai Matsuri Festival

Visitors try the latest technology at the Tokyo Game Show

September

Tokyo Game Show *(mid-Sep)*. Held at the gigantic convention center at Makuhari Messe on Tokyo Bay, the three-day event attracts thousands of visitors.

Hachiman-gu Festival *(Sep 14–16)*. Horseback archery and a procession of floats draw a large crowd to this important Kamakura shrine.
Ningyo-Kuyo *(late Sep)*. Hopeful couples pray for children by offering dolls at the Kiyomizu Kannon-do temple in Ueno Park. Priests make a ritual fire, placing last year's dolls on the pyre.

October

Tokyo International Film Festival *(late Oct)*. The largest in Asia, the focus is on films from Asia and Japan.
Chrysanthemum Viewing *(late Oct–mid-Nov)*. Chrysanthemum pavilions are erected in Shinjuku Gyoen Garden; flower dolls are displayed at Yushima Tenjin shrine.
Edo Tenka Matsuri *(late Oct, alternate, odd-numbered years)*. A parade to commemorate the birth of Edo.

November

Tokyo Designer's Week *(early Nov)*. Art enclaves dotted around the city showcase the latest trends in the field of fashion, video graphics, furniture, and interior design.
Tokyo Jidai Matsuri *(Festival of the Ages, Nov 3)*. Locals in period costumes representing figures from Japanese history parade around Asakusa's Senso-ji temple. This is a great photo opportunity.
Shichi-Go-San *(Seven-Five-Three Children's Festival, Nov 15)*. Children of these ages are dressed up in kimonos for visits to shrines in appreciation of their health and to pray for further blessings.
International Robot Exhibition *(late Nov to early Dec, alternate, odd-numbered years)*. Billed as the world's largest trade show focusing on robotics, it brings together an exciting array of the latest in technology and products.

Sony's humanoid robot exhibit

Average monthly temperature

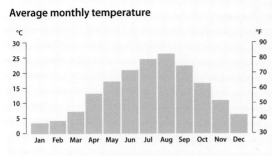

Temperature Chart
Spring is comfortable for most visitors. Summer temperatures can be misleading. June to September are muggy with high levels of humidity. Winter temperatures can drop to freezing. May and October are the most pleasant months with crisp, clear skies.

Winter

Winter can be cold in Tokyo, however there is usually only a day or two of snowfall. The return of *mochi* (rice cakes) and little jars of warmed up sake are seasonal signs. An exodus takes place at Oshogatsu (New Year), which is one of the year's peak travel times. For those who remain at home, it is a chance to enjoy traditional New Year dishes and to offer prayers for the coming year.

Kabuki actor in costume

December
Hagoita Ichi *(Racket Fair, Dec 17–19).* Ornate rackets, sold in the precincts of Senso-ji temple, feature the faces of famous Kabuki actors, celebrities, and sports stars.

Joya-no-Kane *(midnight Dec 31).* Temple bells begin to toll at midnight, 108 rings representing the 108 human sins that must be expunged.

January
Oshogatsu *(New Year's Day).* Japan's most important festival. The first few days are family-oriented. People visit Shinto shrines to offer their wishes for the coming new year.

Water Purification Rituals *(Jan 10–12).* A ritual cleansing by both young and old. The best places to catch this event are at Kanda Myojin and Teppozu Inari shrines.

Seijin no hi *(Coming-of-Age Day, 2nd Mon in Jan).* Young people turning 20 this year celebrate their passage to adulthood.

February
Setsubun *(Feb 3 or 4).* Marking the first day of spring on the old lunar calendar, temple priests and celebrities throw dried soy beans into crowds of onlookers, symbolizing the casting out of bad spirits.

Plum Viewing *(late Feb).* Yushima Tenjin shrine is a famous spot, though there are few plum trees here. Open-air tea ceremonies and floral exhibits are displayed, and plum bonsai are sold.

Public Holidays

If a public holiday falls on a Sunday, the following Monday is also a holiday.

New Year's Day (Jan 1)

Coming-of-Age Day (2nd Mon in Jan)

National Foundation Day (Feb 11)

Vernal Equinox Day (around Mar 20)

Showa Day (Apr 29)

Constitution Memorial Day (May 3)

Greenery Day (May 4)

Children's Day (May 5)

Marine Day (3rd Mon in Jul)

Respect-for-the-Aged Day (3rd Mon in Sep)

Fall Equinox Day (around Sep 23)

Health-Sports Day (2nd Mon in Oct)

Culture Day (Nov 3)

Labor Thanksgiving Day (Nov 23)

Emperor's Birthday (Dec 23)

Braving the icy waters during a purification ritual

TOKYO AREA BY AREA

Tokyo at a Glance

Japan's capital is situated on the banks of the Sumida River, by Tokyo Bay. As the fishing village of Edo it became the shogunate's center of power in 1590. The Shitamachi (low city) of merchants and artisans served the political and intellectual elite in the Yamanote (high city) on the hills to the west. Renamed Tokyo and made capital in 1868, the city was devastated by the Great Kanto Earthquake of 1923, followed by World War II bombing. It has since reinvented itself as one of the world's most modern, exciting, and energizing cities. Transportation is efficient – the easy-to-use JR Yamanote Line circles the city, subway lines crisscross the center (*see* Back Endpaper), and *shinkansen* lines link it with the rest of the country. It can be difficult to find individual buildings by their addresses (*see p171*). The Tokyo Street Finder (*see pp176–85*) locates all the sights, restaurants, and hotels mentioned in this guide.

Locator Map

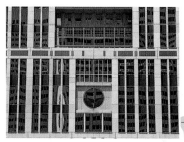

West Shinjuku (*see pp64–5*) is an area of soaring skyscrapers, providing a visible manifestation of the corporate wealth of Tokyo. The most impressive buildings are the Tokyo Metropolitan Government Offices, designed by Kenzo Tange.

SHINJUKU-DORI

EXPRESSWAY NO. 4

WESTERN TOKYO
(See pp60–71)

AOYAMA-DORI

EXPRESSWAY NO 3

Shibuya (*see pp68–9*) is a mixture of large department stores and smaller shops, all catering to young consumers. Adjacent to Shibuya are the equally fashion-oriented areas of Harajuku and Minami-Aoyama.

East Shinjuku (*see pp62–3*) comes alive when West Shinjuku shuts down. It encompasses a red-light area, countless bars, and various forms of entertainment from movies to *pachinko* parlors.

◀ Tokyo's Shibuya district, a famous youth and nightlife center

Ueno Park *(see pp50–51)* is one of Tokyo's most extensive green spaces, always crowded with locals. Spectacular in the cherry blossom season, it also merits an unhurried visit at other times of the year for its boating ponds and many temples, shrines, and museums.

Tokyo National Museum *(see pp52–5)* consists of four main buildings, dominating the northern reaches of Ueno Park, which exhibit a stunning array of Japanese art, and archaeological artifacts. It is the largest such collection in the world and includes some fascinating items from elsewhere in Asia including China and Korea.

NORTHERN TOKYO
(See pp48–59)

EXPRESSWAY NO. 1

EXPRESSWAY NO. 9

CENTRAL TOKYO
(See pp38–47)

DA DORI

EXPRESSWAY NO. 1

Senso-ji Temple *(see pp58–9)* offers an insight into the traditional side of Tokyo. Still attracting thousands of worshipers daily, it also has many craft shops lining its main approach.

| 0 kilometers | 2 |
| 0 miles | 1 |

Ginza *(see pp40–41)* provides the archetypal Tokyo shopping experience, with its venerable department stores and small, exclusive shops, which have been joined by various international designer boutiques. Some excellent restaurants are also located here.

CENTRAL TOKYO

Situated to the north and west of the Sumida River, this area has been at the heart of Tokyo since the first shogun, Ieyasu, built his castle and capital where the Imperial Palace still stands today. Destroyed by a series of disasters, including the Great Kanto Earthquake of 1923 and the Allied bombing in World War II, the area has reinvented itself several times over. Ginza and Nihonbashi were commercial centers and are still prosperous, offering a mix of department stores and side-street boutiques.

The Shiodome skyscraper development is another prominent commercial center. For more down-to-earth shopping, there is the Jimbocho area for books, Akihabara for electronics, and the early-morning Tsukiji Fish Market. Central Tokyo's continuing political importance is evident in the Hibiya and Marunouchi districts, and the area is also home to two very different shrines – Kanda and Yasukuni. A selection of green spaces provides a respite from the bustle elsewhere.

Sights at a Glance

Notable Districts

1. Ginza *see pp40–41*
7. Nihonbashi District
8. Marunouchi District
10. Hibiya District
14. Jimbocho Booksellers' District
17. Akihabara Electronics District

Historic Buildings

2. Kabuki-za Theater
10. Diet Building
11. Imperial Palace

Shrines

13. Yasukuni Shrine
16. Kanda Myojin Shrine

Modern Architecture

5. Shiodome
6. Tokyo Tower
9. Tokyo International Forum

Parks and Gardens

4. Hama Detached Palace Garden
6. Shiba Park

12. Kitanomaru Park
15. Koishikawa Korakuen Garden

Market

3. Tsukiji Fish Market

0 kilometers 1

0 miles 0.5

See also Street Finder
maps 2, 3, 4, 5 & 6

◄ Tokyo's Imperial Palace, with the landmark Nijubashi bridge in the foreground

For keys to symbols *see back flap*

❶ Street-by-Street: Ginza

銀座

When Ieyasu moved his military capital to Edo in 1590, Ginza was all swamp and marshland. Once filled in, the area attracted tradesmen and merchants. The silver mint that provided Ginza's name, "silver place," was built in 1612. In 1872 fire destroyed everything and, with the Meiji Restoration in full swing, the government ordered English architect Thomas Waters to rebuild the area in red brick. From then on it was the focus for Western influences and all things modern, and is still one of Tokyo's prime market centers. Tiny shops selling local crafts mix with galleries, department stores, and the ultra-modern Sony showroom for an unrivaled shopping experience.

Shoppers at the landmark Ginza Yon-chome crossing

Hankyu and Seibu department stores focus on fashions, with a mix of Japanese and international labels.

Mullion Building, housing Hankyu and Seibu department stores

Gallery Center Building
On the second floor of this modern building are a number of exclusive galleries showcasing Japanese and Western art. On the fifth is an auction house, and the sixth has the Youkyo Art Hall, with exhibits by artists working in different media.

HARUMI-DORI

SOTOBORI-DORI

NAMIKI-DORI

MIYUKI-DORI

SUZU...

Ginza Noh Theater

Namiki-Dori and Chuo-Dori are now called "Brand Street" with boutiques such as Gucci, Dior, Louis Vuitton, and Cartier.

The Asahi Building contains a traditional kimono shop, silversmiths, and several boutiques.

Sony Showroom
Sony's latest technology and electronic gadgets are on display on several floors here, and many can be tried out.

Key

— Suggested walk route

▬ Train line

For hotels and restaurants see pp112–15 and pp130–37

Printemps is a branch of the French department store. Parisian influence came to Ginza in the 1930s and can also be seen in the nearby French cafés and boutiques.

Locator Map
See Tokyo Street Finder map 5

Wako Department Store
Opposite the San'ai Building, this enduring landmark was originally built in 1894. Its clocktower is a popular symbol of Ginza, and the window displays are always entertaining.

Matsuya department store is another huge store stocking everything from food to bonsai plants. Restaurant City offers a large range of cuisines.

Nihonbashi

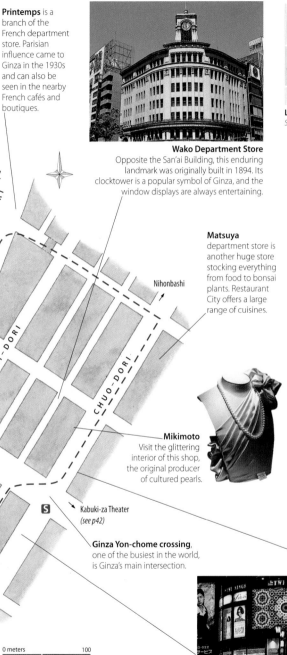

Mikimoto
Visit the glittering interior of this shop, the original producer of cultured pearls.

Mitsukoshi Department Store
This classic Tokyo store retains an aura of glamor – some people still dress up to shop here. Do not miss the particularly luxurious kimono department.

S Kabuki-za Theater
(see p42)

Ginza Yon-chome crossing, one of the busiest in the world, is Ginza's main intersection.

0 meters   100
0 yards   100

San'ai Building
Made of glass, this building is at its best at dusk when the lights and neon signs inside shine through the glass, creating a magical effect.

Kabuki actors performing at the Kabuki-za Theater

❷ Kabuki-za Theater
歌舞伎座

Map 5 C3. 4-12-15 Ginza. **Tel** (03) 3541-3131. **S** Higashi-Ginza stn, Toei Asakusa & Hibiya lines. 🗺
w shochiku.co.jp/play/kabukiza/theater/index.html

Tokyo's principal theater for Kabuki (see p19) opened in 1889 during the reign of Emperor Meiji – a part of Kabuki's shift from popular daytime entertainment for the Shitamachi masses in Asakusa to a more highbrow art form.

The building was one of the striking examples of the use of Western building materials and techniques in traditional Japanese style. Partially destroyed by the Allied bombing of 1945, the theater was rebuilt in 1951, only to be demolished completely in 2010. A brand-new structure re-opened in March 2013 (see pp150–51).

❸ Tsukiji Fish Market
築地中央卸売市場

Map 5 C4. **S** Tsukijishijo stn, Toei Oedo line; Tsukiji stn, Hibiya line. **Open** 5am–1pm Mon–Sat.

Officially known as Tokyo Central Wholesale Market, the world's largest fish market moved to this location from Nihonbashi in 1935, after the 1923 Great Kanto earthquake and its subsequent fires destroyed the old one.

Auctions are held daily (except Sunday), from about 5:30 to 10am. During this time, 15,000 restaurateurs and food sellers from all over the city buy 450 types of sea produce from about 1,700 stalls. The market itself resembles a huge hangar filled with a maze of tiny stalls, each crammed with fish. Despite the rush, people are tolerant of casual visitors. On the same site is a large wholesale vegetable market.

A small bridge marks the entrance to the market. Just before the bridge is **Namiyoke Inari Jinja** (Wave-repelling Fox Shrine), where fishermen and traders come to pray for safety and prosperity. Opposite is a street lined with shops selling everything from dried tuna to porcelain dishes. In the alleys to the right are more shops and food stalls selling excellent sushi and tempura.

When leaving the market, turn left before the bridge for a line of shops and small restaurants. The river wharf, where boats unload, is over the bridge to the left.

The wholesale fish market has moved partly to the Toyosu district; however, there are plans to keep a fish market at this location.

A box of fish from Tsukiji market

❹ Hama Detached Palace Garden
浜離宮庭園

Map 5 B4. **Tel** (03) 3541-0200. **S** Shiodome stn, Oedo line. **R** Shimbashi stn, Yamanote line. **⛴** Sumida River Trip. **Open** 9am–4pm. (Last adm 30 mins before closing.) 🗺

Situated where the Sumida River empties into Tokyo Bay, this 62-acre (25-ha) garden was built in 1654 as a retreat for the shogun's family and opened to the public in 1945. Former US President Ulysses S. Grant stayed in a villa in the gardens during his visit in 1879 and sipped green tea with Emperor Meiji in Nakajima teahouse.

Tuna Fish Supplies

Tsukiji Fish Market specializes in *maguro* (tuna) from as far away as New Zealand and the North Atlantic. Japan consumes about 30 per cent of the annual global 1.7 million ton tuna catch, and eats 80 per cent of its tuna raw, as sashimi, which requires the best cuts of fish. Suppliers can demand prices of up to 10–20 times that of the lower-grade tuna. The Pacific Ocean's Southern Blue Fin tuna, a favorite for sashimi, is endangered. The catch is managed and tuna numbers currently seem stable, although reduced tuna sales may be due to the recession of the 1990s and the late 2000s. If the economy in Japan starts to boom, Southern Blue Fin stocks could once again be put under pressure.

Rows of frozen tuna at Tsukiji Fish Market

The lovely garden grounds surrounding the duck ponds are still a pleasant place to stroll and sit. All of the original teahouses and villas, trees, and vegetation burned down after a bombing raid on November 29, 1944. **Nakajima Teahouse** has been rebuilt, seeming to float over the large pond. Green tea and Japanese sweets are available here.

Nakajima teahouse in Hama Detached Palace Garden

❺ Shiodome

汐留

Map 5 C4, 4 F3. 🟥 Shiodome stn, Toei Oedo line. 🟥 Shimbashi stn, Yamanote line, Toei Asakusa line. 🟥 Shiodome stn, Yurikamome line.

Before industrialization, the ocean-facing parts of Tokyo Bay were famous for their *nori* (seaweed) cultivation. In the late 1980s, waterfront development became Tokyo's new frontier. The **Shiodome City Center** complex, opened in 2003, is one of the more successful of these waterfront developments. Within this grove of ultra-modern skyscrapers are the impressive, triangular **Shiodome Media Tower**, headquarters of Kyodo News, and **Acty Shiodome**, the tallest residential building in Japan.

Indoor malls and a spacious outdoor piazza provide exciting places to dine or shop. Nearby is **ADMT**, the Advertising Museum of Tokyo, located in the basement of the **Caretta Shiodome**, which has the offices of the world's largest advertising agency – Dentsu. Beyond the northern boundary of Shiodome is the **Nagakin Capsule Tower**, a curious apartment complex built in 1972 and inspired by the space race. For greater exploration of the Tokyo Bay area, take the Yurikamome Line from Shiodome Station toward **Rainbow Bridge**, and enjoy great views of the Sumida River and the futuristic island of Odaiba *(see p77)*.

❻ Shiba Park and Tokyo Tower

芝公園と東京タワー

Map 5 A4, 2 F5. 🟥 Shiba-Koen stn, Toei Mita line. Tokyo Tower: 🟥 Akabanebashi stn, Oedo line. **Tel** (03) 3433-5111. **Open** 9am–10pm daily. 🟥 (extra for higher viewpoint).

Shiba Park is a rather fragmented green space. A large part of it is a golf driving range, but a portion in the east is pleasantly landscaped with woods and a water course. The park used to be the Tokugawa family's graveyard and at its center is **Zojo-ji**, the family temple. It was founded in 1393, and Ieyasu moved it here in 1598 to protect

The soaring Tokyo Tower, inspired by the Eiffel Tower in Paris

his new capital. The present-day temple dates from 1974; nearby are the rebuilt Daimon (big gate) and the Sanmon (great gate), built in 1622, the oldest wooden structure in Tokyo.

To the west of the park, on the edge of the Roppongi District *(see pp70–71)*, is the striking **Tokyo Tower**. Completed in 1958, at 1,093-ft (333-m) tall, it is higher than the Eiffel Tower in Paris, on which it is based. The ground floor has an aquarium and elevators to the observation deck. Other floors house amusements. Two viewpoints – the main one at 492 ft (150 m) and a higher one at 820 ft (250 m) – offer spectacular views of Tokyo Bay, the nearby districts of Shimbashi and Ginza, and Mount Fuji on a clear day. As a lofty symbol of the city, Tokyo Tower has been usurped by the 2,080-ft (634-m) Tokyo Sky Tree, in Sumida.

The Shidome skyline from the vantage point of the Sumida River

Mitsukoshi's central hall in Nihonbashi

❼ Nihonbashi District

日本橋地区

Map 5 C1–2, 6 D1. **S** Tokyo stn, Marunouchi line; Nihonbashi stn, Ginza, Tozai & Toei Asakusa lines; Mitsukoshimae stn, Ginza & Hanzomon lines. **R** Tokyo stn, many lines. Tokyo Stock Exchange: **Tel** (03) 3666-1361. **Open** 9am–4pm Mon–Fri. Kite Museum: **Tel** (03) 3271-2465. **Open** 11am–5pm daily. Bridgestone Museum of Art: **Tel** (050) 3377-7254. **Open** 10am–6pm Tue–Sun (to 8pm Fri).

Nihonbashi, meaning "Japan's bridge," after the expansive bridge over the Nihonbashi River that marked the start of the five major highways of the Edo period, was once the trade center of Edo and Meiji Tokyo. After the destruction of the 1923 earthquake, shops, businesses, and banks started relocating to Marunouchi and Ginza.

Although the area never regained its original stature, it is still a thriving commercial center, with dozens of bank headquarters as well as huge department stores and smaller traditional shops. **Mitsukoshi** (see p138) has its main store here, on Mitsukoshimae. It started as a kimono shop in 1673. Head for the basement food market with its free samples, and the sixth-floor bargain counters where you can jostle with Tokyo's thrifty elite. To the west of the store, the **Bank of Japan**, built in 1896 and modeled on the Neo-Classical

Berlin National Bank, was the first Western-style building designed by a Japanese architect, Kingo Tatsuno.

On the north bank of Nihonbashi River, just before **Nihonbashi Bridge**, is the bronze marker from which distances to and from Tokyo are still measured. The bridge here today dates from 1911.

On the south bank of the river, east of the bridge, is the **Tokyo Stock Exchange**, which lists more than 2,000 companies, and is one of the world's top five. This is a great place to see how important commerce remains in Tokyo. The visitors' observation deck overlooks the trading floor and has interesting exhibits comparing stock markets worldwide.

West of the Stock Exchange is the **Kite Museum**, located on the fifth floor of a well-known eatery, Tameikan. The restaurant's former owner, a kite enthusiast, founded the museum which exhibits kites from China and other Asian countries. To the south of Nihonbashi bridge, the **Bridgestone Museum of Art** holds one of Japan's best collections of Western art, including works by Manet, Picasso, Rouault, and Brancusi. To its north, the **Pokemon Center** is a shop devoted to the famous animation characters.

South of the museum, the **National Film Center** (see p147) hosts regular screenings of Japanese and foreign films. There are permanent exhibits of film equipment, and other film-related items. Books, film posters, and archival material are easily available in the center's bookstore and public library.

❽ Marunouchi District

丸の内地区

Map 5 B1–2. **S** Tokyo stn, Marunouchi line. **R** Tokyo stn, many lines. Tokyo Station Gallery: **Tel** (03) 3212-2485. **Open** 10am–5:30pm daily.

During the Edo era, this district earned the name "Gambler's Meadow" as its isolation made it an ideal place to gamble secretly. In the Meiji period it was used by the army, who sold it to Mitsubishi in 1890. The arrival of the railroad increased Marunouchi's appeal as a business site.

Tokyo Station, designed by Kingo Tatsuno and completed in 1914, is based on the design of Amsterdam station. Its dome was damaged in the 1945 air raids and later replaced by the polyhedron here today. The original reliefs adorning the domes over the North and South exits are worth a look, as is the Tokyo Station Hotel. The station also houses the small **Tokyo Station Gallery**.

Facing the station, the striking **Marunouchi Building** is an important local landmark, housing shops, restaurants, and offices. A short walk west of the station over Wadakura Bridge leads to the **Wadakura Fountain Park**, with interesting water features. Returning over the bridge, cross Hibiya-dori and turn right to the **Meiji Seimeikan Building** (1934), with its huge Corinthian columns. Hiroshige, the wood-block print artist, was born on this site in 1797. Beyond, the **Imperial Theater** (see p177), founded in 1910, shows Broadway musicals and Japanese popular dramas.

Tokyo Station's Western-style facade

❾ Tokyo International Forum

東京国際フォーラム

Map 5 B2. **S** Yurakucho stn, Yurakucho line; Tokyo stn, Marunouchi line. **R** Tokyo & Yurakucho stns, many lines. **Open** 7am–10:30pm daily. **W** t-i-forum.co.jp/en

Designed by New York-based architect Rafael Viñoly, and completed in 1996, the Forum is one of downtown Tokyo's most distinctive buildings *(see p17)*. A cultural center, it is made up of two buildings – a curved, glass atrium soaring 200 ft (60m), and a cube-like, white structure housing four halls (the largest seating 5,012). A tree-shaded courtyard separates the two, while glass walkways provide an overhead link.

The interior of the huge atrium has a ceiling resembling a ship's hull. Inside the Forum are a number of shops, cafés, and restaurants, all with state-of-the-art facilities. The Cultural Information Lobby within the complex offers Internet facilities and has an audio-visual library highlighting Tokyo's attractions.

The airy glass-and-metal interior of Tokyo International Forum

The imposing granite exterior of the Diet Building

❿ Hibiya District and the Diet Building

日比谷地区と国会議事堂

Map 2 F3, 5 A2, 5 B2. **S** Kokkai-Gijidomae stn, Chiyoda & Marunouchi lines; Hibiya stn, Toei Mita, Chiyoda & Hibiya lines. Hibiya Park: **Open** 24 hrs daily. Diet Building: **Open** 9am–5pm Mon–Fri. **C** (compulsory, by reservation). Idemitsu Museum of Arts: **Tel** (03) 5777-8600. **Open** 10am–5pm Tue–Sun (to 7pm Fri). **W** sangiin.go.jp/eng/index.htm

Central Tokyo's only Western-style park, **Hibiya Park** is the focus of Hibiya district. The park's location, close to political centers, makes it a favorite place for public protests. The large bandstand is also used for concerts.

Completed in 1936, the **Diet Building** houses the legislature of the Japanese government, originally established as the Imperial Diet in the Meiji era. Tours (in Japanese only) cover the Diet chamber, where you can see the deliberations of Diet members, and the extravagantly decorated rooms used by the emperor for official functions. Overlooking the Imperial Palace, in the Tei Geki building, the **Idemitsu Museum of Arts** features one of the city's finest displays of Japanese and Asian art.

⓫ Imperial Palace

皇居

Map 3 A5, 3 B5, 5 A1, 5 B1. **S** Nijubashi stn, Chiyoda line. **R** Tokyo stn, many lines. Imperial Palace: **Open** Jan 2, Dec 23. East Garden of the Imperial Palace: **Tel** (03) 3213-1111. **Open** 9am–4:30pm Tue–Thu, Sat, Sun (Nov–Feb: to 4pm). **Closed** Mon, Fri.

Ieyasu, the first Tokugawa shogun, started building his castle here in 1590. In the Edo period his successors made this into the world's largest castle; now only the inner circle remains. The emperor and his family still live in the western part of the grounds in the **Imperial Palace**, rebuilt after the previous one was bombed during World War II. Public access is allowed twice a year – at New Year and on the emperor's birthday. The rest of the grounds, bounded by the moat, are divided into public parks.

The most famous landmark is the **Nijubashi**, a double-arched stone bridge, east of the palace. Completed in 1888, it was the palace's main entrance. The huge **Otemon** (Big Hand Gate), rebuilt in 1967, was the main gate before Nijubashi was built. Now it is the entrance to the **East Garden of the Imperial Palace**. Just inside is **Sannomaru Shozokan**, a collection of art and artifacts of the Showa Emperor. Beyond is the Edo-era **Hyakunin Basho**, where 100 samurai lived while standing guard in shifts. Behind is the **Honmaru**, the castle's main keep, only massive stone walls remain with good views from the top. To the east of the Honmaru is the **Ninomaru** garden, landscaped by Shogun Iemitsu in 1630.

A glimpse of the Imperial Palace over the stone bridge Nijubashi

Tokyoites enjoying an outdoor summer picnic in Kitanomaru Park

⓬ Kitanomaru Park

北の丸公園

Map 3 A5. **S** Kudanshita stn, Hanzomon, Toei Shinjuku & Tozai lines; Takebashi stn, Tozai line. National Museum of Modern Art: **Tel** (03) 5777-8600. **Open** 10am–5pm Tue–Sun. 🖪 🖾 momat.go.jp/english Crafts Gallery: **Tel** (03) 3211-7781. **Open** 10am–5pm Tue–Sun. 🖾 Science Museum: **Tel** (03) 3212-8544. **Open** 9:30am–4:50pm daily. 🖾 🖾 jsf.or.jp/eng

Lying to the north of the Imperial Palace, Kitanomaru Park is reached through the massive **Tayasumon** gate. A former ground for the Imperial Palace Guard, the area became a park in 1969. Before entering, keep Tayasumon on your left and walk past it to reach **Chidorigafuchi** (the west moat), one of Tokyo's most beautiful cherry blossom-viewing spots. Row boats can be rented here.

Within Kitanomaru's pleasant grounds are a number of buildings. Near Tayasumon is the **Nippon Budokan** (see p148). Built for the 1964 Olympics martial arts competition, it is now used mostly for rock concerts. A short walk farther on is the **Science Museum**. Some of the interactive exhibits are fun, including virtual bike rides

and electricity demonstrations (all explanations are in Japanese).

Five minutes beyond, over a main road, and left down the hill, is the **National Museum of Modern Art**. The permanent collection comprises Japanese works from the 1868 Meiji Restoration to the present day; visiting exhibits are often excellent. Nearby is the National Museum of Modern Art's **Crafts Gallery**. Inside this 1910 Neo-Gothic brick building is an exquisite collection of modern workings of traditional Japanese crafts – pottery, lacquerware, and damascene (inlaid metal artifacts). Some pieces are for sale.

⓭ Yasukuni Shrine

靖国神社

Map 2 F1. **Tel** (03) 3261-8326. **S** Kudanshita stn, Hanzomon, Tozai & Toei Shinjuku lines. **Open** 24 hours daily. 🖾 yasukuni.or.jp/english Yushukan: **Open** 9am–5pm daily. 🖾

The 2.5 million Japanese, soldiers and civilians who have died in war since the Meiji Restoration are enshrined at Yasukuni Jinja (Shrine of Peace for the Nation), which was dedicated in 1879. Its history makes it a sobering place to visit.

Until the end of World War II, Shinto was the official state religion, and the ashes of all who died in war were brought here regardless of the families' wishes. Unsettling for some of Japan's neighbors, the planners and leaders of World War II and the

colonizers of China and Korea are also enshrined here, including wartime prime minister, Tojo Hideki, and eight other Class-A war criminals. Visits by cabinet ministers are controversial.

Beside the shrine is the **Yushukan**, a museum dedicated to the war dead. Many exhibits put a human face to Japan at war; under a photograph of a smiling young officer is a copy of his last letter home, and there are mementos of a nurse who died from overwork. Romanticized paintings of Japanese soldiers in Manchuria and displays of guns, planes, and even a locomotive from the Thai-Burma Railroad may be disturbing to some.

⓮ Jimbocho Booksellers' District

神保町古本屋街

Map 3 B4–5. **S** Jimbocho stn, Toei Mita, Hanzomon & Toei Shinjuku lines.

Three of Japan's prestigious universities, Meiji, Chuo, and Nihon, started out in this area in the 1870s and 1880s, and soon booksellers sprang up selling both new and used books. At one time 50 per cent of Japan's publishers were based here. Although only Meiji University is still here, dozens of bookshops, several selling *ukiyo-e* prints, remain, all clustered around the junction of Yasukuni-dori and Hakusan-dori. For books in English on Oriental subjects try **Kitazawa Books** or **Issei-do**; for *ukiyo-e* prints, visit **Oya Shobo** – all are on the south side of Yasukuni-dori, walking away from Hakusan-dori.

The change in the economic status (and priorities) of students is evident

Browsing in one of Jimbocho's bookshops

here. Shops selling surf- or snowboards are everywhere. Music shops selling electric guitars seem as numerous as the bookshops.

Tsutenkyo bridge in Koishikawa Korakuen Garden

⑮ Koishikawa Korakuen Garden

小石川後楽園

Map 3 A3–4. **Tel** (03) 3811-3015. Ⓢ Korakuen stn, Marunouchi & Nambo-ku lines. **Open** 9am–5pm daily.

Meaning "garden of pleasure last," Korakuen is one of Tokyo's best traditional stroll gardens, a delightful place to spend a few restful hours. The name Korakuen comes from the Chinese poem "Yueyang Castle" by Fan Zhongyan – "Be the first to take the world's trouble to heart, be the last to enjoy the world's pleasure."

Construction of the garden started in 1629 and finished 30 years later. Once four times its present size of almost 20 acres (8 ha), it belonged to the Mito branch of the Tokugawa family. An exiled Chinese Scholar, Zhu Shun Shui, helped design the garden including the **Engetsukyo** (full-moon) **Bridge**, a stone arch with a reflection resembling a full moon. **Tsukenkyo Bridge** is a copy of a bridge in Kyoto; its vermilion color is a striking contrast to the surrounding deep green forest.

The garden represents larger landscapes in miniature. Rozan, a famous Chinese sightseeing mountain, and Japan's Kiso River are two famous geographic features recreated here. In the middle of the large pond is **Horai Island**, a beautiful composition of stone and pine trees.

⑯ Kanda Myojin Shrine

神田明神

Map 3 C4. **Tel** (03) 3254-0753. Ⓢ Ochanomizu stn, Marunouchi line. Ⓙ Ochanomizu stn, Chuo & Sobu lines. **Open** 24 hours daily. Museum: **Open** 10am–4pm Sat, Sun & public hols. Kanda Matsuri (Sat & Sun closest to May 15 in alternate, odd-numbered years).

Myojin is over 1,200 years old, although the present structure is a reproduction built after the 1923 earthquake. The gate's guardian figures are two beautifully dressed archers – Udaijin on the right and Sadaijin on the left. Just inside the compound on the left is a large stone statue of Daikoku, one of the *shichi-fuku-jin* (seven lucky gods). Here, as always, he is sitting on top of two huge rice bales.

The vermilion shrine itself and its beautiful interior, all lacquer and gold and ornate Chinese-style decoration, are impressive. Early morning is the best time to glimpse the Shinto priests performing rituals. The Kanda Matsuri (see p30) is one of Tokyo's grandest and greatest of Tokyo's festivals – come early and be prepared for crowds.

Behind the main shrine is a **museum** containing relics from the long history of Myojin. There are also several small shrines, hemmed in by the surrounding office blocks.

Lions on the gate to Kanda Myojin Shrine

⑰ Akihabara Electronics District

秋葉原電気店街

Map 3 C4. Ⓢ Akihabara stn, Hibiya line. Ⓙ Akihabara stn, Yamanote, Chuo & Sobu lines.

Akihabara Electronics District surrounds Akihabara Station. Under the station are tiny shops along narrow aisles selling any electronic device, simple or complex. The market grew out of the ruins of World War II, when the Japanese army had surplus radio equipment it wanted to dispose of on the black market. Akihabara and electronics have been synonymous ever since. The focus then changed to house-hold electronic goods, and now the emphasis is on computers, cell phones, and video games. On Chuo-dori, **Laox** (see p138) is a great source of tax-free goods. **Radio Kaikan**, the site that housed the original radio spare parts dealers, remains with small operators. A redevelopment north and east of the station features flagship stores such as the Akihabara UDX and the Yodobashi Akiba Building.

The **Tokyo Anime Center** is a showcase for the very latest in Tokyo's popular anime culture. Its 3D digital theater holds regular screenings, live concerts, and other anime-related events.

Colorful shop fronts and advertisements in Akihabara district

NORTHERN TOKYO

The northern districts of Ueno and Asakusa contain what remains of Tokyo's old Shitamachi (low city). Once the heart and soul of Edo culture *(see p27)*, Shitamachi became the subject of countless *ukiyo-e* wood-block prints *(see p57)*. Merchants and artisans thrived here, as did Kabuki theater *(see p19)* and the Yoshiwara pleasure district near Asakusa. One of the last great battles in Japan took place in Ueno in 1868, when the Emperor Meiji's forces defeated the Tokugawa shogunate. Ueno and Asakusa are the best parts of Tokyo for just strolling and observing. Life in Asakusa still revolves

around the bustling Senso-ji temple, its main approach packed with shops. Ueno is dominated by its huge park containing, among others, the National and Shitamachi museums. It is still possible to find pockets of narrow streets lined with tightly packed homes, especially in the Yanaka area, which escaped destruction by war and earthquake. Shopping is a pleasure in Northern Tokyo. As well as the traditional arts and crafts shops near Senso-ji temple, there are specialists in plastic food in Kappabashi-dori, religious goods in neighboring Inaricho, and electronic items at Ameyoko Market.

Sights at a Glance

See also Street Finder maps 3 & 4

0 meters 500
0 yards 500

For keys to symbols *see back flap*

❶ Ueno Park

上野公園

Ieyasu, the first Tokugawa shogun, built the Kanei-ji temple and subtemples here in the 17th century to negate evil spirits that might threaten from the northeast. Judging by how long the Tokugawas lasted, it was a wise move. In 1873, five years after the Battle of Ueno, when the last supporters of the shogun were crushed by imperial forces, the government designated Ueno a public park. A favorite since its earliest days, the park has figured in many popular wood-block prints and short stories. Shinobazu Pond (actually three ponds) is an annual stop for thousands of migrating birds. Several museums and temples are dotted around the park, and Japan's oldest zoo, which is also one of the country's best, is here.

Boating on the Shinobazu pond

★ Pagoda
This landmark five-story pagoda dates from the 17th century and is a survivor from the original Kanei-ji temple complex. Today it stands in the grounds of Ueno Zoo, a popular destination for Japanese schoolchildren, among others, thanks to its giant pandas.

★ Tosho-gu Shrine
This ornate complex of halls is one of Tokyo's few remaining Edo-era structures. Ieyasu was enshrined here and later reburied at Nikko *(see pp100–1)*.

KEY

① **Shitamachi Museum** *(see p56)*

② **Gojo shrine** is reached through a series of red *torii* (gates).

③ **The Great Buddhist Pagoda** was built in 1967.

④ **The Tokyo Metropolitan Art Museum** has a large collection of contemporary Japanese art.

⑤ **Tokyo National Museum** *(see pp52–5)*

⑥ **The main walkway** is lined with hundreds of cherry trees.

⑦ **The Tomb of the Shogi Tai** is dedicated to the many samurai who died in the 1868 Battle of Ueno.

Ueno Zoo

Benten Hall

Shinobazu Pond

KANEI-JI
TEMPLE

Uguisudani
Station

Rinno-ji
Temple
Imperial
Cemetery

Baseball
ground

Tokyo Metropolitan
Festival Hall

Ueno Station

Japan Art
Academy

Ueno Royal
Museum

0 meters   100

0 yards   100

VISITORS' CHECKLIST

Practical Information
Map 3 C2–3, 4 D2. Ueno Zoo:
Open 9:30am–5pm Tue–Sun.
Tokyo Metropolitan Art Museum:
Open 9am–5pm Tue–Sun.
National Museum of Nature and
Science: **Open** 9am–5pm Tue–Sun.
National Museum of Western
Art: **Open** 9:30am–5:30pm Tue–
Sun (mid-Dec–Mar: to 5pm).

Transport
Ⓢ Ueno stn, Hibiya & Ginza lines.
Ⓡ Ueno & Uguisudani stns,
many lines.

National Museum of Nature and Science
A steam engine and life-sized model
of a blue whale mark this museum's
entrance. Exhibits cover natural
history, science, and
technology.

National Museum of Western Art
Rodin's massive *Gate of Hell*
stands outside this building
by Le Corbusier. On display
are various Impressionist
works, plus paintings by
Rubens, Pollock, and others.

Saigo Takamori Statue
The leader of the
victorious Meiji
forces, Saigo
subsequently
instigated the
Satsuma rebellion
against the
emperor in 1877,
but killed himself
when it failed. He
was posthumously
pardoned, and
this statue was
erected in 1899.

Kiyomizu Hall
Part of the original Kanei-ji
temple, this dates from
1631 and is dedicated to
Senju (1,000-armed)
Kannon. Kosodate Kannon,
the *bosatsu* of conception,
is also here, surrounded by
numerous offerings of dolls.

❷ Tokyo National Museum
東京国立博物館

The group of buildings that makes up the Tokyo National Museum is in a compound in the northeast corner of Ueno Park; tickets to all buildings are available at the entrance gate. The Honkan is the main building. To its east is the Toyokan *(see p54)*. The 1908 Beaux-Arts Hyokeikan is mainly used for special exhibitions. Behind it is the Gallery of Horyu-ji Treasures, containing stunning objects from Horyu-ji temple, near Nara, and the Heiseikan *(see p55)*. More than 110,000 items make up the collection – the best assembly of Japanese art in the world – and the displays change frequently.

Museum Complex Locator Map

Noh and Kabuki
One of the exquisite kimonos that form part of the textile and mask collection, this dates from the 16th century, when it was used in a Noh play *(see p18)*. The kimono depicts lilies and court vehicles.

Heiseikan

First floor

The museum shop in the basement can be reached via twin staircases outside and a central one inside.

This building dates from 1938 and combines Japanese and Western features.

Gallery of Horyu-Ji Treasures

When the estates of the Horyu-ji temple complex near Nara were damaged during the Meiji reforms, the impoverished temple gave a number of its exquisite treasures to the imperial family in exchange for money to finance its repairs. Over 300 of those priceless treasures, including rare and early Buddhist statues, masks used for Gigaku dances, and beautifully painted screens, are housed in this gallery designed by architect Yoshio Taniguchi.

Entrance

Steps down to museum shop

Rikishi mask, used for Gigaku dances, 8th century

7th-century gilt-bronze Kannon statue

★ Ukiyo-e and Costumes
Popular from the mid-17th through the 19th century, these wood-block prints depicted everything from Kabuki stars to famous landscapes, details of market life to scenes from the pleasure quarters, like this 18th-century print of "Two Beauties."

Courtly Art
This collection includes scrolls, wood-block prints, and screens. This 16th-century gold screen is illustrated with a procession of noblemen, a scene from the *Tale of Genji* (see p24).

★ National Treasures
The themed exhibition in the National Treasures room changes about every five weeks. Exhibits may be of calligraphy, Buddhist statues, tea utensils, or even armor, like this 16th-century Muromachi period *domaru* armor.

Second floor

★ Sculpture
This serene, wooden 12th-century sculpture of the Juichimen Kannon *Bosatsu* (11-faced goddess of mercy) is about 10 ft (3 m) high. Mainly Buddhist, the pieces in the sculpture collection range from miniature to monumental.

Key to Floor Plan
- Donations Gallery
- Thematic Exhibition
- Sculpture
- Lacquerware and Ceramics
- Swords and Metalwork
- Folk Culture and Historic Materials
- Modern Art
- Japanese and Buddhist Art
- National Treasures
- Courtly and Tea Ceremony Art
- Military Attire
- Interior Furnishings and Painting
- Ukiyo-e Costumes, Noh, & Kabuki

Gallery Guide: Honkan
The collection is on two floors. The second floor is a counterclockwise, chronological arrangement of Japanese art as it developed from Jomon-era (from 10,000 BC) clay figures to 19th-century ukiyo-e wood-block prints. In between is everything from calligraphy and tea utensils to armor as well as textiles used in Noh and Kabuki. The first floor also works best when viewed counterclockwise. Its rooms are themed, with stunning exhibits of sculpture, lacquerware, swords, and Western-influenced modern art.

Tokyo National Museum: Toyokan

The Toyokan (Asian Gallery) has an eclectic collection of non-Japanese Eastern art, including textiles, sculpture, and ceramics. Many exhibits are from China and Korea – a result of their long ties with Japan. The layout of the three floors is in a rough spiral; a well-marked route takes visitors from the sculpture on the first floor up to the Korean collection at the top.

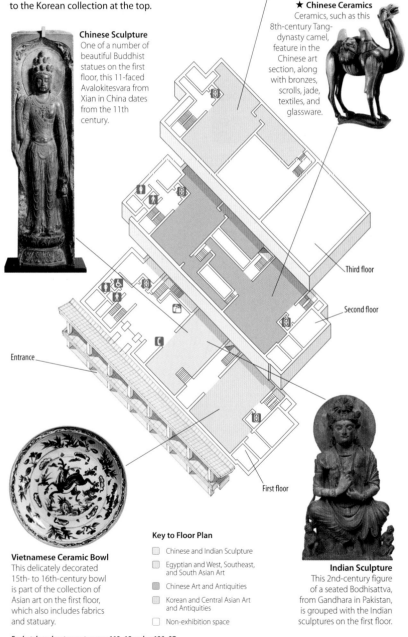

★ Korean Art
Dating from the Bronze Age (100 BC–AD 300), this dagger is one of the older pieces on display in the Korean collection.

★ Chinese Ceramics
Ceramics, such as this 8th-century Tang-dynasty camel, feature in the Chinese art section, along with bronzes, scrolls, jade, textiles, and glassware.

Chinese Sculpture
One of a number of beautiful Buddhist statues on the first floor, this 11-faced Avalokitesvara from Xian in China dates from the 11th century.

Third floor

Second floor

Entrance

First floor

Vietnamese Ceramic Bowl
This delicately decorated 15th- to 16th-century bowl is part of the collection of Asian art on the first floor, which also includes fabrics and statuary.

Key to Floor Plan
- Chinese and Indian Sculpture
- Egyptian and West, Southeast, and South Asian Art
- Chinese Art and Antiquities
- Korean and Central Asian Art and Antiquities
- Non-exhibition space

Indian Sculpture
This 2nd-century figure of a seated Bodhisattva, from Gandhara in Pakistan, is grouped with the Indian sculptures on the first floor.

Tokyo National Museum: Heiseikan

The Heiseikan was purpose-built to house major temporary exhibitions and a superb collection of Japanese archaeological artifacts. Its modern facilities do full justice to the fascinating displays. The first floor houses the Japanese archaeology gallery, with items from 10,000–7,000 BC onward. The temporary exhibitions on the second floor are of mainly – but not only – Japanese art. Captions are in English and Japanese.

★ Haniwa Horse
Haniwa (meaning "clay ring") is used to describe earthenware sculptures that were made for 4th- to 7th-century tombs and were thought to protect the dead. Many forms have been found, including horses and other animals.

First floor

Second floor

★ Haniwa Male Figure
This *haniwa* is dressed as a warrior. Other human figures that have survived include singers, dancers, and farmers.

Entrance

Key to Floor Plan

- Archaeological exhibits
- Temporary exhibitions
- Non-exhibition space

↘ Honkan

Fukabachi Bowl
This large cooking pot is a fine example of Jomon pottery, which is among the oldest in the world. The curved, deep sides allowed the fire to be built up around it, while the flattened base ensured it could be balanced when in the hearth.

★ Jomon Figures
The prehistoric Jomon period (14,500–300BC) produced Japan's first pottery, including *dogu*. This figurine is one of several female figures characterized by bulging eyes.

❸ Shitamachi Museum
下町風俗資料館

2-1 Ueno-koen, Taito-ku. **Map** 3 C3. **Tel** (03) 3823-7451. **S** Ueno stn, Hibiya & Ginza lines. **R** Keisei-Ueno stn, Keisei line; Ueno stn, many lines. **Open** 9:30am–4:30pm Tue–Sun.

Dedicated to preserving the spirit and traditional artifacts of Shitamachi *(see p49)*, this hands-on museum is both fascinating and fun. On the first floor are re-creations of Edo-era shops such as a candy store and a coppersmith's. Second-floor exhibits include traditional toys, tools, and photographs. All the exhibits were donated by Shitamachi residents. *Kamishibai* performances (storytelling using large, hand-painted cards) take place on weekends. The nearby **Shitamachi Museum Annex** (north of Ueno Park) is in the traditional style of shop-houses of the mid-Edo period (late 17th century).

❹ Ameyoko Market
アメ横

Map 3 C3. **S** Ueno stn, Hibiya & Ginza lines; Ueno-Okachimachi stn, Oedo line. **R** Okachimachi stn, Yamanote line; Ueno stn, many lines.

One of the great bazaars in Asia, Ameyoko is a place where almost anything is available, at a discount. In Edo times, this was the place to come and buy *ame* (candy). After World War II black-market goods, such as liquor, cigarettes, and nylons, started appearing here, and *ame* acquired its second meaning as an abbreviation for American (*yoko* means alley). An area of tiny shops packed under the elevated train tracks, Ameyoko is no longer a black market, but it is still the place for bargains on foreign brands. Clothes and accessories are concentrated under the tracks, while food stalls, notably seafood, line the street that follows the tracks. Tropical fruits and exotic imports fill the stalls inside the **Ameyoko Center Building**.

Appetizing colorful beer and food models on display, Kappabashi-dori

❺ Inaricho District and Kappabashi-dori
稲荷町地区とかっぱ橋通り

Map 4 D3, 4 E2–3. **S** Inaricho & Tawaramachi stns, Ginza line.

Inaricho District is the Tokyo headquarters for wholesale religious goods. Small wooden boxes to hold Buddhas and family photos, paper lanterns, bouquets of brass flowers (*jouka*), Shinto household shrines, and even prayer beads can be found here. Most of the shops lie on the south side of Asakusa-dori, between Inaricho and Tawaramachi stations.

Kappabashi-dori, named after the mythical water imps (*kappa*) who supposedly helped build a bridge (*bashi*) here, is Tokyo's center for kitchenware and the source of the plastic food displayed in most restaurant windows. Connoisseurs hold two Kappabashi stores, **Maizuru** and **Biken**, in high esteem.

❻ Drum Museum
太鼓館

Map 4 E3. **S** Tawaramachi stn, Ginza line. **Tel** (03) 3844-2141. **Open** 9am–6pm daily.

Over 600 drums from across Japan and the world are on display at this museum.

None of the text describing the instruments is in English, but a world map on the wall shows the provenance of each drum, including *diembe* drums from Mali, *cuicas* from Brazil, chimes of Chinese origin, and wedding drums from Benin.

All the unmarked drums can be played with the sticks and mallets provided. A blue dot warns that a more delicate handling is required; a red dot signifies "do not touch." The museum's first-floor gift shop sells a good selection of local handicrafts, traditional souvenirs, and even a few drums.

❼ Tokyo SkyTree
東京スカイツリー

1-1-2 Oshiage, Sumida. **Map** off 4 F3. **Tel** (03) 5302-3470. **S** **R** Tokyo SkyTree stn & Oshiage stn, Tobu line. **Open** 8am–10pm daily.

At 634 m (2,080 ft), this is the tallest building in Japan. While its main function is broad-casting, it also hosts a large mall, restaurant, aquarium, and planetarium. The Tembo Deck, at 350 m (1,150 ft) above ground level, offers 360-degree views across Tokyo, and another viewing deck, Tembo Galleria, is at 450 m (1,475 ft).

A worldwide collection of traditional drums, Drum Museum

The Floating World of Ukiyo-e

In the Edo period, wood-block prints, called *ukiyo-e*, or pictures of the pleasure-seeking "floating world," became the most popular pictorial art of Japan. They had a profound influence on artists such as Matisse and Van Gogh. Although today they are credited to individual artists, they were in fact a cooperative effort between the publisher, responsible for financing and distributing the work; the artist, who produced a fine line drawing; the carver, who pasted the drawings onto blocks of wood and carved away what was not to appear on the print, making one block for each color; and the printer, who inked the wooden blocks and pressed them onto the paper – one for each color, starting with the lightest. Editions were limited to 100–200 copies. The first artist known by name was Moronobu, who died in 1694. The golden age of *ukiyo-e* lasted from about 1790 to the 1850s. Beautiful women, Kabuki actors, scenes from Tokyo, including Shitamachi, and the supernatural were recurring themes.

A full-color calendar of beautiful women published by Suzuki Harunobu in 1765 marked a transition from the earlier black-and-white techniques. The calendar was a great success and attracted both financiers and artists to the medium.

Depictions of women were eroticized by artists such as Kitagawa Utamaro and Torii Kiyonaga, after Harunobu's calendar. This print is by Utamaro.

Landscape prints were dominated by Hokusai (1760–1849) and his younger rival Hiroshige (1797–1858). This print is from the latter's *Fifty-Three Stations of the Tokaido*.

This 1825 print by Hokusai shows the carving and printing stages of wood-block print making. Printers relied on vegetable dyes, some of which were very expensive. The red dye *beni*, derived from safflowers, could be worth more than its weight in gold. Some prints required up to a dozen colors.

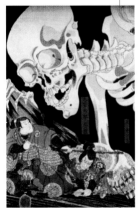

Ghosts and goblins were a favorite theme, especially in summer (to be scared was thought to be cooling). Utagawa Kuniyoshi (whose print is shown here), Taiso Yoshitoshi, and Kobayashi Kiyochika were masters of the genre, which marked the end of *ukiyo-e*'s golden age.

❽ Senso-ji Temple

浅草寺

Popularly known as Asakusa Kannon, this is Tokyo's most sacred and spectacular temple. In AD 628, two fishermen dragged a small gold statue of Kannon, the Buddhist goddess of mercy, from the Sumida River. Their master built a shrine to Kannon, then in 645, the holy man Shokai built a temple to her. Its fame, wealth, and size grew until Tokugawa Ieyasu bestowed upon it a large stipend of land. The Yoshiwara pleasure quarter moved nearby in 1657 only increasing its popularity. The temple survived the 1923 earthquake but not World War II bombing. Its main buildings are therefore relatively new, but follow the Edo-era layout. Though the buildings are impressive, it is the people following their daily rituals that make this place so special.

Five-Story Pagoda
This replica of the original was constructed in 1973.

★ Nakamise-dori
This alley is a treasure trove of traditional wares, including specialists in obi sashes, hair combs, fans, dolls, and kimonos.

KEY

① **For more details about individual shops here, see pages 138–41**

② **The garden** of Dembo-in (abbot's residence) is a tranquil stroll garden used as a training center for monks. It is a masterly arrangement of trees, bamboo groves, lawns, and water.

③ **Awashima Hall** is dedicated to a deity who looks after women.

④ **This hexagonal temple** is a rare survivor from the 15th or 16th century.

⑤ **Yogodo Hall** houses eight Buddha statues.

⑥ **Asakusa Jinja**, built in 1649, is a shrine dedicated to the fishermen who found the Kannon statue.

⑦ **Niten-mon gate** was built in 1618 as the entrance to the original Tosho-gu shrine.

⑧ **Statues donated by a wealthy Edo merchant**

⑨ **Benten-yama Shoro** belfry stands amid a group of temple buildings. The bell used to ring on the hour in Edo.

Kaminarimon Gate
"Thunder Gate" burned down in 1865 and was not rebuilt until 1960. The guardian statues of Fujin *(right)* and Raijin *(left)* have old heads and new bodies.

To Asakusa Station and tourist information office

★ Main Hall
Inside the hall (1958) the gold-plated main shrine houses the original Kannon image. Worshipers come to pay their respects by throwing coins and lighting candles.

★ Main Hall
Several large paintings hang inside the main hall. The painting of angels with lotus flowers is a 20th-century work by Insho Domoto.

Incense Burner
One of the temple's focal points, this incense burner (jokoro) is constantly surrounded by people wafting the smoke over them to keep them healthy.

Nade Botokesan Buddha
This delicate statue has been polished smooth by the hands of those hoping for good luck and help with ailments.

Hozo-mon Gate
Built in 1964 of reinforced concrete, this two-story gate has a treasure house upstairs holding a number of 14th-century Chinese sutras.

WESTERN TOKYO

Shinjuku and Shibuya, the dual centers of Western Tokyo, three stops apart on the Yamanote Line, started to boom only after the 1923 earthquake. This part of the city is modern Tokyo – all vitality and energy, fast-paced, constantly changing, and challenging the more traditional pleasures of Central and Northern Tokyo. Modern architectural landmarks are dotted around, from the Olympic Stadiums of Yoyogi Park to the magnificent twin-towered home for the city government in West Shinjuku.

Shibuya, along with neighboring Harajuku and Minami-Aoyama, is the epicenter of both young and haute-couture Japanese fashion. Nightlife is also in diverse and plentiful supply with Roppongi's cosmopolitan clubs, bars, and music venues, and the neon lights and *pachinko* parlors of East Shinjuku. In these overwhelmingly modern surroundings, historical sights are few and far between but include the popular Meiji Shrine and the nearby Sword Museum.

Sights at a Glance

Notable Districts
1 *East Shinjuku pp62–3*
2 *West Shinjuku pp64–5*
8 Harajuku District
9 *Shibuya pp68–9*
10 Minami-Aoyama District
11 Roppongi District
12 Akasaka District

Shrines
6 Meiji Shrine

Museums
4 Bunka Gakuen Costume Museum
5 Sword Museum

Stations
3 Shinjuku Station

Parks
7 Yoyogi Park

See also Street Finder maps 1 & 2

❶ Street-by-Street: East Shinjuku
東新宿

East Shinjuku is where Tokyo plays. The area has been a nightlife center from Edo times on, when it was the first night stop on the old Tokaido road to Kyoto. Since Shinjuku Station opened in the 19th century, entertainments have been targeted at commuters (mainly men) en route back to the suburbs. Amusements are focused in the tiny bars of Golden Gai and in the red-light district of Kabukicho. Daytime attractions include several art galleries, a tranquil shrine, and some department stores. A late-afternoon stroll as the neon starts to light up on both sides of this fascinating, bustling area would be rewarding.

The Koma Theater specializes in Japanese historical melodramas.

Seibu-
Shinjuku
Station

Movie Houses
This corner of Kabukicho is dominated by cinemas, many showing the latest blockbusters.

West Shinjuku ←
(see pp64–5)

SAKURA-D

YASUKUNI-DORI

Kabukicho
Hostess bars and *pachinko* parlors *(see p69)* flourish here alongside cafés and restaurants. In this area of contrasts, prices range from ¥500 for a bowl of noodles to ¥10,000 for a drink.

Shinjuku
Station
(see p65)

↓ Yoyogi

Studio Alta
Instantly recognizable by its huge TV screen, Studio Alta stands opposite the crossing from Shinjuku Station and is a favorite place for meeting up or just hanging out.

Kinokuniya bookstore has one of Tokyo's best selections of foreign books.

Key

— Suggested walk route

▪▪▪ Train line

For hotels and restaurants see pp112–15 and pp130–37

Golden Gai
Viewed in the daytime these scruffy alleys look anything but golden. Most of the bars here are just wide enough for a bar, a counter, and a row of stools. Each has a set of regulars – from writers to bikers – and quite a few welcome strangers inside.

Locator Map
See Tokyo Street Finder Map 1

Hanazono Shrine
Founded in the mid-17th century, this Shinto shrine is a calm and surprising oasis among the concrete towers. In the tree-filled compound are a reconstructed traditional vermilion-and-white building and several Inari fox statues.

→ Imperial Palace

0 meters 100
0 yards 100

Isetan Department Store
Top Japanese and Western designer boutiques make this stylish store a favorite with Tokyo's affluent young. The food hall in the basement is also worth a visit. On the 8th floor of the Shinkan annex building, the Isetan Art Museum has interesting special exhibitions.

Flags café is a convenient coffee stop opposite Mitsukoshi department store.

❷ West Shinjuku

西新宿

Most of Tokyo's skyscraper office blocks (and some of its most expensive land) are clustered just to the west of Shinjuku Station. About 250,000 people work here each day. Many of the hotels and some office blocks have top-floor restaurants with views of the city. In 1960, the government designated Shinjuku a *fukutoshin* ("secondary heart of the city"); in 1991, when the city government moved into architect Kenzo Tange's massive 48-story Metropolitan Government Offices, many started calling it *shin toshin* (the new capital). Tange's building was dubbed "tax tower" by some, outraged at its US$1 billion cost.

West Shinjuku seen from Tokyo Metropolitan Government Offices

Island Tower

Mitsui Building

Hilton Tokyo

KITA-DORI

GIJIDO-DORI

Sumitomo Building
Inside this block are a shopping center and, at the top, a free observatory.

Dai-Ichi Seimei Building

Century Hyatt Hotel

CHUO-DORI

KOEN-DORI

TOCHO-DORI

FUREAI-DORI

Tokyo Metropolitan Government Offices
This huge complex of two blocks and a semi-circular plaza is unified by the grid-detailing on its facades, recalling both traditional architecture and electronic circuitry. An observatory gives views from Mount Fuji to Tokyo Bay on a clear day.

Shinjuku Central Park

The Washington Hotel has flowing curves (inside land out) and tiny windows in its white facade.

MINAMI-DORI

Keio Plaza Hotel

The NS Building is recognizable by its rainbow-hued elevator shafts. In the 30-story atrium is a 29-m (95-ft) high water-powered clock.

For hotels and restaurants see pp112–15 and pp130–37

NORTHERN TOKYO

WESTERN TOKYO

CENTRAL TOKYO

Locator Map
*See Tokyo Street
Finder Map 1*

Nomura
Building

**The Yasuda
Kasai Kaijo
Building**, with
its graceful
curving base, is
one of the area's
most distinctive
buildings.

Shinjuku Center
Building

Shinjuku Station
and East Shinjuku

**Monolith
Building**
An imposing
building, as its
name suggests,
this block has a
pleasant courtyard
garden on the
north side.

KDD
Building

0 meters 100
0 yards 100

❸ Shinjuku Station
新宿駅

Map 1 B1–2.

With over two million people
passing through each day, this
is the busiest train station in
the world. As well as being a
major stop on both the JR and
metropolitan subway systems,
Shinjuku Station is the starting
point for trains and buses into
the suburbs. On the Yamanote
and Chuo line platforms during
the morning rush hour (from
about 7:30 to 9am), staff are
employed to gently but firmly
push those last few commuters
onto the train, making sure the
odd body part is not slammed
in the closing doors.

The corridors connecting all
the lines and train networks are
edged with hundreds of shops
and restaurants. It is easy to lose
your way in this maze of
seemingly identical passages, and
it may often be simpler to find
your bearings at ground level.
Look for the nearest escalator
or staircase up, and then get
oriented once on the street.

❹ Bunka Gakuen Costume Museum
文化学園服飾博物館

Map 1 A2. **Tel** (03) 3299-2387.
🚇 Shinjuku stn, JR, Odakyu, Keio
Shinjuku, Oedo lines. **Open** 10am–
4:30pm Mon–Sat. 🔖

Opened in 1979, the museum
has been building up its
collection of costumes
and accessories to over,
20,000 exhibits that it
holds today.

Clothing and dyed articles
from such countries and
regions as Africa, the Middle
East, China, and India are
exhibited throughout
the year. Western attire
is represented by a
selection of dresses
typifying fashions of the
18th to 20th centuries.
Among the permanent
items of interest in the Japanese
collection are modern court
dresses, *kosode* (short-sleeved
kimonos), the lavish costumes

worn for Noh dramas, and bags.
The museum also exhibits the
creations of Japanese haute
couture designers.

Late 19th-century Western wear,
Bunka Gakuen Costume Museum

❺ Sword Museum
刀剣博物館

4-25-10 Yoyogi. **Map** 1 A3.
Tel (03) 3379-1386. 🚉 Sangubashi
stn, Odakyu line. **Open** 10am–4:30pm
Tue–Sun. 🔖

A little out of the way, this
museum is full of fine Japanese
swords dating back to the
12th century. On the first floor
is an interesting display of
the process by which a
sword is produced.

The swords themselves are
exhibited on the second floor,
every detail carefully refined,
even down to the pattern of
burnishing on the blade's
face. There is also a display
of decorated hilts. English
explanations trace the history
of the sword, and the processes
of sharpening, handling, and
maintenance. Beautifully
illustrated old Japanese texts
explain the finer points of
sword-making. Among the
ancient samurai swords
are examples of works
by modern master
swordsmiths, who have
kept alive the tradition
of refining steel from
pure iron sand,
painstakingly
manipulating the carbon
content, then hammering,
and cross-welding the steel
for maximum strength.

Ornate sword
handle

Minami Shinmon gateway through a wooden *torii*, Meiji Shrine

❻ Meiji Shrine

明治神宮

Map 1 B3. **Tel** (03) 3379-5511.
🚇 Harajuku stn, Yamanote line.
Treasure Museum Annex: **Open**
9am–4pm daily. Treasure Museum:
Open 9am–4pm Sat, Sun, and public
hols. & Meiji-Jingu Gyoen Garden:
Open daily (times vary). 🎏 🎏 Spring
Festival (May 2–3), Fall Festival (Nov
1–3). 🔡 meijijingu.or.jp

The most important Shinto
shrine in Tokyo, Meiji Jingu
(Imperial shrine) dates from
1920. Emperor Meiji (who
reigned 1868–1912) and his
wife, Empress Shoken, are
enshrined here. A focal point for
right-wing militarists during
Japan's colonial expansion prior
to World War II, the shrine was
destroyed by Allied aerial
bombardment in 1945 but
rebuilt with private donations
in 1958. During the New Year
holidays it is the most heavily
visited place in Japan, with over
three million people worshiping
here and buying good-luck
charms for the year ahead.
    A wide graveled road under
a huge *torii* (gate) and shaded
by cedars leads into the shrine
grounds. On the right is an
abandoned entrance to the JR
Harajuku Station. Just beyond
is a small entrance used by the
emperor when he visits by train.
Next on the right is the
Treasure Museum Annex.
The annex holds changing
exhibitions of the royal couple's
artifacts, including clothes,
lacquerware, and furniture. A
left turn takes you under the
massive **Otorii** (big gate), built
in 1975 of huge logs that came

from a 1,500-year-old Japanese
cypress on Mount Tandai in
Taiwan. A short distance beyond
the gate, on the left, is the
entrance to the **Meiji-jingu
Gyoen Garden**, a favorite of the
Meiji imperial couple. It is said
that Emperor Meiji designed it
himself for his empress. Inside
there is a teahouse overlooking
a pond stocked with water lilies
and carp. To the right of the
pond, a path leads to the
beautiful **Minami-ike Shobuda**
(iris garden), containing over
150 species.
    Past the entrance to the
garden, the road turns to the
right and enters the **main
shrine** area, set in the middle
of a grove of cedars. Another
large wooden *torii* leads to the
Minami Shinmon (outer gate)
through which is a spacious
outer courtyard. Gracefully
curving, the roof is in the Shinto
style of architecture. Through a
gateway to the right is the
Kaguraden, a modern hall built
for sacred music and dance.
To reach the **Treasure Museum**,

either return to the Otorii and
turn left, following the signs,
or walk through the woods
to the left of the shrine. Lining
the walls of the single high-
vaulted room of the Treasure
Museum are portraits of every
emperor going back more
than 1,000 years. Objects on
display include the gorgeous
kimonos worn by Emperor
Meiji and Empress Shoken
for court functions.

❼ Yoyogi Park

代々木公園

Map 1 A4, 1 B4. 🚇 Harajuku stn,
Yamanote line.

Kenzo Tange's two **Olympic
Pavilions** *(see p17)*, the landmark structures in Yoyogi Park,
were completed in 1964 for
the Tokyo Olympics and are
still used for national and international sports competitions.
The impressive curves of the
shell-like structures are
achieved by using steel
suspension cables.
    For almost three decades the
park filled with a fantastic array
of performers and bands every
Sunday. These events were
stopped by the authorities in
the mid-1990s, supposedly due
to worries about the rise in
criminal activities. The weekly
flea market on Sundays is worth
a visit. At the entrance to the
park you can see members of
the *zoku* (groups) who used to
perform here, from punks to
hippies and break-dancers.
    South of the park, on
Inokashira-dori, **NHK Studio
Park**, run by Japan's leading
broadcaster, offers free tours
of its TV studios.

The main Olympic Stadium in Yoyogi Park

❽ Harajuku District
原宿地区

Map 1 B4, 1 C4. **S** Meiji-jingumae stn, Chiyoda line. **R** Harajuku stn, Yamanote line. Ukiyo-e Ota Memorial Museum of Art: **Tel** (03) 3403-0880. **Open** 10:30am–5:30pm Tue–Sun. **Closed** 27th–end of each month.

Large advertising screens in Harajuku

Harajuku Station was the main station for the 1964 Tokyo Olympic village; that concentration of international culture left a great impact on the area, attracting the young and innovative of Tokyo. Today Harajuku remains a fashion center from high-end international stores to bargain boutiques. The neighboring chic and expensive Omotesando and Minami-Aoyama areas *(see p70)* cater to the more urbane shopper.

Takeshita-dori, a narrow alley between Meiji-dori and Harajuku Station, is the place to find what is hot in teen fashion and culture. Prices range from cheap to outrageous, as do the fashions. Starting from the Harajuku Station end, about 660 ft (200 m) down, a left turn leads up some stairs to **Togo Shrine**, founded for Admiral Togo, the commander who defeated the Russian fleet in the Battle of Tsushima, which took place during the Russo-Japanese War. It was a huge naval victory, the first of an Asian country over a Western one. Admiral Togo remains a hero in Japan, and his shrine has a beautiful garden and pond. A **flea market** is held in the grounds of the shrine on the first, fourth, and fifth Sundays of the month.

Running parallel to, and south of, Takeshita-dori is the more sophisticated **Omotesando**. With its wide, tree-shaded sidewalks and dozens of boutiques showcasing top fashion designers and brands such as Celine, Fendi, and Dior, this is one of the best strolls in Tokyo. More fashion can be found in the **Omotesando Hills** mall

Street performer in Harajuku

complex, designed by renowned architect Tadao Ando. The central atrium is encircled by a spiraling walkway, which replicates the angle and incline of the outside pavement, creating an effective interior-exterior flow of line and form. Many top-brand stores such as Yves Saint Laurent are represented here. The complex's trendy restaurants and cafés provide respite from the intensive shopping experience. As you walk from Harajuku Station, just before the intersection with Meiji-dori, a small street off to the left leads to the **Ukiyo-e Ota Memorial Museum of Art**, which houses one of the best collections of *ukiyo-e* prints *(see p57)* in Japan. A vivid image of a Kabuki leading actor by Sharaku and a masterful program of a memorial Kabuki performance by Hiroshige are among many familiar works. There is a small restaurant and a shop selling prints and other *ukiyo-e* related souvenirs. Just to the left down Meiji-dori is **LaForet**, a fashion mecca, with more than 150 boutiques.

Past the pedestrian bridge to the right is the landmark **Hanae Mori Building**. Designed by Kenzo Tange in 1974, it resembles a stack of glass blocks. Just before it is the **Oriental Bazaar**, many shops full of real and fake antiques and handicrafts *(see p139)*. After checking out the attractions along Omotesando, it is a good idea to walk along the narrow lane that leads off the main street, just before the pedestrian bridge. The lane is lined with a growing number of small stores and boutiques, including those of up-and-coming designers, and extends almost all the way to Shibuya.

Unique fashion of lolitas in Harajuku district

❾ Street-by-Street: Shibuya

渋谷

Shibuya is the *sakariba* (party town) for Tokyo's youth. It has been so since the 1930s, when facades featured rockets streaking across the sky. Today this is the place to see the latest in fashion, food, music, and gadgets. Shibuya really started to grow after the 1964 Tokyo Olympics, and its continuing expansion has been spurred by the affluent youth of the world's third-biggest economy. The area, which lies to the northwest of Shibuya station and south of Yoyogi Park, is a mix of trendy boutiques, fashionable department stores, and record shops, plus a couple of interesting museums, and the Bunkamura cultural center. Adjoining this area is Dogen-zaka, a jumble of sloping streets and alleyways lined with nightclubs, bars, and love hotels *(see p109)*.

Locator Map
See Tokyo Street Finder Map 1

Center Gai
The focus for youth entertainment in Tokyo, Center Gai is lined with shops, *pachinko* parlors, restaurants, and karaoke bars full of high-school and college-age kids.

Tokyu Hands is a huge store full of housewares and handicrafts.

Bunkamura
A popular site for rock and classical concerts, this cultural center has movie theaters, an art gallery, and a theater.

Dogen-zaka
Named after a bandit who retired here as a monk, this nighttime destination includes old houses, now art galleries.

Key

— Suggested walk route

▬ Train line

Tower Records

A popular haunt for music lovers, Tower Records has a good stock of Japanese and international music CDs at reasonable prices.

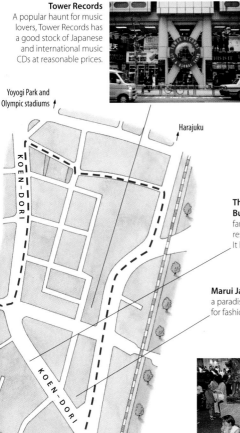

Yoyogi Park and Olympic stadiums ↑

Harajuku

KOEN-DORI

KOEN-DORI

The Humax Pavilion Building is one of the more fanciful buildings in the area, resembling a cartoon rocket. It houses the Disney Store.

Marui Jam department store is a paradise for clothes – the place for fashionable under 25s.

Statue of Hachiko

A favorite meeting place, this 1934 statue depicts the dog who waited for his master at the station every night for more than a decade after his death. Another popular meeting point nearby is the Statue of Moyai.

🅁 🆂
Shibuya Station

Pachinko

One of Tokyo's most popular forms of recreation, *pachinko* is similar to pinball, but without the flippers and requiring little skill. Players buy some steel balls to feed into the *pachinko* machine, winning more steel balls; these are traded in for a prize (gambling for money is illegal). The prize in turn can be exchanged for money, usually in a small shop nearby. Shibuya and Shinjuku have hundreds of *pachinko* parlors.

A typical *pachinko* machine

0 meters 100
0 yards 100

For symbols *see back flap*

The Spiral Building, Minami-Aoyama

❿ Minami-Aoyama District

南青山地区

Map 1 C4–5, 2 D4–5. **S** Gaienmae stn, Ginza line. Watari Museum of Contemporary Art: **Tel** (03) 3402-3001. **Open** 11am–7pm Tue–Sun (to 9pm Wed). 🏛 Nezu Museum: **Tel** (03) 3400-2536. **Open** 10am–5pm Tue–Sun. **Closed** New Year holidays. 🏛 National Children's Castle: **Tel** (03) 3797-5666. **Open** 12:30–5:30pm Tue–Sun (from 10am Sat, Sun, public hols, & school vacations). 🏛 **W** kodomono-shiro.or.jp

Favored by artists, writers, and young entrepreneurs, this district lies between the large Aoyama Cemetery and Shibuya. Aoyama-dori, the wide street at its heart, is a center for boutiques and upscale life. Omotesando crosses it just about in the middle.

On Gaien-Nishi-dori, a fashionable street nicknamed "Killer-dori," is the **Watari Museum of Contemporary Art**. Exhibits are by international and Japanese artists, and change regularly. The bookstore stocks an excellent range of art books.

Back on Omotesando-dori, follow the road southeast away from Omotesando subway station where, on the right, the stunning **Prada Aoyama** fashion store looms into view (see p16). Designed by the dynamic Swiss firm Herzog and de Meuron, the striking building is a six-story chrysalis of diamond-shaped transparent glass blocks that appears to move as the building is circled. Continue in the same direction to the end of the road, and cross the street for the **Nezu Museum**, which houses Japanese, Chinese, and Korean art and is situated in landscaped gardens containing traditional teahouses. A short walk from here is Kotto-dori, another fashionable street, which is full of antique shops selling scrolls, paintings, and porcelain, among many other items.

This street is one of the hottest in Tokyo, with some notable boutiques, cafés, and shops springing up. Returning to Aoyama-dori, near the Omotesando junction toward Shibuya, the next landmark is the white, geometric **Spiral Building**, which owes its name to the large, spiral ramp inside. Designed by Fumihiko Maki in 1985, this building is one of the most popular places in Minami-Aoyama. There is nothing in it that cannot be described as hip and trendy (torendi in Japanese), and that includes most of the people seen here. Attractions inside comprise a first-floor exhibition and performance space, the Spiral Hall (on the third floor), also used for exhibitions and performances, an Italian café, a French restaurant, a stationery and housewares boutique, and a beauty salon.

Farther along, the **National Children's Castle** (see pp10–11) is marked by a large, moon-faced sculpture by Okamoto Taro. There are many activities for kids here, open to Japanese and non-Japanese speakers alike, including areas for free play with toys, computers, music and art classes, and even a child-friendly hotel.

⓫ Roppongi District

六本木地区

Map 2 E5. **S** Roppongi stn, Hibiya & Toei-Oedo lines. Roppongi Hills: **Tel** (03) 6406-6100. Mori Art Museum: **Tel** (03) 5777-8600. National Art Center: **Tel** (03) 6812-9900. Suntory Museum of Art: **Tel** (03) 3479-8600. **Open** 10am– 6pm Wed–Mon (to 8pm Fri & Sat).

Roppongi is famed for its hedonistic club scene and is particularly popular with expats. You can find just about any music you want here – jazz, blues, ska, hip-hop, classic disco, and country and western.

Nighttime scene in the district of Roppongi

Entrance to the contemporary Mori Art Museum, Roppongi

This is also the place for big-name international restaurant chains such as the Hard Rock Café, Spago, and Tony Roma's.

Unveiled in 2003, **Roppongi Hills** aspires to be an all-purpose mini-city. The 54-story Mori Tower forms the focus of the hills. Over 200 shops, restaurants, and bars occupy the complex, which also boasts cinemas, interconnecting walkways, the Grand Hyatt Tokyo (see p112), and the richly imaginative and daring exhibits of the **Mori Art Museum**. Admission to the museum includes access to the **Tokyo City View**, a 52nd-floor observation deck (open later than the museum). *Maman*, the giant, spiny, spider sculpture by Louise Bourgeois outside the main tower, is a major draw.

The **National Art Center** is part of an effort to reinvent Roppongi as something more than just a nightlife zone. The work of renowned architect Kisho Kurokawa, the rippling facade of the building is based on computer-generated rhythmic images inspired by waves and hills. The largest exhibition space in Japan, the art center does not have a permanent collection of its own, but regularly features prominent Japanese as well as overseas exhibitions. **Almond** (*Amando* in Japanese), at the intersection of Roppongi-dori

and Gaien-Higashi-dori, is the main rendezvous spot in Roppongi. The area to the south is where the action is. Clubs come in all shapes and sizes, some just wide enough for a counter and stools. Check the prices of drinks as they vary hugely. West of Almond is the **Square Building**, full of more trendy restaurants and clubs, including the intimate Birdland jazz club.

To the north of Almond lies the complex known as Tokyo Midtown, which houses the **Suntory Museum of Art**. The museum has an unrivaled collection of Edo-era screens, depicting scenes from the Edo court; one particularly fine example is *Namban* (Westerners in Japan). Traditional decorative arts are also well represented here, with ceramics, lacquerware, textiles, and tea utensils. There is also a tea ceremony room, café, and a museum shop.

Ironware kettle in the Suntory Museum of Art

⑫ Akasaka District

赤坂地区

Map 2 E3–4, 2 F3–4. **S** Akasaka-Mitsuke stn, Ginza & Marunouchi lines; Nagatacho stn, Yurakucho, Namboku & Hanzomon lines. ⛩ Sanno Matsuri (Jun 16, Hie Jinja).

With the Diet Building (see p45) and many government offices just to the east, Akasaka is a favorite place for politicians

to socialize. Limousines carry dark-blue-suited men to the many exclusive establishments lining the streets here.

About 656 ft (200 m) along Aoyama-dori from Akasaka Mitsuke Station is the **Toyo-kawa Inari Shrine** (also called Myogon-ji). With its red lanterns and flags, and dozens of statues of foxes (the messengers of Inari, a Shinto rice deity), this is a pleasant place to linger for a while.

Going back past Akasaka Mitsuke Station and over the moat leads to a large building that some may recognize from the James Bond film *You Only Live Twice*. This is the luxurious Hotel New Otani. On the 17th floor is the revolving Blue Sky restaurant, serving Chinese food and offering stunning views across central Tokyo and the Imperial Palace. In the vast grounds and open to all is a 17th-century Japanese garden.

South of Akasaka-Mitsuke Station is the **Hie Jinja**, a shrine with a history dating back to 830. Shogun Ietsuna moved it here in the 17th century to buffer his castle; the present-day buildings are all modern. Each year in mid-June the Sanno Matsuri is celebrated here with a grand procession of 50 *Mikoshi* (portable shrines) and people in Heian-era costumes (see pp30–32).

A *shinowa* circle, erected for good luck, at Hie Jinja in Akasaka

FARTHER AFIELD

Due to Tokyo's expansion in every conceivable direction, the area around the Imperial Palace is just one among several widely dispersed sights of interest around the city. Seeking them out, though, poses few problems in a city with a superb transport system. The Japan Folk Crafts Museum and the Goto Art Museum are small gems in pleasant surroundings that give an idea of Tokyo life as well as its rich heritage. Ryogoku, home to sumo wrestling, also features the fascinating Edo-Tokyo Museum. The impressive Tomioka Hachiman-gu shrine in downtown Fukagawa dates from the 17th century. To the northwest, Rikugi-en, near Ikebukuro, is one of the Edo period's last great stroll gardens. The atmospheric Sengaku-ji temple, in the south, reconstructs the final scenes in the story of the 47 *ronin*, a real-life tale of samurai loyalty and revenge. In contrast, Ikebukuro and Ebisu are modern urban centers. Daikanyama, the chic fashion district, and the futuristic man-made island of Odaiba, with its innovative architecture, offer a contemporary experience.

Sights at a Glance

Notable Districts
1. Ikebukuro District
2. Sugamo
3. Komagome
6. Zoshigaya
7. Ryogoku District
8. Downtown Fukagawa
9. Odaiba
11. Ebisu District
12. Daikanyama District
14. Shimokitazawa

Temples and Shrines
5. Gokoku-ji Temple
10. Sengaku-ji Temple

Museums and Galleries
13. Japan Folk Crafts Museum
15. Goto Art Museum

Scenic Transport Routes
4. Arakawa Tram Line

Key
Main sightseeing area
Expressway
Main road

0 km   1.5
0 miles   1.5

◀ The suspended titanium dome at the Fuji TV Building, Odaiba

The striking exterior of the Tokyo Metropolitan Theatre, Ikebukuro

❶ Ikebukuro District

池袋地区

🚇 Ikebukuro stn, Marunouchi, Yurakucho & Fukutoshin lines. 🚃 Ikebukuro stn, Yamanote & many other lines. Ancient Orient Museum: **Tel** (03) 3989-3491. **Open** 10am–5pm daily. 🎭 Tokyo Metropolitan Theatre: **Tel** (03) 5391-2111. 🎵 for some concerts.

With the second-busiest train station in Japan (after Shinjuku), Ikebukuro is a designated *fukutoshin* (sub-center) of Tokyo. Devoid of the pretensions of other entertainment districts such as Shinjuku and Shibuya, it is a relaxed place, even when seething with people who are drawn by the area's moderately priced restaurants and bars.

A short walk east of the station lies Ikebukuro's main attraction, **Sunshine City**, a four-block complex whose core building is the iconic **Sunshine 60**, one of Asia's tallest buildings. It is built on top of what was Sugamo Prison, where seven World War II war criminals, including Prime Minister Hideki Tojo, were convicted and hanged. There is a planetarium, aquarium, and 60th-floor observatory here. The often-overlooked **Ancient Orient Museum**, on the 7th floor of the

A statue in front of Ikebukuro Station

Bunka Kaikan Center, is Sunshine City's high-culture component featuring pre-Islamic art from the Middle East and Silk Road. Also located on Sunshine 60-dori, **Toyota Amlux**, a five-floor car showroom with a designer studio and a virtual driving simulator, is worth a look. Over on the west side, visitors can watch craftsmen create ceramic objects, paper, lacquer, knives, and kimonos at the **Japan Traditional Craft Center** *(see p140)*. Besides its free art exhibitions on the fifth floor, the nearby **Tokyo Metropolitan Theatre** is famous for its unusually long glass escalator and the world's biggest pipe organ. Built in 1921, **Jiyu Gakuen Myonichikan** (School of Freedom) is a private school building designed by the famous architect Frank Lloyd Wright in his characteristic geometric style.

❷ Sugamo

巣鴨

🚇 Sugamo stn, Mita line. 🚃 Sugamo stn, Yamanote line. Shinsho-ji Temple: **Tel** (03) 3918-4068. **Open** daily. Kogan-ji Temple: **Tel** (03) 3917-8221. **Open** daily.

Sugamo has two temples of interest. **Shinsho-ji temple**'s courtyard is dominated by a large bronze figure. Worshipped as a protector of children and travelers, it is one of the six

roadside statues cast between 1708 and 1720. Sugamo's best-known temple, **Kogan-ji**, is dedicated to the thorn-removing deity Togenuki Jizo, believed to have curative powers. Street markets outside the temple selling traditional souvenirs and Chinese cures add character to this old quarter.

❸ Komagome

駒込

🚇 Komagome stn, Namboku line. 🚃 Komagome stn, Yamanote line. Rikugi-en Garden: **Tel** (03) 3941-2222. **Open** 9am–5pm daily. 🌳 Kyu Furukawa Teien: **Tel** (03) 3910-0394. **Open** 9am–5pm daily.

The celebrated **Rikugi-en Garden** was constructed by Yanagisawa Yoshiyasu, grand chamberlain of the fifth shogun, in seven years, starting in 1695. Yataro Iwasaki, Mitsubishi's founder, oversaw its Meiji-era renovation. The design recreates 88 landscapes in miniature from famous *waka* (31-syllable poems), so the view changes every few steps.

Komagome's other garden of note is the **Kyu Furukawa Teien**. Its main building, a charcoal-grey stone residence designed by British architect Josiah Conder, resembles a small Scottish manor house. The mansion and its English-style rose garden sit on a ridge above steps leading down to a landscaped area, replete with a tea ceremony pavilion and a heart-shaped pond.

Manicured shrubs in the landscaped Rikugi-en garden

Minowabashi stop, a terminal of the Toden Arakawa Line

❹ Arakawa Tram Line

荒川都電

S Edogawabashi stn, Yurakucho line; Otsuka stn, Yamanote line. Sumida River trips: **ℹ** (03) 5608-8869.

Back in 1955, 600,000 people a day were riding the dozens of tram lines that crisscrossed the city. Now, the 8-mile (13-km) Arakawa Line is one of only two that remain. The others were eliminated as old-fashioned in the modernization for the 1964 Olympics.

The Arakawa tram line runs from Waseda in the west to Minowabashi in the east and costs ¥170 for each trip, short or long. Near the Waseda end of the line is the quiet stroll garden of **Shin Edogawa**. A short walk from Arakawa Yuenchimae stop is a modest amusement park, **Arakawa Yuen Park**; Sumida River tourboat trips leave from here. Opposite the Arakawa Nanachome stop is **Arakawa Nature Park**.

The line takes in sections of Shinjuku, Toshima, and Arakawa wards, providing easy access to city sights within walking distance of its stations. These include the historically important **Kishimojin** (Pomegranate Temple) in Zoshigaya, and the **Kyu Furukawa Teien** (*see p74*) in Kita Ward. **Jokan-ji temple**, the last resting place of destitute prostitutes from the old Yoshiwara pleasure quarter, is a short stroll from the line's eastern terminus at Minowabashi.

❺ Gokoku-ji Temple

護国寺

S Gokoku-ji stn, Yurakucho line. **Tel** (03) 3941-0764.

Given Gokoku-ji's historical credentials as one of Edo's most important temples, and its survival in the face of earthquakes, fires, and air raids during World War II, the absence of visitors, especially on weekdays, is surprising.

Before entering the spacious grounds of the temple, visitors pass through the arresting **Niomon gate**. The gate takes its name from the statues of two fierce-looking, red-faced Deva kings positioned at either side of the entrance. The statues are meant to ward off malevolent spirits. The right-hand figure's mouth is open, while his companion's is closed. This symbolizes exhalation and inhalation, creation and dissolution; the harmony of opposites encountered in many of Japan's arts.

Stunningly well preserved, the complex's main hall, dating from 1681, with its sweeping copper roof and massive pillars, is a treasure house of Buddhist statuary. Foremost among the deities here are Kannon, the goddess of mercy. Eight celestial maidens dance across the ceiling in paintings that float over transoms covered with colorful carvings of peonies.

Completing the ensemble of buildings that have been designated Important Cultural Properties are an imposing bell tower and a rare two-tiered pagoda, a popular subject for painters.

Seventeenth-century two-story pagoda, Gokoku-ji temple

❻ Zoshigaya

雑司ヶ谷霊園

S Higashi-Ikebukuro stn, Yurakucho line. **R** Ikebukuro stn, Yamanote line.

To the left of Gokoku-ji temple's rear exit at Higashi-Ikebukuro, just beyond the Shuto Expressway underpass, **Zoshigaya Cemetery** is the resting place of several important literary figures, including Japanese novelists such as Soseki Natsume and Kafu Nagai. The Greek-Irish writer Lafcadio Hearn, whose books helped to introduce Japan to the West in the Meiji era, is also buried here. Scenic tree-endowed graveyards such as Zoshigaya can get crowded during the spring cherry-viewing season. Another little-visited spot, the **Zoshigaya Missionary Museum** built in 1907 by an American missionary John Moody McCaleb, is a well-preserved colonial house open to visitors.

Monks praying inside the well-preserved main hall, Gokoku-ji temple

❼ Ryogoku District
両国地区

Map 4 E4–5. **S** Ryogoku stn, Toei-Oedo line. **R** Ryogoku stn, JR Sobu line. Sumo Museum: 1-3-28 Yokoami, Sumida-ku. **Tel** (03) 3622-0366. **Open** 10am–4:30pm Mon–Fri. **Closed** public hols. Edo-Tokyo Museum: 1-4-1 Yokoami, Sumida-ku. **Tel** (03) 3626-9974. **Open** 9:30am–5:30pm Tue–Sun (7:30pm Sat).

Interior of the Fukagawa Edo Museum

On the east bank of the Sumida River, Ryogoku was a great entertainment and commerce center in Edo's Shitamachi. These days it is a quiet place but it still has its most famous residents – sumo wrestlers. Many *beya* (sumo stables) are here, and it is not unusual to see huge young men walking the streets in *yukata* (light cotton kimonos) and *geta* (wooden sandals).

The **National Sumo Stadium** has been here since 1945; the current building dates from 1985. During a tournament *(see pp20–21)* many of the wrestlers simply walk from their *beya* just down the street. Inside the stadium is a **Sumo Museum** lined with portraits of all the *yokozuna* (grand champions) dating back to the early 19th century.

Beside the stadium is the huge **Edo-Tokyo Museum**, built to resemble an old style of elevated warehouse. One of Tokyo's most imaginative and interesting museums, it has an exhibition space that is divided into two zones on two floors tracing life in Edo and then

Kabuki actor, Edo-Tokyo Museum

Tokyo, as Edo was renamed in 1868. The exhibits, some of which are interactive, appeal to both adults and children and have explanations in Japanese and English.

The historic route around the museum starts at a traditional arched wooden bridge, a replica of Nihonbashi *(see p44)*. There are life-sized reconstructed buildings, including the facade of a Kabuki theater. Marvelous scale-model dioramas, some of which are automated, show everything from the house of a *daimyo* (feudal lord) to a section of Shitamachi. Beside a scale model of Tokyo's first skyscraper is rubble from the 1923 earthquake. There is a rickshaw and Japan's first "light" automobile – a three-seater Subaru with a 360 cc engine. In the media section is a step-by-step example of how *ukiyo-e* wood-block prints *(see p57)* were produced. Models of the boats that once plied the Sumida River give some idea of how important the river was to

Edo life. Just up from the bridge, **Kyu Yasuda Teien**, a tiny Japanese stroll garden replete with traditional stone lanterns, an orange-colored bridge over a carp pond, azalea bushes, and topiary, is located next to the **Earthquake Memorial Park**. The park is dedicated to the victims of the Great Kanto Earthquake, which struck at precisely one minute before noon on September 1, 1923. Today, incense is burnt before the three-story pagoda and memorial hall to mark the catastrophe. The park's Yokami Gallery displays an odd collection of melted metal objects – a broken water pipe, the burnt chassis of a car, and a mass of melted nails.

❽ Downtown Fukagawa
深川

R Monzen-Nakacho stn, Tozai, Kiyosumi-Shirakawa Oedo & Hanzomon lines. Fukagawa Edo Museum: **Tel** (03) 3630-8625. **Open** 9:30am–5pm daily. **Closed** 2nd & 4th Mon. Kiyosumi Teien: **Tel** (03) 3641-5892. **Open** 9am–4:30pm daily.

This area is situated east of the Sumida River and squarely within what was known as Shitamachi, or the "low city" *(see p56)*. It took centuries to reclaim the land from Tokyo Bay and the estuary of the Sumida River. To get a good historical grip on the neighborhood, visit the **Fukagawa Edo Museum**. The museum recreates an old area of Fukagawa circa 1840, with 11 original buildings, homes, shops, a theater, a boathouse, a tavern, and a 33-ft (10-m) high fire tower.

Reconstruction of a Kabuki theater in Ryogoku's Edo-Tokyo Museum

For hotels and restaurants see pp112–15 and pp130–37

The interiors of the re-created houses have an authentic atmosphere with fishing nets and workman's clothing casually hung on the walls, and empty shells strewn on the floor of a reproduced clam peddler's home.

Built within the grounds of a large estate in the area of present-day Monzen Nakacho, the **Kiyosumi Teien** is a beautifully landscaped garden in this down-to-earth district of east Tokyo. A wealthy trader, Kinokuniya Bunzaemon, built the large estate and the grounds were later taken over by the Iwasaki family, founders of the Mitsubishi group. The Kiyosumi Teien is a classic Edo-era *kaiyushiki teien*, or "pond walk around garden," with plants that bloom at different times of the year. An exquisite teahouse floats majestically above the water and 55 rare stones, brought from all over Japan by Mitsubishi steamships, are the highlight of this spacious garden.

Nearby, the **Tomioka Hachiman-gu shrine** dates from the 17th century. The current building is a 1968 reconstruction, but its prayer and spirit halls, and towering, copper-tiled roof are very impressive. The shrine is dedicated to eight deities, including the ever-popular Benten, goddess of beauty and the arts. The famed **Flea Market**, the Fukagawa *ennichi*, is another attraction. A lively event, it is held in the shrine grounds on the first two Sundays of the month, from around 8am to sunset.

Crammed balconies of multi-storied apartments

Living in Small Spaces

Land, and therefore housing, is very expensive in Tokyo. The average home costs 7–8 times the family's yearly income, and space is at a premium. A traditional design has closets for storing rolled-up futons; in the morning the bedding is swapped for a low table at which the family sits cross-legged to eat meals. More and more families are opting for a semi-Western style with raised beds, table, and chairs, resulting in homes being even more cramped.

❾ Odaiba 台場

🚃 Yurikamome Line from Shimbashi stn to Odaiba-kaihinkoen stn; Rinkai line to Tokyo Teleport. 🚢 from Hinode Pier 10:10am–7:10pm, every 20–25 mins. National Museum of Emerging Science and Innovation: **Tel** (03) 3570-9151. **Open** 10am–5pm Wed–Sun. 🚻 Oedo Onsen Monogatari: **Tel** (03) 5500-1126. **Open** 11am–9am. 🚻

The artificial island of Odaiba across the middle of Tokyo Bay, is both a trendy entertainment zone and an ideal location for cutting-edge architecture. Driverless Yurikamome Line trains cross the bay, offering a majestic view of one of the island's most striking constructions, the **Fuji TV Building** (*see p85*). **Odaiba Marine Park** and its artificial beach lies on the other side of the building. The **Rainbow Bridge** can be seen from the outdoor wooden boulevards, cafés, and eateries of **Decks Tokyo Beach** (*see p85*).

A short distance from the Telecom Center, the **National**

Statue, Tomioka Hachiman-gu

The futuristic Fuji TV Building with its suspended dome

Museum of Emerging Science and Innovation (Miraikan) is dedicated to Japanese high-tech creations. Just across the road from the museum is the **Oedo Onsen Monogatari** (Great Edo Hot-Spring Tales), which combines thermal springs with a historical look at Edo in an attractive theme-park setting. In addition to having a choice of 16 different bathing options, visitors can check out old-style shops and restaurants along the main street and try their hand at traditional games.

Nearby is Tokyo Fashion Town, an enclosed complex of retail shops, boutiques, and cafés. **Palette Town**, a few blocks farther, is home to the giant ferris wheel and the **Mega Web** (*see p84*), supposedly the world's largest automobile showroom. It also boasts the opulent **Venus Fort** (*see p84*), a highly original fashion shopping experience. Not far away, the megalithic **Tokyo Big Sight** (*see p84*) houses a convention center, cafés, and restaurants.

The lively flea market outside Tomioka Hachiman-gu shrine

⑩ Sengaku-ji Temple
泉岳寺

🚇 Sengaku-ji stn, Toei Asakusa line. Museum: **Tel** (03) 3441-5560. **Open** 9am–4pm daily (Apr–Sep: 4:30pm). 🈂

This temple is the site of the climax of Japan's favorite tale of loyalty and revenge, retold in the play *Chushingura* and many movies. Lord Asano was sentenced to death by *seppuku* (suicide by disembowelment) for drawing his sword when goaded by Lord Kira. Denied the right to seek revenge, 47 of Asano's samurai, now *ronin* (masterless samurai), plotted in secret. In 1703, they attacked Kira's house and beheaded him, presenting the head to Asano's grave at Sengaku-ji. They in turn were sentenced to *seppuku* and are buried here. Inside the temple gate and up the steps on the right is the well where the samurai washed Kira's head. Farther ahead on the right are the samurai's graves, still tended with flowers. Back at the base of the steps is an interesting **museum** with artifacts from the incident and statues of some of the 47 *ronin*. Overshadowed by the drama, the temple grounds, approached through a small gate with a traditional guard house, merit attention. The temple's original main hall dates from 1612; the current building is a faithful reconstruction. The oldest structure, the Sanmon gate, dates from 1836.

Beer Museum Ebisu, with a Tasting Room for cheap draughts

⑪ Ebisu District
恵比寿地区

🚇 Ebisu stn, Hibiya line. 🚉 Ebisu stn, Yamanote line. Tokyo Metropolitan Museum of Photography: **Tel** (03) 3280-0099. **Open** 10am–6pm Tue–Sat (to 8pm Thu & Fri). 🈂 **W** syabi.com Beer Museum Ebisu: **Tel** (03) 5423-7255. **Open** 11am–7pm Tue–Sun (last adm 1 hr before closing).

The completion in the mid-1990s of **Ebisu Garden Place**, a commercial and residential center, brought this area to life. The superb **Tokyo Metropolitan Museum of Photography**, to the right of the entrance, has a permanent collection of work by Japanese and foreign photographers, and excellent special exhibitions. In the heart of Ebisu Garden Place are a Mitsukoshi store, boutiques, two cinemas, a theater, and restaurants, including Chateau Restaurant Joël Robuchon, a French restaurant that looks like a 19th-century chateau.

The crowded central plaza is a great spot for people-watching. To the left of Mitsukoshi is the small **Beer Museum Ebisu** with exhibits and videos about beer worldwide and in Japan, and free samples.

⑫ Daikanyama District
代官山

🚉 Daikanyama stn, Tokyu Toyoko line. Art Front Gallery: **Tel** (03) 3476-4868. **Open** 10am–5pm Tue–Sun. 🈂

An important archaeological site, where ancient pit dwellings and well-preserved burial mounds have been discovered, Daikanyama is better known these days as a classy, low-rise neighborhood. It is more popular with the smart set, who come here to explore its trendy boutiques, restaurants, patisseries, and alfresco pavement cafés.

Some big name international fashion brands, such as Jean Paul Gaultier, have outposts here, adding more class and distinction to an already chic district. The area, with its back lanes, shops, and home court-yards full of greenery, makes for a pleasant stroll. Interest in the area first grew when Japanese architect Fumihiki Maki began his ongoing **Hillside Terrrace**, an apartment, gallery, and shopping project along leafy Kyu Yamate-dori, in 1969. Buildings have been added over the decades. The **Art Front**

Ebisu Garden Place skyscraper complex, lined with restaurants, shops, and museums

Exhibition of flag models by various artists, Japan Folk Crafts Museum

Gallery hosts interesting art exhibitions. Closer to the station **Daikan'yama Address** (see p142) and **La Fuente** complexes house boutiques, ritzy restaurants, and trendy cafés.

⑬ Japan Folk Crafts Museum

日本民芸館

4-3-33 Komaba, Meguro-ku. **Tel** (03) 3467-4527. 🚃 Komaba-Todaimae stn, Keio Inokashira line. **Open** 10am–5pm Tue–Sun (last adm: 4:30pm). 🏛

Known to the Japanese as Mingeikan, this small but excellent museum was founded by art historian Yanagi Sosetsu. The criteria for inclusion in the museum are that the object should be the work of an anonymous maker, produced for daily use, and representative of the region from which it comes. The museum building, designed by Yanagi and completed in 1931, uses black tiles and white stucco outside.

On display are items ranging from woven baskets to ax sheaths, iron kettles, pottery, and kimonos; together they present a fascinating view of rural life. There are also special themed exhibits, such as 20th-century ceramics or Japanese textiles, and a room dedicated to Korean Yi-dynasty work. A small gift shop sells fine crafts and some books.

Back carrier, Japan Folk Crafts Museum

⑭ Shimokitazawa

下北沢

🚃 Shimokitazawa stn, Inokashira & Odakyu lines. Honda Theater: **Tel** (03) 3468-0030. **Open** daily (times vary according to program).

The really distinguishing character of this region – more popularly known as Shimokita – is its atmosphere. The seeds of the area's relaxed and well-established bohemian image were sown in the 1960s when a number of small, fringe theaters opened here. Some of these have survived. Underground establishments, such as the famous **Honda Theater**, provide small but convivial spaces for modern, experimental productions.

While this youthful, soulful district's north side is a colorful congestion of ethnic restaurants, cafés, fashion boutiques, and music and game stores, the south exit of the station leads to bars and the best concentration of live music venues in Tokyo, most hosting an array of eager emerging bands.

This grungy art village, a haphazard mixture of ramshackle, late 20th-century buildings, and pop art facades covered in graffiti, is unquestionably one of the city's fashion towns, though it remains light years away from the chic and sophisticated streets of Omotesando or Akasaka. Its numerous shops and stalls offer an eclectic selection.

⑮ Goto Art Museum

五島美術館

3-9-25 Kaminoge, Setagaya-ku. **Tel** (03) 3703-0662. 🚃 Tokyu Denentoshi line from Shibuya stn to Futako-Tamagawaen, then Tokyu Oimachi line to Kaminoge. **Open** 10am–5pm Tue–Sun. **Closed** when exhibitions change. 🏛

Set in a pleasant hillside garden, this museum showcases the private collection of the late chairman of the Tokyu Corporation, Keita Goto. Avidly interested in Zen, he was originally attracted to Buddhist calligraphy called *bokuseki*, particularly that of 16th-century priests. Also included are ceramics, paintings, and metalwork mirrors; items are changed several times a year. The museum's most famous works, however, are scenes from 12th-century scrolls of the *Tale of Genji*, painted by Fujiwara Takayoshi, which have been designated National Treasures. They are shown once a year, usually during Golden Week (see p156).

Women in kimonos outside a teahouse at the Goto Art Museum garden

THREE GUIDED WALKS

For all its cosmopolitan sprawl and congestion, Tokyo is a feet-friendly city. Its streets, slopes, temples, shrines, cubby-hole stores, parks and gardens, and architecturally stunning buildings are best experienced on foot. From modern, man-made, sea-facing expanses, and spacious boulevards to the narrow streets of the past, the walks in this book have been designed to maximize time and space by directing you through a concentration of sights, each route presenting different facets of the city's vibrant character. The first walk guides you from the high ground of the Yamanote hills, past Shinto and Confucian institutions to the bustling plebian districts of Ochanomizu and Jimbocho. The second walk is a step back in time to the stone courtyards of garden temples, craft shops, and the crumbling tombs of Yanaka, one of the best-preserved older quarters of Tokyo. The final walk introduces useful vantage points from which to take in the monumental scale and novelty of the artificial island of Odaiba. Food and refreshment recommendations are factored into each itinerary providing enjoyable stopping-off points.

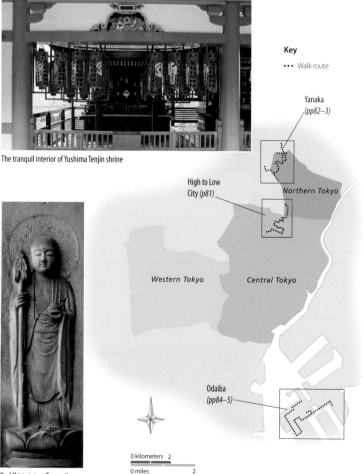

The tranquil interior of Yushima Tenjin shrine

Buddhist statue, Tenno-ji temple, Yanaka

Key

••• Walk route

Yanaka *(pp82–3)*

High to Low City *(p81)*

Northern Tokyo

Western Tokyo

Central Tokyo

Odaiba *(pp84–5)*

0 kilometers 2

0 miles 2

A 45-Minute Walk from the High City to the Low City

The walk follows the slopes of the Yamanote, or High City, down to the flat, river lands of the Shitamachi, the Low City. Starting from Yushima Tenjin, the great shrine of learning, this route includes Kanda Myojin, one of the foremost places of worship in the city, and a rare Confucian temple sitting on a bluff above the Kanda River. It takes in a Russian Orthodox Cathedral, before ending at the lively streets of Ochanomizu.

⑧ The Archeological Museum of Meiji University

② *Torii* (gate) at the entrance to Kanda Myojin shrine

Start at Yushima Tenjin shrine ①, dedicated to a 9th-century scholar deified as Tenjin, the patron of learning. Walk down the gentle slope south of the shrine, crossing Kuramaebashi-dori. A copper-plated *torii* (gate) set at the foot of a slight incline off Hongo-dori announces the entrance to Kanda Myojin shrine ②, the site of the Kanda Matsuri (see p30), one of the city's grandest festivals. Just across the road is the Yushima Seido temple ③, dedicated to the spirit of the Chinese sage Confucius. Shady temple gardens are situated at the base of a bluff above the banks of the Kanda River ④. Walk down to the river and the stone ramparts of Hijiribashi

(The Bridge of the Sages). Pause here to peer west along the river for a good view of the 19-story Century Tower ⑤, one of Tokyo's impressive office buildings; the twin towers boast innovative air-conditioning strips, and a 19-floor atrium that allows extra light to pour in. Cross the bridge to reach the

Russian Orthodox Nikolai Cathedral ⑥, with its deep green onion dome looming over the Ochanomizu cityscape. It is just a few blocks east from here to Kanda Yabu Soba (see p132) ⑦, a legendary buckwheat noodle restaurant just off Shoheibashi-dori. Walk directly west from here to Ochanomizu's main street, Meidai-dori. The Archeological Museum of Meiji University ⑧ appears on the right. It has one of the best collections of ancient objects and artifacts found on digs around Japan. In the same building, check

out the university's Criminal Museum ⑨. Casals Hall ⑩ on the left is a smart auditorium designed by world-famous Japanese architect Arata Isozaki. Turn right at the end of Meidai-dori into Yasukuni-dori and the heart of the famous Kanda-Jimbocho book store district ⑪. The walk ends on this street near Jimbocho subway station.

Tips for Walkers

Starting point: Yushima Tenjin shrine.
Length: 2.5 km (1.5 miles).
Getting there: The start of this walk is the Yushima metro station on the Chiyoda Line.
Stopping-off points: A tea stop at the entrance to Kanda Myojin shrine; lunch at Kanda Yabu Soba, a local institution.

For keys to symbols see back flap

0 meters 400
0 yards 400

Key

••• Walk route

A 90-Minute Walk in Yanaka

One of the best-preserved old quarters of Tokyo that has survived both the Great Kanto Earthquake of 1923 and the fire bombings of 1945 relatively unscathed, Yanaka is a rare enclave of the old city. Its famous graveyard, with mossy tombs, Buddha stones, and cherry trees, is the resting place of famous literati, actors, and former shoguns. A reclusive retreat for artists, writers, and designers, Yanaka's narrow streets do not allow for heavy traffic, making it ideal for walking.

④ The picturesque Kyoji temple housing a wooden hall

Start this walk by turning left just after exiting JR Nishi-Nippori Station's south exit. The quiet road here, sitting on a ridge known as the Suwa Plateau, is a good introduction to the old world charms of Yanaka. Follow the sloping road until a row of ginkgo trees and a well-weathered Suwa shrine ① appear on the left. Founded in 1322, the shrine is home to the deity who protects Nippori and Yanaka districts.

It is just a few steps along to Joko-ji temple ②, known as the "Snow-Viewing Temple." Once a popular spot to watch snowflakes and compose poetry, it has a rock in the temple garden where the shogun Iemitsu rested while admiring the view. Today only a mass of railway tracks and love hotels can be seen. More interesting are the well-carved stone Buddhas near the temple's entrance, and a bronze figure of Jizo, protector of children, carved in 1691 by a Buddhist priest-artist Kumu-shonin.

① Lion sculpture outside Suwa shrine

Walk past the small road known as Fujimi-zaka or "Fuji-Viewing Slope," a narrow road lined with old red-brick walls. Directly opposite a row of old tenements, the main attraction at Yofuku-ji temple ③ is the Nioman gate. The two guardian statues within the gate were built at the beginning of the 18th century.

Take a left at the end of the road and Kyoji temple ④ comes into view, its zelkova wood gate pitted with bullet holes from an ancient battle. Return to the main road, and continue to the Asakura Choso Museum ⑤, a sculpture gallery dedicated to the work of renowned Japanese sculptor, Fumio Asakura. Return

to the main road, turn left, and continue walking until you see a flight of stone steps descending to a narrow shopping street called the Yanaka Ginza ⑥, selling traditional crafts and foods. Follow the smell of roasting tea to Chaho Kanekichi-en, an old-fashioned teashop near the entrance to the street. Return up the stone

steps, and continue past Kyoji temple. Turn right up a short flight of steps to enter Yanaka Cemetery ⑦. With its mossy tombstones, leafy walks, wrought-iron gates, and worn stone lanterns, Yanaka Cemetery is almost Gothic in character. Head to Tenno-ji temple ⑧, adjoining the cemetery ground. The statue of the Great Buddha of Yanaka, a bronze figure cast in 1691 is the focal point.

Return to the road, bear left and then take the first right, reaching a T-junction at the end. It is easy to miss, but on the right corner, the Gamo residence ⑨ is a fine example of *dashigeta-zukuri* (projecting girder style) design. Turn left at

⑧ Seventeenth-century bronze statue of Buddha, Tenno-ji temple

Tips for Walkers

Starting point: Nishi-Nippori station, south exit.

Length: 1.5 miles (2.5 km).

Getting there: Arrive via the JR Yamanote Line train or Chiyoda Line metro.

Stopping-off points: A range of original tea blends at Chaho Kanekichi-en, and plenty of Japanese restaurants.

the T-junction, away from Nishi Nippori Station. Turn right down Sansakizaka and walk to the entrance of Zensho-en temple ⑩. Meditation sessions are held here on Sunday mornings, but the main point of interest is a 20-ft (6-m) high, gold-leaf-covered statue at the rear of the main hall; this is known as the Yanaka Kannon, after the goddess of mercy. Continue down the slope for about 100 meters (100 yards) or so for Daien-ji temple ⑪. Two adjoining halls, one Buddhist and the other Shinto, have fine wooden carvings of dragons, nymphs, and Chinese phoenixes. Across the road from Daien-ji is one of Tokyo's oldest and most exquisite paper arts shops, Isetatsu ⑫. View well-crafted fans, combs, dolls, and colorful chests of drawers. Take the lane next to the shop and walk until you reach a small road. Turn left and then bear right until the T-junction. The Daimyo Clock Museum ⑬ to your right displays a fascinating collection of timepieces made exclusively for Japan's feudal lords.

⑭ The ornate exterior of Nezu Shrine

Follow the road down to busy Shinobazu-dori. Turn right and walk up to the traffic lights, then turn left for Nezu Shrine ⑭. Enter through the impressive vermilion Zuishinmon gate, then to a second portal, Karamon gate, with some fine lacquered partitions. You will then reach the main sanctuary, a superb Momoyama-style structure with vivid carvings. Return to Shinobazu-dori, turn right, and walk a few blocks. Cross Kototoi-dori until you see a unique three-story wooden Meiji-era building that houses the popular Hantei ⑮ (see p132), an atmospheric Japanese-style restaurant. This walk ends near Nezu metro station.

GUBASHI-DORI

Nippori

④
⑤
⑦
⑧
⑨
YANAKA CEMETERY
YANAKA
⑩
SANSAKIZAKA
⑪
⑫
SHINOBAZU-DORI
⑬
KOTOTOI-DORI
NEZU
⑮
S Nezu
UENO PARK
SHINOBAZU-DORI
NICHI-DAI-TSUTSUI-DORI
⑭
KOTOTOI-DORI
HONGO

0 meters   200
0 yards   200

Key

••• Walk route

⑫ Isetatsu shop, renowned for Edo-style paper with colorful patterns

A 90-Minute Walk in Odaiba

The post-modernist buildings, art installations, and shopping malls that constitute Odaiba (see p77) seem to hail from another world. Odaiba's sheer audacity, its flamboyant marriage of design, technology, commercialism, and fun, epitomizes Japan's fascination with blending high kitsch into a concoction that is both refined and brashly artificial. In this pleasure quarter for the city savvy, a walk through this island comes with restaurant and café stops to recover from the sheer over-stimulation.

① The futuristic Tokyo Big Sight building, a remarkable piece of architecture

Start the walk at Tokyo Big Sight ①, which is accessed by overhead walkways from Kokusai-Tenjijo Station, or by climbing the steps from the Suijo water bus, Tokyo Big Sight Station. One of Tokyo's prominent architectural marvels, Tokyo Big Sight combines a convention center, exhibition halls, cafés, and restaurants in a pyramidal structure that appears to be upside down. Large atriums and an eighth-floor observation gallery provide superb views of the Tokyo waterfront development and the bay.

Return to the elevated tracks of the Yurikamome Line, following them in the direction of Aomi Station and the Palette Town complex. The gigantic

Tips for Walkers

Starting point: Kokusai-Tenjijo-Seimon Station on the Yurikamome Line.
Length: 1 mile (2 km).
Stopping-off points: Recuperate at a table with a view of the goings on at Venus Fort at Thé Chinois Madu. Daiba Little Hong Kong typifies the island's ersatz fun, and the food is good.

ferris wheel, the Stream of Starlight ②, comes into view on the right. The views from the top are worth the dizzy sensation some passengers may experience as they rise above the picturesque bay. Also in the Palette Town development, Mega Web ③, a state-of-the-art automobile showroom, is run by Toyota. Look out for Toyota City Showcase, with a driving simulator, test-drive area, and a History Garage Museum.

Cross to the next block of Palette Town and enter the unreal world of the Renaissance-themed shopping mall Venus Fort ④, a complex

④ The opulent interiors of Venus Fort shopping mall

of retail shops and cafés lined with designer boutiques such as Jean Paul Gaultier and Vanessa Bruno. Windows have been eliminated for the sake of striking optical illusions, including an artificial overhead sky that permanently re-creates the ambience of twilight. Soak in the scenery, sitting at the authentic Chinese-style teashop, Thé Chinois Madu.

DAI-SAN DAIBA HISTORICAL PARK

Key

••• Walk route

Odaiba Sea Park Sta

⑨

Daiba

SHIOKAZE PARK

0 meters   400
0 yards   400

Fune-no-kagakukan

Walk to the rear of Palette Town, turn left and move along the Central Promenade, until you reach the 88-ft (27-m) high statue of Flame of Freedom in the form of a golden needle, the work of modern sculptor Marc Coutelier. Turn left here and walk along the West Promenade until the Miraikan ⑤, the National Museum of Emerging Science and Innovation, appears on the right. This museum is dedicated to displays of Japanese high-tech designs, and one of its most popular attractions is the diminutive running robot Asimo. Experimental kits, robots, and interesting space goods are on sale at the gift shop.

Walk from the Miraikan past the Telecom Center to reach Oedo Onsen Monogatari ⑥, a hot-spring theme park that features various kinds of traditional amusements in an old-world atmosphere, in addition to spa facilities. Follow the Yurikamome Line north toward Daiba Station. Ocean-facing Shiokaze Park, a good

⑪ Rainbow Bridge and the Tokyo skyline

picnic spot with lots of trees, is on the left. Just beyond the station, the spectacular Fuji TV Building ⑦ *(see p16)* looms

into view. Designed by master Japanese architect Kenzo Tange, the building's two main sections are linked by walkways and a silver sphere containing a restaurant and an observation gallery. Aqua City ⑧, the complex next door, houses countless restaurants, cafés, fashion stores, a video arcade, and a multiplex cinema. Visitors are usually surprised when they glimpse the remarkable replica of New York City's Statue of Liberty ⑨ at the edge of the concourse. Stroll along the outdoor wooden boulevards, cafés, and eateries of Sunset Beach Restaurant Row. This forms the exterior part of Decks Tokyo Beach, a shopping and amusement complex. The Decks Tokyo Brewery, on the fifth floor, is notable for the Daiba brand micro-beer brewed on the premises. Sega Joyopolis, a virtual reality arcade, occupies the third to fifth floors. Odaiba Marine Park ⑩, a sliver of green abutting a sandy, artificial beach, lies below Decks. Visitors peer over the strip to the graceful lines of the expansive Rainbow Bridge ⑪, atmospherically illuminated at night. Duck back into the main building of Decks Tokyo Beach. Daiba Little Hong Kong ⑫ up on the sixth and seventh floors consists of several "streets" that simulate a downtown Chinese area. With speakers emitting sounds of feral cats fighting in narrow lanes and the roar of planes descending over washing lines, it is more a romantic throwback to mid-20th-century Hong Kong than the modern city's skyscraper districts. Chinese dumplings and dim sum at Shi An Gyoza in Little Hong Kong are a treat. The walk ends here. Odaiba Kaihin-koen Station is nearby.

⑤ The Miraikan, showcasing Japan's high-tech wonders

For keys to symbols *see back flap*

BEYOND TOKYO

Some of the country's most famous sights are just a short train trip away from Tokyo. Foremost among these are the historic temple towns of Nikko, Narita, and Kamakura, and bustling Yokohama, Japan's second-largest city. Hakone is a mountainous hot-spring town and on a clear day, it offers picturesque views of the soaring peak of Mount Fuji – one of the great icons of Japan.

It takes less time than one would imagine to leave behind the sprawling suburbs, dormitory towns, and industrial fringes of Tokyo to reach breathtaking natural habitats and environs. Fine hiking trails, wildlife, and flora are easily accessed at Chichibu-Tama National Park and the Fuji Five Lakes area, while the volcanic hills and gorges of Hakone and the Izu Peninsula have been hot-spring destinations for foreign visitors since the 19th century.

Yokohama, a cosmopolitan city with a vibrant port area, delightful museums, and a large, atmospheric Chinatown district combines history, ethnicity, and modernity. Yokohama's neighbor Kamakura, sitting snugly between green hills and the Pacific, is a treasure-house of spectacular Zen temples, tranquil gardens, teahouses, and exquisite craft shops. The origins of the magnificent Tsurugaoka Hachiman-gu shrine date from the 11th century, while the Great Buddha, a splendidly realized bronze statue, has survived from when it was first cast in 1252. To the east of Tokyo, Narita-san, an important temple associated with Fudo, the god of fire, is a place of common worship throughout the year. Located a stone's throw from Narita Airport, this temple provides the chance to see how Japanese observe their faith, right down to having new cars blessed and protective amulets hung on them, in a ritual presided over by robed priests. Just an hour north of the capital, the elaborate shrines, rand gates, and tombs of Nikko, where the first shogun Ieyasu is enshrined, are overshadowed by towering forests of cryptomeria, creating a mood of spiritual grandeur.

A row of Buddhist statues, Nikko, Tochigi prefecture

◀ Snow-capped Mount Fuji and the Fuji-Hakone-Izu National Park

Exploring Beyond Tokyo

The areas beyond Tokyo offer great geographical and cultural diversity. Bayside Yokohama, a residential zone, sits just above the Miura Peninsula. Ocean-facing Kamakura is an ancient temple city. Narita-san, one of the most important temples in the Kanto area, lies on the flatlands of Chiba beyond the eastern suburbs. The thermally rich and picturesque Izu Peninsula lies to the west. Topographic diversity continues with Hakone and Mount Fuji and the Fuji Five Lakes. At historically rich Nikko, the low slopes of the Ashio-sanchi range span west toward Chichibu-Tama National Park. Nearby Okutama is a favorite weekend hiking area for Tokyoites.

Daibutsu, the Great Buddha of Kamakura

Sights at a Glance

❶ Narita
❷ Kawagoe
❸ Yokohama
❹ Kamakura *pp92–5*
❺ Chichibu-Tama National Park
❻ Hakone
❼ Izu Peninsula
❽ Mount Fuji and the Fuji
    Five Lakes *pp98–9*
❾ Shizuoka
❿ Nikko *pp100–5*

Key

═══ Expressway
▬▬ Major road
▬ Main railroad
— Minor railroad
△ Peak

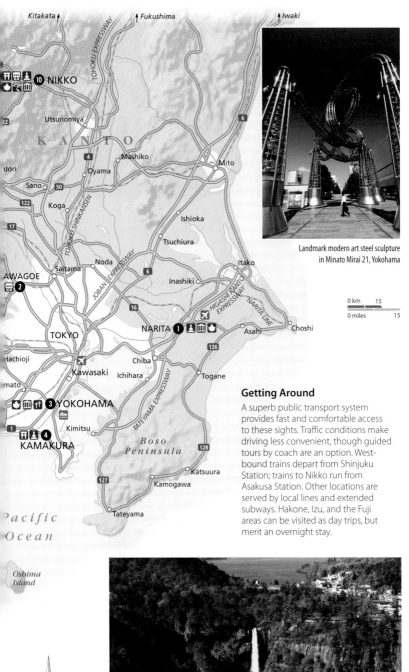

Kitakata ↑   ↑ Fukushima   ↑ Iwaki

TOHOKU EXPRESSWAY

10 NIKKO

Utsunomiya

K   A   N   T   O

Mashiko

Oyama

Mito

Sano

dori

50

122

Koga

17

Ishioka

Tsuchiura

TOHOKU SHINKANSEN

Saitama

Noda

Itako

AWAGOE 2

Inashiki

JOBAN EXPRESSWAY

6

HIGASHI KANTO EXPRESSWAY

NARITA LINE

16

NARITA 1

Asahi

Choshi

TOKYO

126

Chiba

Hachioji

Kawasaki

Ichihara

Togane

mato

TATEYAMA EXPRESSWAY

3 YOKOHAMA

Kimitsu

1

Boso

Peninsula

128

4

KAMAKURA

127

Katsuura

Kamogawa

Tateyama

Pacific

Ocean

Oshima
Island

Landmark modern art steel sculpture
in Minato Mirai 21, Yokohama

0 km   15

0 miles   15

Getting Around

A superb public transport system
provides fast and comfortable access
to these sights. Traffic conditions make
driving less convenient, though guided
tours by coach are an option. West-
bound trains depart from Shinjuku
Station; trains to Nikko run from
Asakusa Station. Other locations are
served by local lines and extended
subways. Hakone, Izu, and the Fuji
areas can be visited as day trips, but
merit an overnight stay.

A panoramic view of the Kegon Falls, Nikko National Park

For keys to symbols see back flap

❶ Narita
成田

Chiba prefecture. 🏚 100,000.
✈ 🚌 ℹ in front of JR stn (0476)
24-3198. 🅦 **city.narita.chiba.jp/
english** 🎋 Setsubun-e (Feb 3).

A quiet little town, Narita's main
attraction is **Narita-san Shinsho-
ji**, an Esoteric-Shingon-sect
temple founded in 940 and
dedicated to Fudo Myo-o, Deity
of Immovable Wisdom. Several
times daily, the priests burn
wooden sticks to symbolize
extinguishing of earthly
passions. The streets are full of
traditional shops for the 12
million temple visitors a year.

Environs
Near Narita are over 1,000 ancient
burial mounds (kofun); the best
are in **Boso Historical Park**. The
**National Museum of Japanese
History** offers a good survey
of Japan.

🌿 **Boso Historical Park**
15 mins by taxi from Narita stn.
Tel (0476) 95-3126. **Open** Tue–Sun.

🏛 **National Museum of Japanese
History**
15 mins walk from Sakura stn. **Tel**
(043) 486-0123. **Open** Tue–Sun. 🎋

❷ Kawagoe
川越

Saitama prefecture. 🏚 322,000. 🚌
ℹ at JR stn (049) 222-5556. 🅦 **city.
kawagoe.saitama.jp** 🎋 Ashi-odori
(Leg-dancing, Apr 14), Kawagoe
Festival (3rd weekend in Oct).

Nicknamed "Little Edo,"
Kawagoe preserves the
atmosphere

A row of kura buildings in Kawagoe

Yokohama Bay Bridge

of 19th-century Edo (Tokyo) in
its kura buildings. The traditional
kura structure, with thick clay
walls, double doors, and heavy
shutters, was used for
warehouses and shops.

About 30 kura remain, all
within a 10-minute walk north
of Hon-Kawagoe Station. The
Kura-Zukuri Shiryokan, formerly
a kura tobacconist, is now a
museum. Nearby, **Toki-no-kane**
wooden bell tower was built in
1624 to tell the time and warn
of fires. East of the kura streets
is **Kita-in**, a Tendai-sect temple
which includes the only extant
rooms from Edo Castle.

At one time, Kawagoe
possessed its own castle, which
was the dominant structure in
the town. Part of that castle
remains in the shape of
Honmaru Goten, the former
residence of the feudal lord,
which features majestic rooms
and elegant reception halls.

Kura-Zukuri Shiryokan
Tel (049) 225-4287. **Open** Tue–Sun.
Closed 4th Fri of month. 🎋

Honmaru Goten
2-13-1 Kurawa-machi. **Tel** (049) 224-
6015. **Open** 9am–5pm
Tue–Sun.

❸ Yokohama
横浜

Kanagawa prefecture. 🏚 3,690,000.
✈ 🚌 ℹ Sangyo Boeki Center Bldg
(045) 641-4759. 🅦 **city.yokohama.jp**
🎋 Chinese New Year (Feb),
Yokohama Port Festival (May 3)

Japan's second-largest city,
Yokohama has been a center for
shipping, trade, foreign contact,
and modern ideas since the
mid-19th century. Formerly a
small fishing village on the
Tokaido road, it was made a
treaty port in 1859; there
followed an influx of foreign
traders, especially Chinese and
British, making it the biggest
port in Asia by the early 20th
century. The 1923 Kanto
Earthquake wiped out 95 per
cent of the city, killing
40,000 people, then World
War II bombing again destroyed
half the city. After the war,
Yokohama became a base for
US soldiers. By the 1970s, it was
once again Japan's largest port.
The heart of the city is compact
and walkable.

Minato Mirai 21, an area of
redeveloped docks, has some
creative architecture (with high-
tech earthquake-proofing) and
on weekends comes alive with
street performers. Its focal point
is the **Landmark Tower**, built in
1993 under US architect Hugh
Stubbins and, at 971 ft (296 m),
Japan's tallest building.
Reached by the world's fastest
elevator (at 2,500 ft (750 m) per
minute), the 69th-floor public
lounge has a spectacular
360-degree view. To the north,

Kenzo Tange's **Yokohama Museum of Art** houses displays of modern art and photography.

In the older, more attractive part of town, the **NYK Maritime Museum** covers the history of shipping, with detailed models. Created on rubble from the 1923 earthquake, **Yamashita Park** is a pleasant promenade overlooking the futuristic Osanbashi Pier; ships, including the restored moored liner **Hikawa Maru**, which cruised between Yokohama and Seattle in 1930–60; and the 2,800-ft (860-m) long **Yokohama Bay Bridge** (1989).

Chinatown, the largest of Japan's three Chinatowns, has around 2,500 Chinese inhabitants, and a mass of restaurants, food shops, Chinese-medicine shops, and fortune-tellers. At its heart is the Chinese **Kantei-byo temple** (1887), dedicated to ancient Chinese hero Kuan-yu, who was worshiped as a god of war but is now popular as a god of business success and prosperity.

Among the many 4,500 tombs in the early 20th-century **Foreigners' Cemetery** is that of Edmund Morel, the English engineer who helped build Japan's first railroads, with a tombstone shaped like a railroad ticket. The lovely **Sankei-en Garden** belonged to silk-trader Tomitaro Hara (1868–1939). Among the ponds and flowers are 16 architectural treasures, including a three-story pagoda from Kyoto.

Landmark Tower
Tel (045) 222-5015. **Open** daily.

Yokohama Museum of Art
Tel (045) 221-0300. **Open** Fri–Wed.

NYK Maritime Museum
Tel (045) 221-0280. **Open** Tue–Sun.

Hikawa Maru
Tel (045) 641-4362. **Open** Tue–Sun.

Foreigners' Cemetery
Tel (045) 622-1311. **Open** Apr–Nov: Sat, Sun, & public hols.

Sankei-en Garden
10 mins by bus from Negishi stn (JR) to Honmoku Sankei-en Mae.
Tel (045) 621-0634. **Open** daily.

Environs
Outside the center are two entertaining venues – **Kirin Beer Village**, with tasting tours of the automated Kirin brewery; and **Shin-Yokohama Ramen Museum** (see p136). The **Hodogaya Commonwealth Cemetery** (a bus ride from Yokohama, Hodogaya, or Sakuragi-cho stations) contains Allied graves from World War II (including POWs).

Kirin Beer Village
Namamugi stn, Keihin Kyuko line.
Tel (045) 503-8250. **Open** Tue–Sun.

One of the colorful entrance gates to Yokohama's Chinatown

Yokohama City Center

① Minato Mirai 21
② Yokohama Museum of Art
③ Landmark Tower
④ NYK Maritime Museum
⑤ Kantei-byo Temple
⑥ Chinatown
⑦ Yamashita Park
⑧ Hikawa Maru
⑨ Foreigners' Cemetery

For keys to symbols *see back flap*

❹ Kamakura

鎌倉

A seaside town of temples and wooded hills, Kamakura was Japan's administrative capital from 1185 until 1333. As a legacy, today it has 19 Shinto shrines and 65 Buddhist temples, including two of Japan's oldest Zen monasteries (in Kita Kamakura, *see p94*). Many of the temples and gardens nestle against the hills that ring the town and are linked by three hiking trails. Favored by artists and writers, Kamakura has numerous antique and crafts shops. In cherry-blossom season and on summer weekends it can be swamped by visitors. Some parts are best explored on foot, but there are one-day bus passes and bicycles for rent at Kamakura Station.

The path down the center of Wakamiya-oji, Kamakura's main street

🏯 Hase-dera Temple

🚉 Hase stn. ☎ **Tel** (0467) 22-6300. **Open** daily. 📷 **W** **hasedera.jp**

Simple and elegant, Hase-dera is home to a superb 11-faced Kannon, *bodhisattva* of mercy. The Treasure House displays characteristic Muromachi-era carvings of the 33 incarnations of Kannon and a 1421 image of Daikokuten, god of wealth. Beside it is the sutra repository; rotating the sutras is said to earn as much merit as reading them. The 1264 bell is the town's oldest. Below it is a hall dedicated to Jizo, guardian of children, surrounded by countless statues to children who have died or been aborted.

🏯 Great Buddha

🚉 Hase stn. ☎ **Tel** (0467) 22-0703. **Open** daily. 📷

The Great Buddha (Daibutsu) is Kamakura's most famous sight. Cast in 1252, the bronze statue of the Amida Buddha is 44 ft (13.5 m) tall. Having survived tidal waves, fires, earthquakes, and typhoons, it now has shock-absorbers in its base. Its proportions are distorted so that it seems balanced to those in front of it – this use of perspective may show Greek influence (via the Silk Road). The interior is open to visitors.

🏯 Hachiman-gu Shrine

🚉 Kamakura stn. ☎ **Tel** (0467) 22-0315. **Open** daily. Kamakura National Treasure House Museum: **Tel** (0467) 22-0753. **Open** daily. 📷

Hachiman shrines are dedicated to the god of war; this one is also a guardian shrine of the Minamoto (or Genji) clan. Built in 1063, it was moved here in 1191. The approach runs between two lotus ponds: the Genji Pond has three islands (in Japanese *san* means both three and life) while the Heike Pond, named for a rival clan, has four (*shi* means both four and death). The path leads to the Maiden stage for dances and music. The main shrine above was reconstructed in 1828 in Edo style. To the east, the **Kamakura National Treasure House Museum** contains a wealth of temple treasures.

🏯 Myohon-ji Temple

🚉 Kamakura stn. ☎ **Tel** (0467) 22-0777. **Open** daily.

On a hillside of soaring trees, this temple, with its steep, extended roof, is Kamakura's largest of the Nichiren sect. It was established in 1260, in memory of a 1203 massacre.

🏯 Hokoku-ji Temple

☎ **Tel** (0467) 22-0762. **Open** daily. 📷 (for adm to bamboo grove).

The buildings at Hokoku-ji, a Rinzai Zen temple founded in 1334, are modern; its great attraction is its lovely bamboo grove. There is also a pleasant raked gravel and rock garden worth exploring.

YOKOH

Zeni-Arai
Benten Shrine ⑤

Sasuke-no
Inari Shrine

SHIY

**Great Buddha
Hiking Trail**

⑫
Great Buddha
(Daibutsu)

⑪ Hase-dera
Temple

Yuigahai
Statio

Hase 🚉
Station

HIGH

NATIONAL

*Yuigahama
Beach*

↓ ENOSHIMA

The head of the Great Buddha, or *Daibutsu*

The Maiden in front of the main shrine at Hachimangu shrine

Zuisen-ji Temple
Tel (0467) 22-1191.
Open daily.
This secluded temple is known for its naturalistic garden. Created in 1327 by the monk Muso Soseki, it features a waterfall-fed lake, rocks, and sand; a Zen meditation cave is cut into the cliff. Decorative narcissi also bloom here in January, and Japanese plum trees blossom in February.

Sugimoto-dera Temple
Tel (0467) 22-3463.
Open daily.
Founded in 734, this is Kamakura's oldest temple and pleasantly informal. The softly thatched hall contains three wooden statues of 11-faced Kannon, protected by ferocious guardian figures at the temple gateway.

Sights at a Glance
1. Engaku-ji Temple
2. Tokei-ji Temple
3. Meigetsu-in Temple
4. Kencho-ji Temple
5. Zeni-arai Benten Shrine
6. Hachiman-gu Shrine
7. Zuisen-ji Temple
8. Sugimoto-dera Temple
9. Hokoku-ji Temple
10. Myohon-ji Temple
11. Hase-dera Temple
12. Great Buddha

For keys to symbols *see back flap*

Exploring Kita Kamakura

Zen Buddhism came to Japan from China at the end of the 12th century. Its simplicity and accessibility appealed to the ethos of Kamakura samurai warriors as well as to ordinary people. Kita (north) Kamakura, a tranquil area of wooded gullies, includes three of Kamakura's five great Zen temples – Kencho-ji, Engaku-ji, and Jochi-ji (the others are Jomyo-ji and Jufuku-ji). The area is served by its own train station, from which most sights can be reached on foot. Delicate vegetarian food *(see p118)*, which complies with Zen dietary rules, can be tried at Kita Kamakura temples and restaurants.

🔼 Engaku-ji Temple

🚉 Kita Kamakura stn.
Tel (0467) 22-0478.
Open daily. 🔼

Deep in trees, the largest of Kamakura's five great Zen temples, Engaku-ji was founded by the Hojo regent Tokimune in 1282. An influential meditation center since the Meiji era, it now runs public courses.

Although much of Engaku-ji was destroyed by the 1923 Kanto Earthquake, 17 of its more than 40 subtemples remain, and careful rebuilding has ensured that it retains its characteristic Zen layout *(see opposite)*. One of its highlights, in the Shozoku-in subtemple, is the Shariden. Japan's finest example of Chinese Sung-style Zen architecture, it is open only at New Year but can be seen through a gate at other times. Farther on, the Butsunichian, mausoleum of Engaku-ji's founder, serves *matcha* tea. It was the setting for Kawabata Yasunari's 1949 novel *Senbazuru* (Thousand Cranes).

Bosatsu statue at Kencho-ji

🔼 Tokei-ji Temple

🚉 Kita Kamakura stn. **Tel** (0467) 22-1663. **Open** daily. 🔼

This quiet little temple was set up as a convent in 1285, at a time when only men were allowed to petition for divorce. However, if a woman spent three years here she could divorce her husband. Thus Tokei-ji was nicknamed the "divorce temple." In 1873 the law was changed to allow women to initiate divorce; in 1902 Tokei-ji became a monastery. It is still refuge-like, with gardens stretching back to the wooded hillside.

🔼 Meigetsu-in Temple

🚉 Kita Kamakura stn. **Tel** (0467) 24-3437. **Open** daily. 🔼

Known as the "hydrangea temple," Meigetsu-in is a small Zen temple with attractive

Stone monuments in the peaceful cemetery at Tokei-ji temple

gardens. As well as hydrangeas (at their peak in June), there are irises; these bloom in late May, when the rear garden, usually only tantalizingly glimpsed through a round window, is opened to the public.

🔼 Kencho-ji Temple

🚉 Kita Kamakura stn. **Tel** (0467) 22-0981. **Open** daily. 🔼

Kencho-ji is the foremost of Kamakura's five great Zen temples and the oldest Zen training monastery in Japan. Founded in 1253, the temple originally had seven main buildings and 49 subtemples; many were destroyed in fires, but 10 subtemples remain. Beside the impressive Sanmon gate is the bell, cast in 1255, which has a Zen inscription by the temple's founder. The Buddha Hall contains a Jizo *bodhisattva*, savior of souls of the dead. Behind the hall is the Hatto, where public ceremonies are performed. The Karamon (Chinese gate) leads to the Hojo, used for services. Its rear garden is constructed around a pond supposedly in the shape of the kanji character for heart or mind. To the side of the temple a tree-lined lane leads to subtemples and up steps to Hanso-bo, the temple's shrine.

🔼 Zeni-Arai Benten Shrine

🚉 Kamakura stn. **Tel** (0467) 25-1081. **Open** daily.

This popular shrine is dedicated to Benten, goddess of music, eloquence, and the arts, and one of the "seven lucky gods" of folk religion. Hidden in a niche in the cliffs, it is approached through a small tunnel and a row of *torii* (gates). These lead to a pocket of wafting incense, lucky charms, and a cave spring where visitors wash coins in the hope of doubling their value.

Washing coins at Zeni-Arai Benten shrine

The Layout of a Zen Buddhist Temple

Japanese Zen temple layout is typically based on Chinese Sung-dynasty temples. Essentially rectilinear and symmetrical (in contrast to native Japanese asymmetry), Zen temples have the main buildings in a straight line one behind another, on a roughly north-south axis. The main buildings comprise the Sanmon (main gate), Butsuden (Buddha Hall), Hatto lecture hall, sometimes a meditation or study hall, and the abbot's and monks' quarters. In practice, subtemples often crowd around the main buildings and may obscure the basic layout. The temple compound is entered by a bridge over a pond or stream, symbolically crossing from the earthly world to that of the Buddha. Buildings are natural looking, often of unpainted wood, conducive to emptying the mind of worldly illusions, to facilitate enlightenment. The example below is based on Engaku-ji.

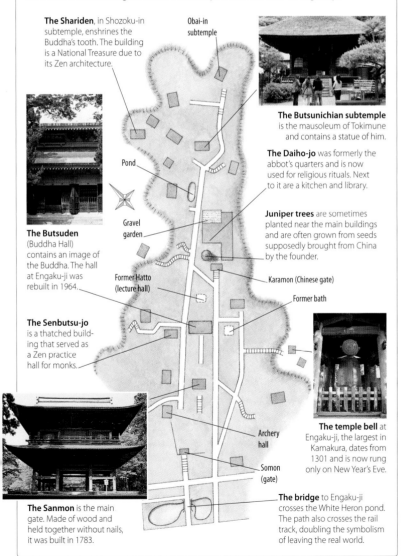

The Shariden, in Shozoku-in subtemple, enshrines the Buddha's tooth. The building is a National Treasure due to its Zen architecture.

Obai-in subtemple

The Butsunichian subtemple is the mausoleum of Tokimune and contains a statue of him.

The Daiho-jo was formerly the abbot's quarters and is now used for religious rituals. Next to it are a kitchen and library.

Pond

Juniper trees are sometimes planted near the main buildings and are often grown from seeds supposedly brought from China by the founder.

Gravel garden

The Butsuden (Buddha Hall) contains an image of the Buddha. The hall at Engaku-ji was rebuilt in 1964.

Former Hatto (lecture hall)

Karamon (Chinese gate)

Former bath

The Senbutsu-jo is a thatched building that served as a Zen practice hall for monks.

Archery hall

The temple bell at Engaku-ji, the largest in Kamakura, dates from 1301 and is now rung only on New Year's Eve.

Somon (gate)

The Sanmon is the main gate. Made of wood and held together without nails, it was built in 1783.

The bridge to Engaku-ji crosses the White Heron pond. The path also crosses the rail track, doubling the symbolism of leaving the real world.

❺ Chichibu-Tama National Park
秩父多摩国立公園

Tokyo, Saitama, Nagano, and Yamanashi prefectures. ⚡ 71,500 (Chichibu city). 🚆 Seibu-Chichibu stn, Seibu-Chichibu line; Chichibu stn, Chichibu line; Okutama or Mitake stns, JR line. 🅸 Chichibu stn (0494) 25-3192. 🎏 Yo Matsuri (Dec 2–3, Chichibu city). 🌐 env.go.jp/en/nature/nps/park/parks/chichibu.html

This remote area of low mountains, rich in traditions and wildlife, stretches from the narrow valleys of Okutama in the south to the basin around Chichibu city in the north. The two parts of the park are separated by mountains, crossed only by a few hiking trails, and are reached by two separate rail networks. Within the park, travel is mostly by bus.

Chichibu was a prime silk-producing region until the early 20th century. Today it is known for its vibrant festivals and its pilgrim route linking 33 Kannon temples. To the north, at **Nagatoro**, the Arakawa River runs past rare crystalline schist rock formations.

In the Okutama area, **Mount Mitake** has good hiking, and an attractive mountaintop shrine village, easily reached by a funicular. Stalactite caves at **Nippara** are worth visiting.

🦇 Nippara Caves
NW of Okutama. **Tel** (0428) 83-8491. **Open** daily. 🖼

Yosegi-Zaiku Marquetry

Originating in the 9th century, this type of marquetry has been a Hakone specialty since the 19th century; today there are about 100 practitioners in the area. Although it looks like inlaid mosaic,

yosegi-zaiku uses a very different technique. Strips are cut from planks of up to 40 varieties of undyed woods and glued together to form patterned blocks. These are in turn glued into larger blocks, which are then either shaped with a lathe into bowls and boxes, or shaved into cross-sectional sheets, used to coat items such as boxes and purses. The paper-thin sheets are flexible and can be laminated. Some of the most popular creations are "magic" boxes, opened in a sequence of moves to reveal a hidden drawer.

Craftsman making a *yosegi-zaiku* box

Environs

South of Chichibu-Tama lies **Mount Takao** (on the Keio train line to Takaosan-guchi). Its slopes have pleasant walks with sweeping views of Tokyo and Mount Fuji.

❻ Hakone
箱根

Kanagawa prefecture. ⚡ 14,000. 🚆 🅸 698 Yumoto, Hakone (0460) 85-8911. 🌐 hakone.or.jp/english/index.html 🎏 Toriiyaki (Aug 5, Lake Ashi), Daimyo Gyoretsu (Nov 3, Hakone-Yumoto).

Hakone is a hilly hot-spring town whose scattered attractions are both cultural and natural. Popular as a resort since the 9th century, it can be very crowded. The Hakone area extends across the collapsed remains of a huge volcano, which was active until 3,000 to 4,000 years ago, leaving a legacy today of hot springs and steam vents.

Although Hakone can be visited as a long day trip from Tokyo, it is worth an overnight stay. Two- or three-day public transportation passes are available on the Odakyu Line from Shinjuku, Tokyo. A convenient circuit of the main sights starts from the *onsen* (hot spring) town of **Hakone-Yumoto**, taking the Tozan switchback train up the hillside to **Hakone Open-Air Museum**, with its modern sculptures. Continue via funicular to **Hakone Art Museum**, which has an excellent Japanese ceramic collection and garden. Via the funicular and then a ropeway over the crest of the hill is the **Owaku-dani** ("Valley of great

Crossing the rocky scree and steaming vents of Owaku-dani valley in Hakone

For hotels and restaurants see pp112–15 and pp130–37

A statue of *The Izu Dancer* by a waterfall near Kawazu, Izu Peninsula

boiling"), an area of sulfurous steam vents.

The ropeway continues to **Lake Ashi**, where replicas of historical Western-style boats run to **Hakone-machi** and **Moto-Hakone**. In clear weather there are breathtaking views of Mount Fuji. At Hakone-machi is an interesting reconstruction of the **Seki-sho Barrier Gate**, a historic checkpoint that used to control the passage of people and guns on the Edo-period Tokaido road between Edo (Tokyo) and Kyoto.

Yosegi-zaiku box, Hatajuku

From Hakone-machi it is a short walk to Moto-Hakone. In a prominent position on a hilltop overlooking Lake Ashi, **Narukawa Art Museum** exhibits 1,500 artworks by modern Japanese masters, and has spectacular views of the surrounding mountains. Over a pass beyond Moto-Hakone is the **Amazake-chaya** teahouse, and **Hatajuku** village, known for *yosegi-zaiku*, a form of decorative marquetry.

🏛 **Hakone Open-Air Museum**
Tel (0460) 82-1161. **Open** daily. ⚐

🏛 **Hakone Art Museum**
Tel (0460) 82-2623. **Open** Fri–Wed. ⚐

Seki-sho Barrier Gate
Tel (0460) 83-6635. **Open** daily. ⚐

🏛 **Narukawa Art Museum**
Tel (0460) 83-6828. **Open** daily. ⚐

❼ Izu Peninsula
伊豆半島

Shizuoka prefecture. 🚃 ℹ Atami, Ito, and Shuzenji stns. 🎆 Daimonji Burning (Jul 22–3, Atagawa), Anjin Festival (Aug 8–10, Ito).

A picturesque, hilly peninsula with a benign climate, Izu is popular for its numerous hot springs. A place of exile in the Middle Ages, in the early 17th century it was home to the shipwrecked Englishman William Adams, whose story was the basis of the James Clavell novel *Shogun*. **Shimoda**, on the southern tip, became a coaling station for foreign ships in 1854, then opened to US traders. Today Shimoda has little of interest besides pretty gray-and-white walls, reinforced against typhoons with crisscross plasterwork.

Izu's east coast is quite developed, but the west has charming coves and fishing villages, such as **Toi** and **Heda**, offering delicious long-legged crabs and other seafood. The center is also relatively unspoiled, with wooded mountains and rustic hot springs, including **Shuzenji onsen** and a chain of villages from **Amagi Yugashima** to **Kawazu**. The latter were the setting for Yasunari Kawabata's short story *The Izu Dancer*, commemorated across Izu. Two-day transportation passes cover parts of the peninsula.

❽ Mount Fuji and the Fuji Five Lakes

See pp98–9.

❾ Shizuoka
静岡

Shizuoka & Yamanashi prefecture. 🚅 713,000. 🚃 ℹ in JR stn (054) 252-4247. 🌐 pref.shizuoka.jp 🎆 Shizuoka Festival (1st w/e Apr).

Settlement in this area stretches back to AD 200–300. Later a stop on the old Tokaido road, and the retirement home of Tokugawa Ieyasu *(see p103)*, Shizuoka is today a sprawling urban center, the city at greatest risk of a major earthquake in Japan. As a result it is probably the only place that is fully prepared.

The **Toro Ruins** near the port have well-explained reconstructions of ancient buildings and an excellent interactive **museum**. The view from **Nihondaira** plateau, in the east of the city, to Mount Fuji and Izu, is superb. Nearby is **Kunozan Tosho-gu**, one of the three top Tosho-gu shrines.

🏛 **Toro Ruins**
Museum: **Tel** (0542) 85-0476. **Open** Tue–Sun. **Closed** last day of month. ⚐

Environs
West of Shizuoka, **Kanaya** has one of Japan's largest tea plantations. Fields and processing plants can be visited, and the elegant **Ocha no Sato** museum portrays tea lore. Nearby, the **Oigawa steam railroad** takes you right into the untamed South Alps.

🏛 **Ocha no Sato**
Tel (0547) 46-5588. **Open** daily. **Closed** Tue. ⚐

A reconstructed dwelling at the Toro site, Shizuoka

❽ Mount Fuji and the Fuji Five Lakes
富士山と富士五湖

At 12,390 ft (3,776 m), Mount Fuji is Japan's highest peak by far, its near-perfect cone floating lilac gray or snow-capped above hilltops and low cloud. Dormant since 1707, the volcano first erupted 8–10,000 years ago. Its upper slopes are loose volcanic ash, devoid of greenery or streams. Before the 20th century, Mount Fuji was considered so sacred that it was climbed only by priests and pilgrims; women were not allowed until 1872. Today pilgrims are greatly outnumbered by recreational climbers. The Fuji Five Lakes area, at the foot of the mountain, is a playground for Tokyoites, with sports facilities and amusement parks.

Lake Sai
This is the least spoiled of the Fuji Five Lakes and offers beautiful views of Mount Fuji.

Lake Kawaguchi is the most accessible and commercialized lake.

Key

- ▰▰▰ Expressway
- ═══ Other road
- ╌╌╌ Trail

Lake Motosu is the deepest lake, reaching a depth of 460 ft (140 m).

Lake Shojin is the smallest lake, and good for fishing.

The Sea of Trees (Aokigahara Jukai) is a primeval forest famed for being easy to get lost in.

Kawaguchi-ko trail is 5–6 hours up from the 5th stage, and 3 hours down. Another trail, the Yoshida, shares most of its route with this one.

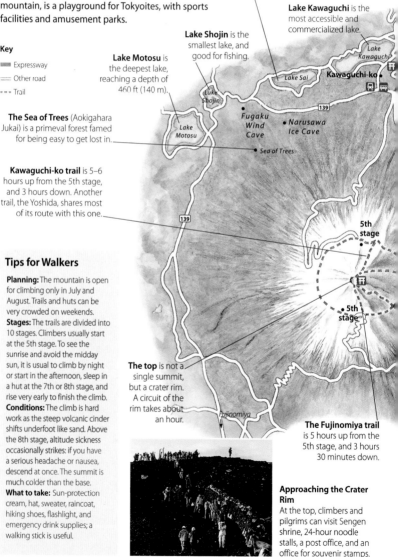

Lake Kawaguchi

Lake Sai

Kawaguchi-ko

Lake Shojin

Fugaku Wind Cave

Narusawa Ice Cave

Lake Motosu

Sea of Trees

139

5th stage

5th stage

Fujiaomiya

Tips for Walkers

Planning: The mountain is open for climbing only in July and August. Trails and huts can be very crowded on weekends.
Stages: The trails are divided into 10 stages. Climbers usually start at the 5th stage. To see the sunrise and avoid the midday sun, it is usual to climb by night or start in the afternoon, sleep in a hut at the 7th or 8th stage, and rise very early to finish the climb.
Conditions: The climb is hard work as the steep volcanic cinder shifts underfoot like sand. Above the 8th stage, altitude sickness occasionally strikes: if you have a serious headache or nausea, descend at once. The summit is much colder than the base.
What to take: Sun-protection cream, hat, sweater, raincoat, hiking shoes, flashlight, and emergency drink supplies; a walking stick is useful.

The top is not a single summit, but a crater rim. A circuit of the rim takes about an hour.

The Fujinomiya trail is 5 hours up from the 5th stage, and 3 hours 30 minutes down.

Approaching the Crater Rim
At the top, climbers and pilgrims can visit Sengen shrine, 24-hour noodle stalls, a post office, and an office for souvenir stamps.

Sengen Jinja
Many Sengen shrines, including this main one at Fuji-Yoshida, can be found around Fuji. The inner sanctum of Sengen shrines is on the crater rim at the summit. They are dedicated to the deity of the mountain.

Otsuki and Tokyo

Fuji-Yoshida, the traditional pilgrim base, has old inns, and waterfalls for ritual cleansing before the climb.

Oshino

Lake Yamanaka is popular for waterskiing and swimming.

Lake Yamanaka

Subashiri trail is 4 hours 30 minutes up from the 5th stage, and 3 hours down.

5th stage

Tokyo

138

h stage

Gotenba

Tomei Expressway

Mishima

Gotenba trail is 8 hours up from the 5th stage, and 3 hours down.

0 kilometers   5
0 miles   3

Mount Fuji in Art

Mount Fuji's graceful, almost symmetrical form, its changing appearance at different seasons and times of day, and its dominance over the landscape have made it both a symbol of Japan and a popular subject for artists. The mountain features in various series of 19th-century wood-block prints: Katsushika Hokusai (1760–1849) and Ando Hiroshige (1797–1858) both published series called *Thirty-Six Views of Mount Fuji*, and Hiroshige also depicted Fuji in his *Fifty-Three Stages of the Tokaido* published in 1833–4. It often appears in the background of prints of Edo (Tokyo); it is still sometimes visible among Tokyo's high-rises even today. In other arts, Mount Fuji is echoed in decorative motifs, for instance on kimonos, in wood carvings, and even in the shape of window frames.

One of Hiroshige's *Thirty-Six Views of Mount Fuji*

Beneath the Wave off Kanagawa from Hokusai's *Thirty-Six Views of Mount Fuji*

⑩ Nikko

日光

Over 1,200 years ago, the formidable Buddhist priest Shodo Shonin, on his way to Mount Nantai, crossed the Daiya River and founded the first temple at Nikko. Centuries later, Nikko was a renowned Buddhist-Shinto religious center, and the warlord Tokugawa Ieyasu *(see p103)* chose it for the site of his mausoleum. When his grandson Iemitsu had Ieyasu's shrine-mausoleum Tosho-gu built in 1634, he wanted to impress upon any rivals the wealth and might of the Tokugawa clan. Since then, Nikko, written with characters that mean sunlight, has become a Japanese byword for splendor.

Bato Kannon, with a horse on the headdress, at Rinno-ji temple

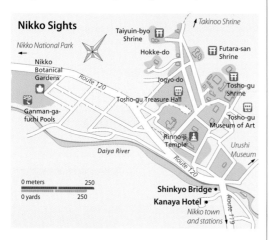

Nikko Sights

Shinkyo Bridge

Open daily.

This red-lacquered wooden bridge, just to the left of the road bridge, arches over the Daiya River where, legend has it, Shodo Shonin crossed the river on the backs of two huge serpents. The original, built in 1636 for the exclusive use of the shogun and imperial messengers, was destroyed by flood. The current bridge dates from 1907.

🏯 Rinno-ji Temple

Open daily. 🎫

The first temple founded at Nikko, by Shodo Shonin in 766, this was originally called Shihonryu-ji. When it became a Tendai-sect temple in the 17th century, it was renamed Rinno-ji. Its **Sanbutsu-do** (Three Buddha Hall) is the largest hall at Nikko. The three gilt images, of Amida Buddha, Senju (thousand-armed) Kannon, and Bato (horse-headed) Kannon, enshrined in the hall correspond to the three mountain deities enshrined at Futara-san shrine. Beyond the hall, the nine-ringed bronze pillar, **Sorinto**, contains 1,000 volumes of *sutras* (Buddhist scriptures) and is a symbol of world peace. The **Treasure Hall** (Homotsuden) has a large and fascinating array

Exploring Nikko Town

Of the two stations in Nikko, the JR station, the oldest in eastern Japan, is a classic. The graceful wooden edifice was built in 1915. Buses to many of Nikko's sights run from here. The half-a-mile- (1-km-) long avenue from the train stations to the Tosho-gu precincts is lined with shops, restaurants, and inns. A good shop for Nikko wood carvings and *geta* (wooden sandals) is Tezuka, on the left halfway up the street. An architectural treat is the venerable 19th-century Kanaya Hotel, situated on a rise to the left, just before the Daiya River.

The Shinkyo Bridge spanning the Daiya River

of temple treasures, mainly dating from the Edo period. Behind it is the **Shoyoen**, a lovely landscaped Edo-style 19th-century stroll garden for all seasons. Its path meanders around a large pond, over stone bridges, and past mossy stone lanterns.

The Sanbutsu-do hall at Rinno-ji

🔒 Tosho-gu Shrine
See pp102–3.

🏛 Tosho-gu Treasure Hall and Museum of Art
Tel (0288) 54-2558 (Treasure Hall); (0288) 54-0560 (Museum of Art). **Open** daily. 🎫

In the Treasure Hall are shrine treasures along with armor and swords used by the Tokugawa shoguns. In the Museum of Art is an outstanding collection of early 20th-century painted doors and panels by Taikan Yokoyama and others.

Hokke-do and Jogyo-do
These two halls belong to Rinno-ji and house Buddhist relics. Linked by a corridor, they are often referred to as the twin halls.

🔒 Futara-san Shrine
Open daily. 🎫
Founded by Shodo Shonin in 782, this shrine is dedicated to the gods of the mountains Nantai (male), Nyotai (female), and Taro, their child. It is actually the main shrine of three; the other two are at Lake Chuzenji and on the summit of Mount Nantai. The bronze *torii* (gate) here is an Important Cultural Property. More interesting is the tall bronze lantern, which was said to take the shape of a monster at night. The gashes in the lantern are from the sword of a samurai.

🔒 Takinoo Shrine
Tel (0288) 21-0765. **Open** daily.
A quiet 30-minute uphill walk through the woods via a stone path to the left of Futara-san Shrine, this peaceful, rustic shrine, thought to be dedicated to a female deity, draws women and those looking for love. Toss a stone through the hole in the top of the *torii* (gate) and into the shrine grounds and your wish, they say, will come true.

Shrine interior at Futara-san

🔒 Taiyuin-byo Shrine
See pp104–5.

⛩ Ganman-ga-fuchi Pools
🚌 to Nishisando bus stop.
Lava flows from an old eruption of Mount Nantai, combines with the limpid waters of the Daiya River to make these unusual scenic pools, a sacred spot to followers of Buddhism. About 70 stone statues of Jizo, the *bodhisattva* of children, line the path by the river. They are known as phantom statues because their numbers always appear to change.

🌿 Nikko Botanical Gardens
🚌 to Rengeishi bus stop. **Tel** (0288) 54-0206. **Open** Tue–Sun. **Closed** Dec 1–Apr 14. 🎫
Some 3,000 varieties of plants and flowers from Japan and around the world can be seen at these gardens, a branch of the Koishikawa Botanical Gardens of the University of Tokyo. Flora from Nikko National Park are showcased. April to July, when skunk cabbages and irises bloom, is a lovely time to visit.

🏛 Urushi Museum
🚌 to Marumi bus stop. **Tel** (0288) 53-6807. **Open** Mar 20–Nov 20: Mon, Sat & Sun. 🎫
This small museum, which opened in 1998 in wooded Ogurayama Park, showcases the lacquerware arts of Nikko and Japan – *urushi* is Japanese for lacquer. Used in Japan for over 5,000 years, lacquer has reached the height of refinement only in the past 1,000 years. The museum collection also includes examples of lacquerware from China, India, and Egypt.

VISITORS' CHECKLIST

Practical Information
Tochigi prefecture. 🗻 17,000. 🛈 at Tobu Nikko stn (0288) 54-2496. 🎉 Tosho-gu Grand Festival (May 17–18); Tosho-gu Fall Festival (Oct 17). 🌐 **city.nikko.lg.jp/fl/index.html**

Transport
🚉 JR and Tobu-Nikko lines.

Painted sliding doors at the Tosho-gu Museum of Art

Nikko: Tosho-Gu Shrine

Tokugawa Iemitsu set out to dazzle with this shrine-mausoleum for his grandfather Ieyasu. For two years some 15,000 artisans from all over Japan worked, building, carving, gilting, painting, and lacquering, to create this flowery, gorgeous Momoyama-style complex. Almost anything that can be decorated is. Although designated a shrine in the Meiji period, it retains many of its Buddhist elements, including its unusual pagoda, sutra library, and Niomon gate. The famed *sugi-namiki* (Japanese cedar avenue) leading to the shrine was planted by a 17th-century lord, in lieu of a more opulent offering.

Sleeping Cat Carving
Over an entrance in the east corridor, this tiny, exquisite carving of a sleeping cat is attributed to Hidari Jingoro (Jingoro the Left-handed).

★ Yomeimon Gate
Lavishly decorated with beasts and flowers, this gate has one of its 12 columns carved upside-down, a deliberate imperfection to avoid angering jealous spirits. Statues of imperial ministers occupy the niches.

KEY

① **The Rinzo** contains a sutra library of Buddhist scriptures in a revolving structure.

② **Drum tower**

③ **The Honji-do**'s ceiling is painted with the "crying dragon," which echoes resoundingly if you clap your hands beneath it.

④ **Bell tower**

⑤ **The Karamon** gate is the smallest at Tosho-gu.

⑥ **Haiden (sanctuary)**

⑦ **Honden (inner sanctuary)**

⑧ **The three sacred storehouses** are built according to a traditional design.

⑨ **The Niomon** (or Omotemon) gate is guarded by two fearsome Nio figures, one with an open mouth to pronounce the first letter of the Sanskrit alphabet (ah), the other with a closed mouth for the last letter (un).

⑩ **Ticket office**

⑪ **Granite torii (gate)**

Sacred Fountain
The granite basin (1618), for ritual purification, is covered with an ornate Chinese-style roof.

Tokugawa Ieyasu

Ieyasu (1543–1616) was a wily strategist and master politician who founded the dynasty that would rule Japan for more than 250 years. Born the son of a minor lord, he spent his life accumulating power, not becoming shogun until 1603, when he was 60. Ieyasu built his capital at the swampy village of Edo (now Tokyo), and his rule saw the start of the blooming of Edo culture. He ensured that after his death, he would be enshrined as a god and *gongen* (incarnation of the Buddha). His posthumous name was Tosho-Daigongen ("the great incarnation illuminating the East").

Ieyasu's treasure tower, containing his ashes

VISITORS' CHECKLIST

Practical Information
Tel (0288) 54-0560.
Open 8am–5pm daily (4pm Nov–Mar).

★ Pagoda
Donated by a *daimyo* (feudal lord) in 1650, this five-story pagoda was rebuilt in 1818 after a fire. Each story represents an element – earth, water, fire, wind, and heaven – in ascending order.

To Ieyasu's tomb and treasure tower

⑧ ⑨ ⑩ ⑪

Entrance

★ Sacred Stable
A carving of the three wise monkeys decorates this unpainted wooden building. A horse given by the New Zealand government is stabled here for several hours a day.

Nikko: Taiyuin-Byo Shrine

Completed in 1653, Taiyuin-byo Shrine is the mausoleum of Tokugawa Iemitsu (1604–51), the grandson of Ieyasu *(see p103)* and powerful third shogun, who closed Japan to foreign commerce and isolated it from the world for over 200 years. Tayuin is his posthumous Buddhist name. If Tosho-gu is splendid, Taiyuin-byo is sublime. Set in a grove of Japanese cedars, it has a number of ornate gates ascending to the Haiden (sanctuary) and Honden (inner sanctuary). The shogun's ashes are entombed beyond the sixth and final gate.

Kokamon Gate
This striking Ming-dynasty Chinese-style massive gate is beside the picturesque path to Iemitsu's tomb.

★ Haiden
Decorated with lovely carvings of dragons, the Haiden (Hall of Worship) also has some famous 17th-century lion paintings by Kano School painters.

Niomon Gate
This marks the main entrance to the shrine. A single Nio warrior god stands guard on each side.

KEY

① **The drum tower** leads to Honji-do hall, with a painting of a dragon on its huge ceiling.

② **The Karamon** gate is adorned with delicate carvings, such as a pair of cranes.

③ **The Ai No Ma** is a richly decorated connecting chamber.

④ **The Honden** (usually closed to the public) holds a gilded Buddhist altar with a wooden statue of Iemitsu.

⑤ **Stone lanterns** were donated over the years by *daimyo* (feudal lords).

Entrance

For hotels and restaurants see pp112–15 and pp130–37

VISITORS' CHECKLIST

Practical Information
Tel (0288) 53-1567.
Open 8am–5pm daily
(4pm Nov–Mar).

Bell Tower
This structure forms a pair with the
drum tower. Though no longer
used, the drum signifies positive/
birth, while the bell negative/death.

Yashamon Gate
The third gate is beautifully gilded and
contains four statues of Yasha, a fierce
guardian spirit. It is also known as
Botanmon, or peony gate, after its
detailed peony carvings.

★ Nitenmon Gate
Four guardian statues occupy
the niches here. At the front are
the gods Komoku and Jikoku,
while at the back are the
green god of wind and
the red god of thunder.

Granite Fountain
On the ceiling above the
basin is a dragon painting
by Kano Yasunobu, which
is sometimes reflected in
the water below.

TRAVELERS' NEEDS

WHERE TO STAY

The choice of accommodation in Tokyo can be truly overwhelming, ranging from five-star skyscraper hotels and well-known foreign brand-name chains to cozy boutique hotels and *ryokan* (see p110), or traditional Japanese inns. A stay at a higher-end *ryokan* – where you sleep on futons (mattresses), soak in aromatic cedar tubs, and enjoy *kaiseki (see p118)* dinners served in private rooms – can be a truly memorable experience. But one thing that all hotels – from opulent establishments to family-run *minshuku (see p111)* – have in common is a concern for comfort combined with a long tradition of hospitality. Most accommodations are fairly central, usually located near the main line and metro stations, but if you can forego designer interiors and spectacular night views, there are cheaper options available on the fringes of the central districts.

Booking and Paying

The **Japanese Inn Group** is a useful organization for finding *ryokan* and hotels geared to receiving foreign visitors, although the number of listings is somewhat limited. The booking website **Jalan**, which is popular locally, offers many more options, including some very reasonable bargains, but, unfortunately, only some of the listings are in English. Booking accommodation in advance is advisable, especially during major public holidays (see p33). Rates quoted are sometimes per person, not per room, especially when wanting to stay at a *ryokan*.

Most hotels accept all major credit cards. The bill is usually payable on departure, but business hotels and some others may request advance payment. In the case of love hotels, advance payment is almost always the norm.

Elegant room with a view at the Grand Hyatt Tokyo *(see p112)*

Deluxe Hotels

Top American chains – such as Hilton, Sheraton, Hyatt, Four Seasons, and Westin – are well established in Tokyo. Japanese-owned hotels range from over-the-top opulence and discreet exclusivity to chic minimalism and quaint eccentricity. "Intelligent" hotels are common; they feature rooms that monitor temperature, computerized toilets, a voicemail message system, MP3 docks, and Wi-Fi.

Deluxe hotels often have popular restaurants and bars, many with spectacular views. Some even have small shopping malls that offer not just restaurants, but also convenience stores and even post offices.

Business Hotels

Many lower- and mid-range hotels in Tokyo fall into the business category *(bijinesu hoteru)*. Although they cater mainly to budget-conscious business travelers, anyone can stay, and since they are generally located within easy reach of stations on the Yamanote Line, they are very convenient. Do not expect English to be spoken.

Rooms are Western-style, functional, small, and spotlessly clean. Slippers and a cotton robe are generally supplied. There is no room service, but there are usually vending machines and often at least one restaurant with a good choice of traditional Japanese or Western-style breakfasts.

Capsule Hotels

Unique to Japan, these hotels feature encapsulated beds in and out of which guests must crawl as there is no room to stand up. Rattan blinds or curtains can be pulled across for privacy. Usually constructed in two tiers, they cater mainly to *salarymen* who are too tired or inebriated to catch the last train home. Most are clustered around major train stations or nightlife areas. Facilities include

Entrance to the 52-story Park Tower, Park Hyatt Tokyo *(see p112)*

◄ A rack full of colorful kimonos in a shop in Tokyo

a personal TV, radio, alarm call system, and air-conditioning. Smoking is not allowed inside the capsule, but there is usually a communal smoking room, usually with vending machines selling beer, sake, soft drinks, and sometimes snacks. Japanese-style baths and often saunas are included in the price; sometimes bathing facilities can be surprisingly extensive, including jet massage and cold-water pools. Most capsule hotels have TV lounges and restaurants selling Japanese food and beverages. Some even have small video arcades.

The size of such hotels varies widely, ranging from 50 capsules to over 600. Most still cater only to men, but the number of capsule hotels catering to female guests is rising. These establishments usually have a women-only floor. Expect to pay ¥3,500–¥5,000 in cash. It is only possible to check into a capsule hotel for one night at a time, although it is common for people to stay for multiple nights in a row. In this case, you must check out in the morning and check in again later in the day. It is usually not possible to store luggage at the reception.

Love Hotels

Designed for dating couples and married partners who live with extended families and feel in need of some privacy, love hotels are mainly found in entertainment areas and along expressways and highways, much like motels. Dual pricing applies – typically ¥3,500 for a two-hour rest, and ¥7,000–¥8,000 for an overnight stay, although the more luxury places will charge more. Love hotels can be an affordable way to stay in a relatively luxurious hotel, though some caution is required. If you check in too early, you may be charged an hourly, rather than overnight, rate. The overnight rate is usually only available after 10pm, but this depends on the hotel. As with capsule hotels, it is only possible to check into a love hotel for one night at a time. Rooms are fairly spacious, clean, and with a private bath.

Couples choose their room from a photo board, then pay either a cashier who sits behind a screen or at a machine. They then receive their key. English is not usually spoken, and room rates and payment instructions are almost always in Japanese. Credit cards are not accepted.

Youth Hostels

Cheap, clean, and open to people of all ages, youth hostels in Tokyo are the cheapest option for travelers. They do not usually require membership, and rates run from ¥2,500 to ¥4,000. Payment is in cash only. All meals come at an additional cost. Many youth hostels have a curfew, so it is worth checking first if you may stay out late.

Sparse but pristine interior of a youth hostel in central Tokyo

Recommended Hotels

The hotels recommended in these listings feature a wide selection to suit every budget and requirement. As well as the best and most luxurious international deluxe hotels, *ryokan* (traditional Japanese inns) are also included, where a relaxing soak in a thermal hot-spring bath is an unforgettable part of the experience. For the more budget-conscious traveler, there is a range of business hotels to choose from and also *minshuku* (family-run B&Bs), often located away from the city center. In Tokyo, a hotel isn't just a place to spend the night – it can also be a unique part of the travel experience. So novel accommodation options such as capsule and love hotels are included; as well as being unusual, these places can also be good value for money. The DK Choice identifies establishments that have one or more exceptional qualities, such as featuring top-class amenities, being great value for money, or having unique style.

For JNTO offices and website see p159.

DIRECTORY

Jalan
🅦 jalan.net/en/japan_hotels_ryokan/

Japanese Inn Group
Tel (06) 6225-3611.
🅦 japaneseinngroup.com

Japan City Hotel Association
🅦 jcha.or.jp/english

The East Lobby at the Mandarin Oriental Tokyo *(see p112)*

Traditional Accommodations

A *ryokan* is a unique fusion of private and communal styles of living. Such Japanese traditions as removing shoes at the right point *(see p161)* are important, no matter what the cost of the room, and the most expensive of these traditional inns may demand a high level of etiquette. A family-run *minshuku* – a type of guesthouse – is an even more intimate way to experience the Japanese lifestyle. There are also options that are *ryokan* at heart, but with Western-style touches, such as private bathrooms or beds rather than futons.

Ryokan Sawanoya, in a quiet neighborhood near Ueno Park *(see p115)*

What is a Ryokan?

A *ryokan* is a traditional inn, often associated with older towns or mountain and hot-spring areas. While top-end Tokyo *ryokan* can be relied on to have many of the traditional graces found in their rural counterparts, mid-range *ryokan*, with modern touches and conveniences, can be a little different. Some are set in Edo-period buildings – confections of wood, glass, bamboo, paper screens, and *tatami* matting.

Certain important Japanese customs apply. The greatest surprise for many foreigners is that bathing facilities are traditionally communal, not private. They may also be quite elaborate, and when it is part of a hot-spring resort, the establishment is called an *onsen*.

Most *ryokan* place emphasis on the quality of their meals, and the room price often includes breakfast and dinner. This can be ideal in quiet areas where few restaurants are open in the evening, but a constraint elsewhere.

Another possible problem, mainly for elderly foreigners,

is the Japanese tradition of living at floor level, using legless chairs and beds.

Note that many *ryokan* impose a curfew around 11pm, so check before you step out, or make arrangements about keys in advance if you plan to stay out late.

Arriving at a Ryokan

Guests usually check into a *ryokan* in the mid- to late afternoon, to allow plenty of time for bathing and dinner. At larger *ryokan*, there may be a doorman to smooth the way, but in smaller establishments, guests should slide open the front door and politely call *"gomen kudasai"* to announce their arrival.

At this point, the *okamisan* (female owner or manager) usually appears, often dressed in an attractive kimono; this is the signal to remove outdoor shoes and step into a pair of waiting house slippers *(see p161)*. Before entering the guestroom, remove the house slippers and leave them outside the door.

Typical Rooms

Guestrooms are floored in *tatami* mats. Normally in one corner of the room is an alcove, called *tokonoma*, which may contain a hanging scroll, flowers, or other artifacts. There will also be a low table surrounded by cushions *(zabuton)* or folding chairs. On the table top will be a tray, bearing a tea set and possibly *wagashi* sweets *(see p128)*.

Your futon mattress and bedding will be stowed in cupboards when you first enter the room. These will usually be laid out discreetly for you in the evening while you are out of the room.

Ordinarily a room will be further supplied with a TV, air conditioner, and/or heater. There is usually a telephone, although it may not have an international connection. You should also find a small towel in a box or basket, which you can take to the communal bathroom to use as a washcloth. A personal outdoor bath *(rotenburo)* counts as a luxury, but it is not uncommon for there to be a small Western-style shower in the bathroom, which one can use as an alternative to the communal bathing areas. A screened-off veranda, with Western-style table and armchairs, is also commonplace.

As is the case everywhere in Japan, you should walk only in bare feet or socks on the *tatami*.

Wearing Yukata

Somewhere in the room will be traditional robes *(yukata)* for you to wear. Most people change into *yukata* for the duration of their stay, since the loose-cotton kimonos

Room with *tatami* mats, low table, and *zabuton*, plus a Western-style daybed

Small communal bath and separate low shower for cleansing

symbolize relaxation and leisure time. In resort towns and hot springs, they are even worn outside on the streets, together with the high wooden sandals called *geta*. A loose jacket may also be provided during the colder months. It is best to follow the example of others as to exactly where and when to wear the robes.

Fold *yukata* left-side over right, as right-side over left is the way a kimono is traditionally folded when a corpse is being dressed for burial or cremation. Use the *obi* sash provided to secure the gown.

Bathing Arrangements

Within the *ryokan* will be at least one communal bath; high-end establishments often have multiple baths, saunas, water-jet massage pools, and even an attractive Japanese-style garden to admire while you bathe.

In smaller *ryokan* with only one bath, bathing times may differ for men and women. In larger establishments, bathing is segregated, with one entrance for men and another for women. Mixed-sex bathing is very rare these days. The size of the bath and bathroom naturally dictates how many people can bathe at any one time. Check with the *okamisan* if you are unsure about the house rules. In the bathroom, there will be an area for undressing, a low shower or tap area, and the large bath itself. The golden rule to observe is that you must shower first and not enter the

hot bath until you are clean. The bath itself is intended only for relaxation. The same bathwater is used by other guests; thus it is considered extremely bad manners to contaminate it either with an unwashed body or soap and shampoo. A wash cloth is often used for modesty purposes while walking around the bathing area, but this should be placed on the shoulder of the bath when you actually enter the water.

Eating Arrangements

Meals are sometimes served in a dining room, but more often in the room by a maid or the *okamisan*. The more exclusive the establishment, the more likely it is that meals will be served in private.

Meal times are usually set quite early in the evening. Depending on the situation,

People wearing *yukata*, the design of which is often specific to each *ryokan*

the *okamisan* may stay for a while, explaining the dishes, demonstrating how they should be eaten, and chatting; or she may leave discreetly, returning only to clear the table.

Staying in a Minshuku or Pension

A *minshuku* is a family-run pension that is opened to travelers as and when demand requires. With rates ranging from ¥5,000 to ¥9,000, this is an economical option, as well as a good opportunity to see how people live. The atmosphere is more homely; guests are treated as part of the family at meal-times and bathtime, and they should fold up and stow away their own bedding.

Western-style pensions are also popular. Located mostly in resort areas, they are rustic and relaxed in style and offer good, hearty meals. Generally managed by married couples, they fall somewhere between a *minshuku* and the more service-oriented pamperings of a small hotel.

Temple Lodgings

Staying at a *shukubo* (on the grounds of a temple) is a great way to experience Japanese culture, but this is mostly confined to areas beyond Tokyo; see **Temple Lodging in Japan** for details. *Shukubo* are more than just places to stay, and many encourage their guests to join *zazen* meditation sessions or participate in other spiritual activities. There is also a chance to try *shojin ryori*, Japan's unique, vegetarian temple cuisine.

DIRECTORY

Japan Minshuku Center
Tel (0120) 07-6556.
ⓦ minshuku.jp

Japan Ryokan Association
Tel (03) 3231-5310.
ⓦ ryokan.or.jp

Temple Lodging in Japan
ⓦ templelodging.com

Where to Stay

Deluxe Hotels

Central Tokyo

Imperial Hotel ¥¥¥
1-1-1 Uchisawaicho, Chiyoda-ku
Tel *(03) 3504-1111* **Map** 5 B2
W imperialhotel.co.jp
First opened in 1890, the Imperial is one of Tokyo's oldest and most prestigious hotels.

InterContinental Tokyo Bay ¥¥¥
1-16-2 Kaigan, Minato-ku
Tel *(03) 5404-2222* **Map** 5 B5
W interconti-tokyo.com
Guests here enjoy stunning views of landmarks such as the Tokyo SkyTree and the Rainbow Bridge.

Mandarin Oriental Tokyo ¥¥¥
2-1-1 Nihonbashi-Muromachi, Chuo-ku
Tel *(03) 3270-8800* **Map** 5 C1
W mandarinoriental.com/tokyo
Tokyo's most luxurious hotel, with a massive Presidential Suite.

The Palace Hotel ¥¥¥
1-1-1 Marunouchi, Chiyoda-ku
Tel *(03) 3211-5211* **Map** 5 B1
W en.palacehoteltokyo.com
The decor in the spacious rooms is inspired by the Imperial Palace.

Peninsula Hotel Tokyo ¥¥¥
1-8-1 Yurakucho, Chiyoda-ku
Tel *(03) 6270-2888* **Map** 5 B2
W peninsula.com
A sophisticated hotel close to the Imperial Palace. The spa facilities are highly regarded.

The Tokyo Station Hotel ¥¥¥
1-9-1 Marunouchi, Chiyoda-ku
Tel *(03) 5220-1111* **Map** 5 C1
W thetokyostationhotel.jp
History, convenience, and elegance all rolled into one at this 1915 hotel located inside the iconic Tokyo Station building.

Northern Tokyo

Asakusa View Hotel ¥¥¥
3-17-1 Nishi-Asakusa, Taito-ku
Tel *(03) 3847-1111* **Map** 4 E2
W viewhotels.co.jp
Comfortable rooms have views of old and new Tokyo – from Senso-ji Temple to the SkyTree.

The Gate Hotel Kaminarimon ¥¥¥
2-16-11 Kaminarimon, Taito-ku
Tel *(03) 5826-3877* **Map** 4 E3
W gate-hotel.jp
The chic modern design of this hotel contrasts with the nearby ancient Senso-ji Temple.

Hotel Parkside ¥¥¥
2-11-18 Ueno, Taito-ku
Tel *(03) 3836-5711* **Map** 3 C3
W parkside.co.jp
Elegant, sophisticated hotel with fabulous views of Ueno Park and the famous Shinobazu Pond.

Western Tokyo

Shinjuku Washington Hotel ¥¥
3-2-9 Nishishinjuku, Shinjuku
Tel *(03) 3343-3111* **Map** 1 A2
W tokyo.grand.hyatt.com
Clean and efficient, featuring a 24-hour convenience store for any late-night needs.

Grand Hyatt Tokyo ¥¥¥
6-10-3 Roppongi, Minato-ku
Tel *(03) 4333-1234* **Map** 2 E5
W tokyo.grand.hyatt.com
Modern rooms have an uncluttered Japanese vibe. A peaceful haven in the hectic city.

Hilton Tokyo ¥¥¥
6-6-2 Nishi-Shinjuku, Shinjuku-ku
Tel *(03) 3344-5111* **Map** 1 A1
W hilton.com/Tokyo
All the style and comfort one expects from a Hilton hotel, with the added benefit of being in Shinjuku's Chuo-koen Park.

Keio Plaza Hotel ¥¥¥
2-2-1 Nishi-Shinjuku, Shinjuku-ku
Tel *(03) 3344-0111* **Map** 1 A2
W keioplaza.com
Fairly reasonably priced, with a range of restaurants and bars.

DK Choice

Park Hyatt Tokyo ¥¥¥
3-7-1-2 Nishi-Shinjuku, Shinjuku-ku
Tel *(03) 5322-1234* **Map** 1 A2
W tokyo.park.hyatt.com
The legendary Park Hyatt, the setting for the famous film *Lost in Translation*, is one of the most luxurious and best-located hotels in Tokyo. Boasting fine views of Shinjuku's Chuo-koen Park, it also has excellent pool and spa facilities. The on-site New York Bar and Grill is a popular spot.

The Ritz Carlton Tokyo ¥¥¥
Tokyo Midtown, 9-7-1 Akasaka, Minato-ku
Tel *(03) 3423-8000* **Map** 2 E4
W ritzcarlton.com/tokyo
Located in Tokyo Midtown, one of the city's more swanky developments, this hotel is close to the action.

Price Guide

Prices are based on one night's stay in high season for a standard double room, inclusive of service charges and taxes.

¥	under ¥8,000
¥¥	¥8,000–¥20,000
¥¥¥	over ¥20,000

Shibuya Excel Hotel Tokyu ¥¥¥
Shibuya Mark City Building, 1-12-2 Dogenzaka, Shibuya-ku
Tel *(03) 5457-0109* **Map** 1 B5
W tokyuhotelsjapan.com
Overlooking Shibuya's famous intersection, this reasonably priced high-end hotel is comfortable and modern.

Farther Afield

Hotel Nikko Tokyo ¥¥¥
1-9-1 Daiba, Minato-ku
Tel *(03) 5500-5500*
W hnt.co.jp
Comfortable and reasonably priced rooms with great views.

The Westin Tokyo ¥¥¥
1-4-1 Mita, Meguro-ku
Tel *(03) 5423-7000*
W westin-tokyo.co.jp
All rooms here are decorated in European design; suites have views over the skyline. Relax in the Japanese-style garden.

Beyond Tokyo

Hilton Tokyo Narita Airport Hotel ¥¥¥
456 Kosuge, Narita, Chiba Prefecture
Tel *(0476) 33-1121*
W hilton.com/Narita-Airport
Located just 10 minutes from Narita Airport, this no-fuss hotel is a good base from which to explore the Boso Peninsula.

The building housing the Mandarin Oriental Hotel at dusk

Hyatt Regency Hakone Resort and Spa ¥¥¥
1320 Gora, Hakone-Machi, Ashigarashimo-gun
Tel *(0460) 82-2000*
w hakone.regency.hyatt.jp
In one of Japan's best-known *onsen* (hot-spring) resort towns, this Hyatt has two large on-site pools where visitors can soak in the thermal, sulphate-rich waters.

InterContinental The Grand Yokohama ¥¥¥
1-1-1 Minato Mirai, Nishi-ku, Yokohama
Tel *(045) 223-2222*
w interconti.co.jp
Luxurious rooms feature all modern conveniences and offer great views of Yokohama Harbor.

Kamakura Prince Hotel ¥¥¥
1-2-18 Shichirigahama-Higashi, Kamakura, Kanagawa Prefecture
Tel *(0467) 32-1111*
w princehotels.com
This classy resort hotel has ocean views, comfortable rooms, a large outdoor swimming pool, and a golf driving range.

Business Hotels
Central Tokyo
APA Hotel Tsukiji-Eki-Minami ¥¥
7-10 Tsukiji, Chuo-ku
Tel *(03) 3549-0111* **Map** 5 C3
w apahotel.com
A stylish and modern business hotel located close to key tourist attractions.

Business Hotel Ban ¥¥
3-17-10 Tsukiji, Chuo-ku
Tel *(03) 3543-8411* **Map** 5 C3
w hotelban.co.jp
Clean, functional rooms offer basic facilities. Breakfast is included in the room price.

Ginza Grand Hotel ¥¥
8-16-15 Ginza, Chuo-ku
Tel *(03) 3572-4131* **Map** 5 B3
w ginzagrand.com
Perfect for the business traveler staying in Ginza, this hotel offers stylish "urban rooms" designed for functionality and relaxation.

Northern Tokyo
Hotel Marutani ¥¥
6-7-6 Ueno, Taito-ku
Tel *(03) 3831-4308* **Map** 3 C3
w hotel-marutani.com
The Marutani offers its guests the option of staying in either Japanese-style *tatami* rooms or Western rooms. With communal baths.

Understated elegance at The Tokyo Station Hotel *(see p112)*

Ochanomizu St. Hills Hotel ¥¥
2-1-19 Yushima, Bunkyo-ku
Tel *(03) 3831-0081* **Map** 3 B4
w sthills.co.jp
Friendly, no-frills hotel in one of the quieter parts of central Tokyo.

remm Akihabara ¥¥
1-6-5 Kanda Sakumacho, Chiyoda-ku
Tel *(03) 3254-0606* **Map** 3 C4
w remm.jp/akihabara
Modern rooms with a range of services, from massages to newspaper deliveries.

Super Hotel Asakusa ¥¥
2-33-1 Asakusa, Taito-ku
Tel *(03) 5806-9000* **Map** 4 F2
w superhoteljapan.com
A modern hotel in an old Tokyo neighborhood, close to the sights.

Ueno First City Hotel ¥¥
1-14-8 Ueno, Taito-ku
Tel *(03) 3831-8215* **Map** 3 C3
w uenocity-hotel.com
Simple, functional rooms with basic amenities in one of Tokyo's more lively neighborhoods.

Western Tokyo
Akasaka Yoko Hotel ¥¥
6-14-12 Akasaka, Minato-ku
Tel *(03) 3586-4050* **Map** 2 E4
w yokohotel.co.jp/english/stay
Clean, tidy, and modest-sized rooms in a quiet part of Tokyo.

Best Western Shinjuku ASTINA Hotel ¥¥
1-2-9 Kabuki-cho, Shinjuku-ku
Tel *(03) 3200-0220* **Map** 1 B1
w eng.bw-shinjuku.com
Modern accommodations in this chain hotel that also offers Ladies Rooms for women traveling alone.

Hotel Ark Tower Roppongi ¥¥
Roppongi, Minato-ku
Tel *(03) 3404-5111* **Map** 2 E5
w arktower.co.jp/en
Standard rooms at this hotel near Roppongi have basic facilities.

Hotel Sunroute Plaza Shinjuku ¥¥
2-3-1 Yoyogi, Shibuya-ku
Tel *(03) 3375-3211* **Map** 1 B2
w hotelsunrouteplazashinjuku.jp
Modest-sized rooms have large, comfortable beds. Easy access to shopping and dining in Shinjuku.

Kadoya Hotel ¥¥
1-23-1 Nishi-Shinjuku, Shinjuku-ku
Tel *(03) 3346-2561* **Map** 1 A1
w kadoya-hotel.co.jp
All rooms here have memory-foam mattresses and pillows. Close to Shinjuku Station.

Shibuya City Hotel ¥¥
1-1 Maruyama-cho, Shibuya-ku
Tel *(03) 5489-1010* **Map** 1 A5
Modest but tidy rooms in this hotel located just a five-minute walk from Shibuya Station.

Farther Afield
The b Ikebukuro ¥¥
1-39-4 Higashi-Ikebukuro Toshima-ku
Tel *(03) 3980-1911*
w theb-hotels.com
A smart business hotel in lively Ikebukuro, a bustling district that is little visited by tourists.

Kichijoji Tokyu Inn ¥¥
1-6-3, Kichijoji-Minamicho, Musashino-shi
Tel *(0422) 47-0109*
w kichijoji-i.tokyuhotels.co.jp
This contemporary hotel has good-sized, well-maintained rooms. The on-site restaurant is popular. Good service.

Beyond Tokyo
West Inn Fujiyoshida ¥¥
Matsuyama 1205, Fujiyoshida, Yamanashi Prefecture
Tel *(0555) 23-8465*
w westinn.jp
Stylish hotel with large rooms, most of them featuring breathtaking views of Mt. Fuji.

For more information on types of hotels *see page 109*

Capsules and Love Hotels

Central Tokyo

Capsule Value Kanda ¥
1-4-5, Kajicho, Chiyoda-ku
Tel (03) 6206-0724 **Map** 5 B1
Run by English-speaking staff,
this capsule hotel offers a range
of business facilities at no
additional cost, including access
to computers and Wi-Fi.

First Cabin Akihabara ¥
3-38 Kandasakumacho, Chiyoda-ku
Tel (03) 6240-9798 **Map** 4 D4
The decor at this hotel is inspired
by airplane cabins. There are
two types of room available:
first-class cabin and the
smaller business-class cabin.

Northern Tokyo

Capsule Hotel Asakusa River Side ¥
2-20-4 Kaminarimon,
Taito-ku **Map** 4 F3
Located near Asakusa Station,
this no-frills capsule hotel also
accepts female guests; the
eighth floor is reserved
exclusively for women.

Sauna and Capsule Hotel Dandy ¥
Egg Bldg, 6F, 2-6-11 Ueno, Taito-ku
Tel (03) 3839-8100 **Map** 3 C3
Guests here enjoy excellent
bathing facilities, including an
open-air bath and natural-wood
sauna, plus a good restaurant.

Western Tokyo

Capsule and Sauna Century Shibuya ¥
1-19-14 Dogenzaka, Shibuya-ku
Tel (03) 3464-1777 **Map** 1 A5
No-frills hotel with larger-sized
capsules on the tenth floor.

The entrance to Homeikan Honkan,
a ryokan in northern Tokyo (see p115)

DK Choice

Green Plaza Shinjuku ¥
1-29-2 Kabukicho, Shinjuku-ku
Tel (03) 3207-5411 **Map** 1 B1
🆆 hgpshinjuku.jp/en/
Tokyo's first ever capsule hotel
is now the largest in Japan,
with 630 small but surprisingly
comfortable capsules. The
Green Plaza also offers sauna,
hot-spring, and massage
facilities. English-speaking staff.

Ishino Spa Roppongi VIVI Capsule Hotel ¥
5-5-1 Roppongi, Minato-ku
Tel (03) 3403-4126 **Map** 2 E5
Situated just a few minutes from
Roppongi Station, this is the
perfect capsule hotel for those
wanting to party until late.

Shinjuku Kuyakushomae Capsule Hotel ¥
1-2-5 Kabukicho, Shinjuku-ku
Tel (03) 3232-1110 **Map** 1 B1
This well-located capsule hotel
offers its guests the added
attraction of a spacious bathing
area and sauna.

Bali An Island ¥¥
2-1-11 Kabukicho, Shinjuku-ku
Tel (0120) 759-417 **Map** 1 B1
🆆 balian.jp
Modeled on a Balinese holiday
resort, this love hotel is popular
with young Japanese couples.
The first-floor lobby has a pool
table, darts, and a bar. Unlike
other love hotels, Bali An Island
also welcomes parties of four.

Hotel Grand Chariot ¥¥
2-6-1 Kabukicho, Shinjuku-ku
Tel (03) 3208-0005 **Map** 1 B1
🆆 grandchariot.com
Guests can indulge in pure love-
hotel chic at this hotel close to
Shinjuku Station. Modern rooms
have mood lighting.

Hotel Roppongi ¥¥
7-19-4 Roppongi, Minato-ku
Tel (03) 3403-1571 **Map** 2 E5
In the heart of Roppongi, this
attractive love hotel offers a
variety of themed rooms,
including Edwardian chic and
traditional Japanese style.

Hotel Villa Giulia ¥¥
2-27-8 Dogenzaka, Shibuya-ku
Tel (03) 3770-7781 **Map** 1 A5
🆆 hotenavi.com
This love hotel in Shibuya has
decent-sized modern rooms.
To check in, push a button,
take a slip for your room, then
follow the spoken (Japanese)
instructions for payment.

Farther Afield

Private Hotel Aroma (Ikebukuro) ¥¥
2-64-7 Ikebukuro, Toshima-ku
Tel (03) 3988-0890
🆆 hotelaroma.jp
A classy love hotel in the heart of
Ikebukuro, with attractive rooms
in a range of styles, including
Oriental, Japanese, and Balinese.

Minshuku, Pensions & Hostels

Central Tokyo

Anne Hostel Tokyo ¥
2-21-14 Yanagibashi, Taito-ku
Tel (03) 5829-9090 **Map** 4 E4
A good option for low-budget
travelers wanting to stay in
central Tokyo. It offers tatami
rooms, dorms, and private rooms.

Northern Tokyo

Khaosan Tokyo Laboratory ¥
2-1-4 Nishi-Asakusa, Taito-ku
Tel (03) 6479-1041 **Map** 4 E3
🆆 khaosan-tokyo.com
Colorful rooms have a pop-art
theme here. There are both
shared dorms and private rooms.
The staff speak good English.

Retrometro Backpackers ¥
2-19-1 Nishi-Asakusa, Taito-ku
Tel (03) 6322-7447 **Map** 4 E2
🆆 retrometrobackpackers.com
A small, friendly hostel with dorm
rooms only, located in an old,
restored Japanese-style house.

Sakura Hotel Jimbocho ¥
2-21-4 Kanda-Jimbocho,
Tel (03) 3261-3939 **Map** 3 A5
🆆 sakura-hotel.co.jp
A good option for low-budget
travelers. Rooms and dorms are
simple, but with free Wi-Fi.

Toco. Tokyo Heritage Hostel ¥
2-13-21 Shitaya, Taito-ku
Tel (03) 6458-1686 **Map** 4 D1
🆆 backpackersjapan.co.jp
Located in a traditional house
with an attractive Japanese-style
garden, this hostel offers a cheap
night's rest in quiet Ueno.

Farther Afield

Guest House Shinagawa-shuku ¥
1-22-16 Kita-Shinagawa,
Shinagawa-ku
Tel (03) 6712-9440
🆆 bp-shinagawashuku.com
Very reasonably priced hostel
with tidy and minimalist
Japanese-style rooms.

Meg Econo Inn Tokyo ¥
1-56-28 Matsubara, Setagaya-ku
Tel *(03) 3322-5546*
w meg-econoinn-tokyo.com
Quaint *minshuku* with Western-
and Japanese-style rooms.

Tama Ryokan ¥
1-25-33 Takadanobaba, Shinjuku-ku
Tel *(03) 3209-8062*
w tamaryokan.com
A family-run *minshuku* offering
basic accommodation for budget
travelers. Note that all rooms are
on the second floor, and there is
no elevator.

Beyond Tokyo

B&B paSeo ¥¥
1320-634 Gora, Hakone-machi,
Ashigarashimo-gun
Tel *(0460) 82-6100*
w hakone-paseo.com
This Japanese-style B&B with
beautiful, manicured grounds is
attached to a florist and tearoom.

Fuji Hakone Guesthouse ¥¥
912 Sengokuhara, Hakone-machi,
Ashigarashimo-gun
Tel *(0460) 84-6577*
Stay in *tatami* rooms and enjoy
the outdoor *onsen* at this
attractive guesthouse in a
tranquil part of Hakone.

Gasthof Mai ¥¥
100 Kujira-machi, Nikko-shi,
Tochigi-ken
Tel *(0288) 54-1380*
Cute, faux European-style
pension with good breakfasts
and an outdoor Japanese bath.

Villa Revage ¥¥
1800 Kujira-machi, Nikko-shi,
Tochigi-ken
Tel *(0288) 53-6188*
w nikko.or.jp
Attractive pension with both
Japanese- and Western-style
rooms. The elaborate bathing
area includes an outdoor *onsen*.

Ryokan

Northern Tokyo

Homeikan Honkan ¥¥
5-10-5 Hongo, Bunkyo-ku
Tel *(03) 3811-1181* **Map** 3 A3
w homeikan.com
This stylish, wooden *ryokan* has
a manicured Japanese garden.

Ryokan Katsutaro ¥¥
4-16-8 Ikenohata, Taito-ku
Tel *(03) 3821-9808* **Map** 3 C2
w katsutaro.com
A no-frills but cosy *ryokan*
located close to Ueno Park.

Green Plaza Shinjuku, Tokyo's first capsule hotel *(see p114)*

Ryokan Ryumeikan Honten ¥¥
3-4 Kanda Surugadai, Chiyoda-ku
Tel *(03) 3251-1135* **Map** 3 B4
w ryumeikan-honten.jp
Founded in 1899, this historic
ryokan offers guests a traditional
experience – the room decor is
inspired by the tea ceremony
in the Edo period. Japanese
breakfast is available.

Ryokan Sawanoya ¥¥
2-3-11 Yanaka, Taito-ku
Tel *(03) 3822-2251* **Map** 3 B2
w sawanoya.com
Family-run *ryokan* with a library
of English books. Comfortable,
reasonably priced rooms close
to Ueno Park.

Sukeroku no Yado
Sadachiyo ¥¥
2-20-1 Asakusa, Taito-ku
Tel *(03) 3842-6431* **Map** 4 E2
w sadachiyo.co.jp
This elaborate *ryokan* is
decorated in traditional style.
There are two shared public
bathrooms.

Farther Afield

Wakana ¥¥
4-7 Kagurazaka, Shinjuku-ku
Tel *(03) 3260-3769*
Located on a narrow, stone-
paved lane in Kagurazaka,
Tokyo's stylish old geisha quarter,
this small *ryokan* is also known
as the "writers' inn," since many
famous Japanese authors have
stayed here.

Meguro Gajoen ¥¥¥
1-8-1 Shimo-Meguro, Meguro-ku
Tel *(03) 3491-4111*
w megurogajoen.co.jp
A luxurious *ryokan* in one
of Tokyo's more upmarket
neighborhoods. Guests can
opt to stay in Japanese- or
Western-style rooms; the latter
have a *tatami* seating area.

Beyond Tokyo

Kurhaus Ishibashi Ryokan ¥¥
185-1 Rendaiji, Shimoda, Shizuoka
Prefecture
Tel *(0558) 22-2222*
w kur-ishibashi.com
A 140-year-old *ryokan* with
Western-style rooms and
en-suite bathrooms. It serves
excellent seafood dinners.

Nikko Green Hotel, Fuwari ¥¥
9 Honcho, Nikko, Tochigi Prefecture
Tel *(0288) 54-2002*
w nikko-fuwari.com
This traditional *ryokan* has an
attractive *onsen* bathing area.

Fuji Lake Hotel ¥¥¥
1 Funatsu, Fujikawaguchiko-cho,
Minamitsuru-gun
Tel *(0555) 72-2209*
w fujilake.co.jp
A cross between a *ryokan* and
a deluxe hotel, this place offers
great views of Mt. Fuji.

Hakone Setsugetsuka ¥¥¥
1300-34 Gora, Hakone-machi,
Ashigarashimo-gun
Tel *(0460) 861-333*
Overlooking the Hakone
mountains, this luxury *ryokan*
has elaborate Japanese-style
baths – some on the balconies.

Shimoda Central Hotel ¥¥¥
133-1 Aitama, Shimoda-shi,
Shizuoka Prefecture
Tel *(0558) 28-1126*
w shimoda-central-hotel.co.jp
Luxury, resort-style *ryokan*
located amid rice fields. Guests
can relax in the pool or keep
active on the tennis court.

Sunnide Resort ¥¥¥
2549-1 Oishi, Fujikawaguchiko-
machi, Minamitsuru-gun
w sunnide.com
View Mt. Fuji from the comfort
of an *onsen* bath at this luxury
resort beside Kawaguchiko Lake.

For more information on types of hotels *see page 109*

WHERE TO EAT AND DRINK

Tokyo is one of the major gourmet cities in the world, known not only for its sushi and other Japanese delicacies, but also for the remarkable variety of foreign cuisines. Humble taverns or grills that have been in business for centuries nestle side by side with gleaming high-rise malls lined with delis and markets serving foods from around the world. The quality of meals at high-end restaurants is matched by their prices, but eating out does not have to be exorbitant. There are numerous mid- or low-end diners; noodle shops abound, as do fast-food restaurants (both Western and local); and, if pressed for time and money, you can pick up snacks in supermarkets, convenience stores, and mid-range restaurants clustered around train stations. Wherever you go, standards of service and cleanliness are invariably high. It is hard to get a bad meal in Tokyo.

Savoring a sushi meal at a restaurant in Jingumae

Meals and Meal Times

Most *ryokan* (see p110) and some hotels serve a traditional Japanese breakfast from 7 until 9am. If your hotel doesn't, you will easily find a nearby café serving coffee and croissants or Danish pastries. When Japanese eat breakfast out, they usually do so in coffee shops that serve sets called *moningu* (morning), consisting of coffee, toast, a hard-boiled egg, and a small salad. However, breakfast is not a major meal in modern Tokyo.

Tokyoites tend to eat lunch early. Typically, lunch runs from 11:30am to 2:30pm, and dinner starts at 5:30 or 6pm. Although some upscale restaurants stop serving at 9 or 10pm, most stay open until around 11 or 11:30pm (later still in areas such as Roppongi) to cater to the after-hours office crowd.

Reservations and Dress Code

Reservations are advisable at top restaurants in Tokyo and essential at the most exclusive dining places. Elsewhere, you can usually find a table without a reservation, especially if you arrive early in the evening. Some restaurants won't allow phone reservations, but if you show up in person and no tables are free, they will put your name on a list and call you when a space opens up.

There is no dress code in Japan for eating at restaurants, though women may find long, loose clothing advantageous when dining at a place with *zashiki* (low platform) seating. Also, be sure to wear clean socks or stockings without holes if seating on *tatami* mats is involved, as you will have to take off your shoes.

Set Menus (Teishoku)

Most restaurants in Tokyo offer fixed-price menus called *teishoku*. These can be especially good value at lunchtime. Usually there will be a number of menu choices.

Some restaurants have window displays with realistic-looking plastic models of their dishes, or menus with photographs. Point to an item if you do not know its name. At many noodle restaurants, Japanese curry shops, and basic diners or *shokudo*, it may be necessary to obtain a ticket from the vending machine at the entrance before you place an order.

Prices and Paying

Tokyo has restaurants to suit all budgets. You can slurp a bowl of noodles for less than ¥500 or spend an entire week's budget on a single meal. Many upscale restaurants that might charge ¥10,000–¥20,000 per head at dinner often have economical lunch menus for ¥3,000–¥5,000.

A consumption tax of 8 percent is included in the price, but many Western restaurants add a service charge, too. Some traditional Japanese eateries serve an obligatory starter (*otoshi*) in lieu of a table charge.

At coffee shops and many restaurants, the bill is placed on your table. Just take it to the cashier to pay. At some bars and restaurants you will be asked to pay at your table. The amount, written on a slip of paper, will be presented to you on a small tray. Place your payment (cash or card) on this tray; your change will be returned on the same tray. Tipping is not expected and may be refused.

Realistic-looking plastic-food display in a restaurant window

Entering a Restaurant or Bar

A set of *noren* (half-curtains) outside the door indicates that a restaurant is open for business. Duck past the curtain, slide open the door, and pause at the threshold. If you do not have a reservation, indicate how many people are in your group by raising the appropriate number of fingers. In some restaurants, you may be asked to remove your shoes. Slippers will be provided for walking around on the wooden floor areas, or if you need to use the toilet.

Many Japanese restaurants in Tokyo offer Western-style tables and chairs, plus counter seating looking into the open kitchen. They may also have traditional seating, or *zashiki*. This involves sitting at low tables on thin cushions (*zabuton*) on *tatami* mats. Shoes and slippers are never worn on *tatami* mats. Women often sit with their legs to the side, mermaid-style; the most common position for men is cross-legged. The Japanese don't expect foreign guests to sit in these positions, but it is ill-mannered to stretch your legs out under a low table. Special chairs with backs but no legs are often provided, or there may be leg wells under the tables.

The counter is a great place to sit, especially in sushi restaurants, since it gives prime views of the chefs preparing the food. Smoking is discouraged at seats close to the kitchen. Many Japanese restaurants have non-smoking sections, but only a few are entirely non-smoking.

Food Customs, Etiquette and Taboos

After they are seated, diners are often given *oshibori*, or small damp towels. These are used to wipe hands (not the face and neck), and then left on the table top for dabbing fingers and spills; do not place them on your lap. Never blow your nose into the *oshibori* or even a handkerchief in public.

The Japanese say *"itadakimass"* ("I humbly receive") before eating; on leaving, it is polite

Enjoying a meal while sitting on *zabuton* cushions at a low table

to say *"gochiso-sama deshita"* ("it was a feast"). Calling *"sumimasen"* ("excuse me!") is the standard method of attracting the waiter's attention.

Japanese drinking etiquette requires that you pour for the other person and vice versa. When on the receiving end, pick up your glass, supporting the bottom with the other hand. When a toast (*kanpai*) is made, beer and whiskey glasses should be clinked; with sake, cups are raised in a salute.

Japanese meals often comprise numerous courses, each served in separate bowls or plates. In formal situations, each person will have his own individual vessels; more informally, you serve yourself from shared bowls in the middle of the table. Do not eat from communal bowls, but transfer a few bite-sized portions onto a small plate in front of you, using the serving chopsticks, if provided.

It is quite acceptable to pick up small bowls (such as rice bowls) and hold them halfway to the mouth. Soup is slurped directly from the bowl, but any solid morsels should be picked out with chopsticks (*hashi*). If a morsel proves too difficult to handle, you can hold a chopstick in each hand and make a sawing motion to cut it.

Do not use chopsticks to spear food, or to push it straight from the bowl into the mouth. Gesturing and pointing with your chopsticks

are also impolite. Chopsticks should never be stuck upright into bowls of rice or other food; and food should never be passed from one set of chopsticks to another. These gestures are associated with funerary customs and are taboo at the dinner table.

When not using them, lay your chopsticks on the rest (*hashi-oki*) provided, or across the lowest dish, keeping them uncrossed and parallel with your side of the table.

Recommended Restaurants

The listings in this guide cover the rich and diverse spectrum of different cuisines available in Tokyo, from fine-dining *kaiseki* restaurants serving elegant banquets of beautifully arranged traditional food to hole-in-the-wall noodle restaurants where you can slurp some of Tokyo's best *ramen*. Eateries serving classics such as tempura, *nabe, yakitori*, and *tonkatsu* are well covered, as are the places to sample *monjayaki*, the local version of *okinomiyaki*, the Japanese pancake you cook at your own table. World foods haven't been left out as they are a big part of eating out in Japan's most international city. The DK Choice option identifies restaurants that are especially good for a particular reason, be it a unique cultural location, such as a former sumo stable turned into a restaurant, or the chef's unique and novel take on traditional Japanese cuisine.

Delicacies including *maki-zushi* at the counter in a Tokyo sushi bar

Types of Restaurants and Bars

Tokyo has a wide range of restaurants to suit every taste and budget, from hole-in-the-wall noodle stands to havens of refinement serving formal *kaiseki* banquets, not to mention fine French, Italian, and Chinese cuisines. Most Japanese restaurants tend to specialize in specific genres, such as sushi, *sukiyaki*, or tempura, or even in individual ingredients such as tofu and *fugu* (poison blowfish).

Re-created traditional warehouse *(kura)*, Gonpachi restaurant, Ginza

Kaiseki Ryori

Japan's traditional haute cuisine, *kaiseki ryori* is derived from the food served to accompany tea ceremonies, developed in Kyoto some 500 years ago. A typical banquet comprises numerous small courses, each exquisitely arranged, served in a prescribed order, and with careful reference to the season. Typically, *kaiseki* meals are served with great formality in elegant restaurants (sometimes known as *ryoriya*), or at *ryotei*, discreet establishments with courtyard gardens and spare but elegant private rooms.

Izakaya and Dining Bars

Izakaya are down-to-earth places where you eat as you drink (rather than vice versa), ordering a few dishes at a time. At their most basic, these are budget taverns, identified by raucous, smoke-filled interiors, and battered red lanterns by the front door. Others are more refined, and may serve food of considerable quality. Many have large platters of pre-cooked items on their counter tops to pick from. A similar genre, now common in Tokyo,

is the "dining bar." The approach is similar to that of an *izakaya* but with plenty of French and Italian influences.

Cheap *izakaya* seem to be more and more present around Tokyo, many of them part of large national chains. They may offer an all-you-can-drink deal, known as *nomihoudai*, with a fixed price for alcoholic drinks, or *tabehoudai*, or all-you-can-eat, which can be good value for money if you are in the mood to consume a lot in a short space of time.

Specialty Restaurants

Tempura, *sukiyaki*, teppanyaki, and *tonkatsu* are generally served at restaurants that focus on each particular genre. Other areas of specialization worth investigating include *yakitori* (charcoal-grilled skewers of chicken), *unagi* (grilled eel), and *nabe* (winter hotpots cooked at the table). Also worth trying is *okonomiyaki*, the Japanese-style pancake that comes in either Osaka or Hiroshima style. Tokyo also has its own version *(mojayaki)*, which is softer and very tasty. *Fugu* restaurants serve up the delight of the adventurous gourmet, the poisonous blowfish. Japanese-style curry is also popular as a cheap and tasty lunch, and it can be ordered with a range of interesting toppings, including cheese, sausages, and pork.

Sushi Restaurants

Sushi restaurants *(see pp126–7)* vary greatly in style, from low-priced *kaiten-zushi* shops, where the sushi comes to you on a conveyor belt, to astronomically expensive places where everything – from the fish to the ginger – is of optimum quality. As a general rule, if there are no prices listed anywhere, it will be expensive. At expensive sushi restaurants it is usually best to go for an *omakase*, which means the chef can decide what sushi to serve; that way you will get the best ingredients and freshest fish available on any given day.

Counter seating looking into the open kitchen at a sushi restaurant, Ginza

WHERE TO EAT AND DRINK | 119

Vegetarian Food

Although traditional Japanese cuisine includes plenty of vegetables and high-protein soyfoods such as tofu and *natto* (fermented soybeans), it is not a vegetarian's paradise, as most dishes are cooked in a fish-based stock (*dashi*). However, *shojin ryori* restaurants tend to use kelp and mushroom stock instead. *Shojin ryori*, which literally means "devotion food," developed along with Zen Buddhism in the 12th century and is a type of vegetarian temple food. Meals can range from elaborate – and just as expensive – banquets similar to *kaiseki* (but without using any fish, meat, or eggs) to modern versions served in contemporary settings. Although Kyoto is better known for its *shojin ryori*, there are several fine specialist restaurants in Tokyo, as well as around the Zen temples in Kamakura. Tokyo has a growing number of macrobiotic and natural-food eateries. Indian restaurants also offer good vegetarian options, as do some Turkish restaurants.

Noodle Restaurants

Japanese noodles come in two main forms: brown buckwheat *soba*, a favorite in Tokyo since Edo times, and white *udon*, made from wheat flour. These are served cold with a dip or in a hot, savory soup. *Ramen* is a Japanese variant on Chinese noodles, usually served with a

A cozy noodle bar with compact outdoor seating, Shinjuku

meaty broth, although the Japanese have turned it into a dish all of its own. There is a wide range of different types of *ramen* soups, and these have links to various regions of Japan. The main ones are miso, *shouyu* (soy sauce), *tonkotsu* (pork bones), and *shio* (salt). Late-night *ramen* counters are ubiquitous, cheap, and enduringly popular.

Other Asian Restaurants

Chinese and Korean food is hugely popular in Tokyo. *Yakiniku* (Korean-style barbecue with plenty of red meat) diners are found throughout the city, with the most authentic in Shin-Okubo, Tokyo's Korea Town, located in northern Shinjuku. *Yakiniku* is best eaten with friends, as you cook it yourself at the table, and it is often washed down with a shot or two of the Korean liquor *soju*. Good Thai, Vietnamese, Mongolian, and Indian restaurants are also available throughout the city.

Western Restaurants

Yoshoku-ya are restaurants that serve Japanese versions of Western dishes, especially those introduced to Japan in the Meiji period, such as *omu-raisu* (omelet rice) or gratin. Family restaurants, or *famiresu*, specialize in this type of food. Hamburger steak is often the centerpiece, usually served

on a hotplate with a rich demi-glace gravy sauce on top. Most family restaurants are large national chains, for example Volks or Gasuto, and have very reasonably priced beer and wine.

At the high end, Tokyo boasts French and Italian cuisine to rival the finest in Europe and North America. There are also numerous budget bistros and trattorias of remarkable authenticity. Spanish food is catching on fast, and German-style food can be found in beer halls, which are popular places to drink. The British Isles are well represented by many pubs of varying quality, and classics from home, such as fish and chips or bangers and mash, are often on the menu.

Fast Food and Convenience Stores

There are several fast-food chains selling burgers, fried chicken, and the like. Many have familiar names (McDonald's, KFC) but may serve Japanese variations. In addition to Western fast-food chains, there are many selling Japanese-style fast food. Local clones such as Mosburger offer innovative twists, such as burgers between rice patties, served with shreds of cooked burdock. One of the most famous chains is Yoshinoya, which specializes in *gyudon*, thinly sliced beef over a bowl of rice, which is usually eaten on the run. *Takoyaki*, which originate from Osaka, are small grilled balls made from batter and diced octopus. These are also a popular fast food among young people and are usually eaten while piping hot, standing at a counter in front of the store.

Convenience stores offer a good selection of *bento* boxes (see p125), *onigiri* (rice balls), and an extensive range of ready-to-eat meals, which staff will heat up for you in the microwave. They also stock a huge range of dried snacks – everything from the familiar potato crisps to the more exotic, such as dried squid.

The Tanuki

In Japanese folklore badgers are celebrated as lovable buffoons or drunken rascals. This is one of the reasons why the ceramic likeness of the *tanuki* is often found at the entrance of *izakaya* and other drinking places.

Reading the Menu

General vocabulary likely to be useful when eating out is given in the *Phrase Book* on pages 200–4. Individual ingredients are also listed there. A selection of some of the most popular dishes and styles of cooking are listed in this glossary, including Japanese script to help you read menus in Japanese. Further details about some of the dishes follow on pages 122–7.

Donburi: Rice-Bowl Dishes

Katsudon
カツどん
Rice bowl topped with a breaded, deep-fried pork cutlet and semi-cooked egg.

Nikudon
肉どん
Rice bowl with beef, tofu, and gelatinous noodles.

Oyakodon
親子どん
Rice bowl with chicken, onions, and runny, semi-cooked egg.

Tamagodon
卵どん
Rice bowl topped with a semi-cooked egg.

Tendon
天どん
Rice bowl that has one or two shrimp tempura and sauce.

Unadon
鰻どん
Rice bowl with grilled eel.

Other Rice Dishes

Kamameshi
釜飯／かままめし
Rice and tidbits steamed in a clay or metal pot with a wooden lid. Served in the container it was steamed in.

Kare raisu
カレーライス
"Curry rice." This can be *ebi-kare* (shrimp curry), *katsu-kare* (with deep-fried pork cutlet), or a range of other meat, fish, or vegetable options.

Makunouchi bento
幕の内弁当
Classic *bento* (see p125).

Ocha-zuke お茶漬け
Rice in a bowl with a piece of grilled salmon, pickled plum, etc., over which tea is poured.

Omu-raisu オムライス
Thin omelet wrapped around rice mixed with tomato sauce and chicken or pork bits.

Onigiri
おにぎり
Two or three triangular chunks of rice wrapped in strips of dried seaweed (*nori*).

Unaju 鰻重
Grilled eel served over rice in a lacquered, lidded box.

Yaki-onigiri 焼おにぎり
A variation of *onigiri*, this is prepared without seaweed and grilled over a flame.

Zosui
雑炊
Rice soup made with the leftover stock of a one-pot (*nabemono*) meal.

Noodle Dishes

Kitsune soba/udon
きつねそば／うどん
Soba or *udon* noodles in flavored *dashi* broth with pieces of fried tofu.

Nabe yaki udon
鍋焼うどん
Udon noodles simmered in a lidded ceramic pot (*donabe*) with a flavored *dashi* broth, perhaps with shrimp tempura, shiitake mushroom, and egg. Popular in winter.

Ramen ラーメン
Chinese-style noodles in a broth. Usually there are some thin slices of roast pork on top, along with sliced leeks, seaweed, and a slice of fish-paste roll.

Reimen (Hiyashi chuka)
冷麺（冷やし中華）
Chinese noodles topped with strips of ham or roast pork, cucumbers, and cabbage. Dressed with a vinegar and sesame oil sauce. Popular summer dish.

Three pieces of *onigiri*

Somen
そうめん
Very thin white noodles, usually served in ice water. A summer dish.

Tamago-toji soba/udon
卵とじそば／うどん
Soba or *udon* in a flavored *dashi* broth into which an egg has been stirred to cook gently.

Tempura soba/udon
天ぷらそば／うどん
Soba or *udon* in a flavored *dashi* broth with one or two pieces of shrimp tempura.

Yakisoba
焼そば
Soft Chinese noodles sautéed on a griddle with vegetables and some form of meat or fish.

Zarusoba
ざるそば
Soba noodles served cold on a bamboo rack. Variation: *ten-zarusoba* has shrimp and vegetable tempura next to noodles.

Rice Crackers and Nibbles

Crackers (*senbei* or *osenbei*) are sold in supermarkets. Beautifully made and presented, they are also sold at station gift counters and stalls at the popular tourist attractions.

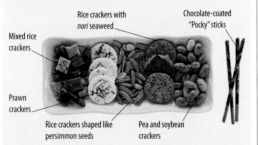

Rice crackers with *nori* seaweed

Chocolate-coated "Pocky" sticks

Mixed rice crackers

Prawn crackers

Rice crackers shaped like persimmon seeds

Pea and soybean crackers

Dishes Prepared at the Table

Mizutaki/Chirinabe
水焚き／ちり鍋
Nabemono (one-pot meal) of vegetables, tofu, and chicken (*mizutaki*) or fish (*chirinabe*).

Okonomiyaki
お好み焼
Thick pancake-shaped mix of cabbage, egg, shrimp, squid, or pork cooked on a griddle.

Shabu-shabu
しゃぶしゃぶ
Nabemono (hot pot) with thinly sliced beef and vegetables cooked in a metal pan.

Table condiments: seven-spice (*shichimi*) powder, jar of soy sauce, and ground chili pepper (*ichimi*)

Sukiyaki
すき焼き
High-quality pan-cooked beef or chicken and vegetables.

Teppanyaki
鉄板焼
Meat and/or shrimp or squid and vegetables grilled on a griddle in front of the diner.

Udon-suki
うどんすき
Udon noodles, chicken, and sometimes clams or shrimp simmered in a soup.

Sushi

Chirashi-zushi
ちらし寿司／鮨
"Scattered" sushi (*see p126*).

Nigiri-zushi
握り寿司／鮨
"Fingers" of sushi (*see p126*).

Maki-zushi
巻寿司／鮨
"Rolled" sushi (*see p127*).

Set Meal

Teishoku
定食
A set meal (*see p116*), with rice, soup, some vegetables, salad, a main meat dish, and pickles.

Menu Categories

Aemono
和え物
Dressed salad dishes.

Agemono
揚げ物
Deep-fried foods.

Nimono
煮物
Simmered foods.

Sashimi (Otsukuri)
刺身（お造り）
Raw fish (*see p127*).

Sunomono
酢の物
Vinegared dishes.

Yakimono
焼き物
Grilled foods.

À La Carte

Agedashi-dofu
揚げだし豆腐
Deep-fried tofu (bean curd) in a stock.

Chikuzen-ni 筑前煮
Vegetables and bits of chicken simmered together.

Eda mame
枝豆
Soybeans steamed in the pod. Popular summer snack.

Hiya-yakko/Yudofu
冷やっこ／湯豆腐
Cold/simmered tofu.

Kinpira
きんぴら
Sautéed burdock and carrot strips seasoned with sauces.

Natto
納豆
Fermented soybeans.

Niku-jaga
肉じゃが
Beef or pork simmered with potatoes and other ingredients.

Oden
おでん
Hot pot with white radish, boiled egg, and fish cake in soy broth.

Ohitashi
おひたし
Boiled spinach or other green leafy vegetable with sauce.

Shio-yaki
塩焼
Fish sprinked with salt and grilled over a flame or charcoal.

Tamago-yaki
卵焼き
Rolled omelet.

Tonkatsu
豚カツ／トンカツ
Breaded, fried pork cutlet.

Grilled eel (*unagi*) basted in a sweet sauce, a *yakimono* dish

Tori no kara-age
鶏の空揚げ
Deep-fried chicken.

Tsukemono no moriawase
漬物の盛り合わせ
Combination of pickles.

Yakitori
焼鶏／やきとり
Marinated chicken grilled on skewers.

Yakiniku
焼肉
Korean-style beef barbecue.

Chinese-Style Dishes

Gyoza
餃子／ギョウザ
Fried dumplings.

Harumaki
春巻
Spring roll.

Shumai
焼売／シュウマイ
Small, pork dumplings crimped at the top and steamed.

Yakimeshi/chahan
焼めし／チャーハン
Fried rice.

Izakaya Snacks

Cucumber and seaweed

Dried squid

Onion and bonito

At *izakaya* (*see p118*) establishments, which are tavern-like places serving food rather than restaurants, dishes such as dried strips of squid and pickles complement the beer, *shochu* and other drinks (*see pp128–9*).

The Flavors of Japan

More so than in most developed countries, where the produce of the entire world is available in supermarkets all year round, Japan is a country in which local and seasonal produce is still highly valued. The traditional cuisine of Tokyo reflects its waterfront location and its easy access to the fertile plains inland. Tokyo is also the focus of the nation's food distribution network, especially through the busy stalls of its central wholesale market in Tsukiji *(see p42)*. The city also boasts numerous restaurants serving the specialties of other regions of Japan. Its modern cuisine reflects influences from all around the world.

Ramen noodles

Chef at work, using chopsticks to arrange exquisite dishes

Edo Cuisine

In the early 17th century, Tokyo, then known as Edo, became the administrative capital of Japan after the powerful Tokugawa family moved there. With them arrived thousands of rich landowning samurai and wealthy merchants. This led to the development of Edo cuisine, a fusion of dishes from diverse parts of the country, that is today the most commonly recognized form of Japanese food.

The story of the ascendancy of Edo cuisine is also that of the decline in dominance of typically delicate flavors from Western Japan. *Soba* (buckwheat noodles) has been a popular food among Edo residents since the late 17th century and is renowned as one of the true tastes of Edo cuisine. As more people from the north of Japan moved to Edo, *udon* noodles, which were popular in the south, were replaced by *soba* noodles. *Soba* is most commonly eaten in the same simple way that it was eaten in the past: in a *zaru*

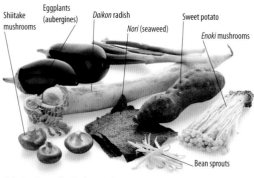

Shiitake mushrooms
Eggplants (aubergines)
Daikon radish
Nori (seaweed)
Sweet potato
Enoki mushrooms
Bean sprouts

Selection of vegetables that feature in Japanese cuisine

Traditional Japanese Specialties

A typical banquet, such as might be served at a *ryotei* (upscale restaurant), may have up to 20 courses. Much is made of seasonal ingredients, with decorative flourishes also chosen to reflect the time of year. *Kaiseki* is a traditional style of cuisine in which a dozen or more dishes are served to each person, categorized according to cooking method, not ingredients. *Sake (see p129)* is the usual accompaniment. Vegetarian cusine, called *shojin ryori*, uses protein-rich tofu rather than meat or fish. It was developed by Zen Buddhists and is now found in many restaurants located in or near the precincts of Zen temples. The Japanese have also elevated tea snacks to an art form – delicate and pretty *wagashi* are usually made from sweet bean paste.

Bonito tuna flakes

Unadon, featuring grilled eel over a bed of rice, is popular as it is thought to have great health benefits.

Tuna being laid out for sale at Tokyo's Tsukiji Fish Market (see p42)

their seafood. Chilly Hokkaido in Northern Japan boasts warming hotpots. Osaka and Hiroshima in Western Japan vie over their respective recipes for *okonomiyaki* pancakes. On the island of Shikoku, Kochi is famous for *katsuo* (skipjack tuna); on the island of Kyushu, Kumamoto is renowned for horsemeat sashimi, while Kagoshima washes its seafood down with copious *shochu* liquor (see p129). The southern islands of Okinawa boast a pork-rich cuisine.

KOBE BEEF

One significant contribution that the Japanese have given to meat connoisseurs across the world is Kobe beef. The black *wagyu* cows of Hyogo prefecture, of which Kobe is the capital, are bred and reared using strictly guarded and time-honoured traditions to make some of the highest-quality beef in the world. Although similar cows are raised in America and Australia, the meat is not considered to be genuine if it is not from Hyogo, which makes authentic Kobe beef an expensive delicacy. Kobe beef is an extremely tender meat, and it is identifiable by the striations of fat that run through it. It is used in a range of Japanese dishes – it can be eaten raw as sashimi, cooked as teppanyaki or, as is popular nowadays, served simply as a big hearty steak or even a luxurious burger.

(a small bamboo sieve). The weaker soy sauce of Western Japan also became less favored when people in Edo adopted a stronger tasting sauce. Even grilled eel, which is thought to be a typical part of Edo cuisine, was originally a dish from Kyoto, but it is the Edo method of cooking the eel and preparing the sauce that we know today. Other foods which feature strongly in Edo cuisine are sushi, tempura, and *oden* (see p121).

Regional Cuisine

As the nation's capital, Tokyo has continued to draw its population from all corners of the country. This has had a significant impact on the way the city eats. There are numerous restaurants serving regional cuisines, and it is quite possible to sample the specialties of every corner of Japan without leaving the city. The cuisine of Kyoto is esteemed for its refinement and exquisite arrangements, especially *kaiseki* and temple cuisine (see p118), featuring tofu and other products based on soybeans. Areas along the Sea of Japan are renowned for

Omoide Yokacho, a lane of restaurants in Shinjuku, Tokyo

Tempura, originally a Portuguese dish, is lightly battered deep-fried vegetables or seafood.

Okonomiyaki is a thick, pancake-shaped mix of egg and other ingredients, cooked on a griddle.

Yakiudon are thick noodles fried with seafood, seaweed, shiitake mushrooms, tuna flakes, and bean sprouts.

The Japanese Meal

Along with the indispensable rice and miso soup (made from fermented soy bean paste), a Japanese meal usually consists of a variety of smaller dishes that are designed to complement each other. Plain ingredients are often given strong flavors, such as a bowl of rice topped off with an *umeboshi* (sour plum) or pickled ginger, or tofu that has been marinated in a strong, vinegary sauce. Two liquid ingredients central to most Japanese dishes are *dashi*, a light stock made from giant kelp *(konbu)* and dried skipjack tuna shavings, and Japanese soy sauce *(shoyu)*.

Firm tofu

Japanese family enjoying breakfast together

The Japanese Breakfast

One of the many attractions of staying in the home of a Japanese family, or in a traditional Japanese hotel, is sampling the Japanese breakfast. Like most other Japanese meals, it consists of different dishes served separately. At its heart is a bowl of rice and some miso soup.

It is polite for the rice to be placed to the left and the soup to the right of the sitter. Not only is it common for there to be variations in miso soup from region to region, individual families tend to have their own idiosyncratic method of producing this most Japanese of soups.

The basic rice and soup are accompanied by a range of side dishes, of which the most common is a portion of grilled fish, often salted salmon or mackerel. Other dishes may include dried seaweed, omelet, and a small portion of pickles.

Natto is a dish made out of fermented soy beans and it is a much-loved breakfast dish among health-conscious Japanese. Usually eaten with rice, it is famous not only for being extremely healthy, but also for its obnoxious smell.

Miso soup

Nori (seaweed)

Grilled salmon

Pickled eggplant (aubergine)

Umeboshi (pickled plums)

Rice

Pickled *daikon* radish

Tofu

Some of the ingredients for a typical Japanese breakfast

Preparation and Portions

A fastidiousness about detail characterizes both the preparation and presentation of Japanese food. Good presentation is vital to a Japanese restaurant's success, but it is not only the highly expensive, multi-course *kaiseki* meals that display this quality; even the cheapest food has a touch of the meticulous about it. This attention to culinary aesthetics naturally favors portions that are small and served individually to maximize the impact that they have on both taste and sight. Vegetables are cooked to remain crisp and retain their colors and, even when fried, food is not allowed to become greasy – the oil is heated high enough to seal the food instantly. The serving of small portions also has health benefits, and it should come as no surprise that obesity is much less of a problem here than in Western developed countries. Nowhere else in the world is healthy eating so attractive, varied, or delicious.

Small portions of a number of complementary dishes

The Bento Box

A *bento* is a take-home meal in a compartmentalized box – office workers buy them for lunch, schoolchildren eat from them at their desk, and business travelers have them with a beer on the bullet train. In its neat, individual compartments there will invariably be a large portion of rice, a main serving of meat or fish, pieces of omelet, some vegetables, and a selection of pickles. But part of the charm of the *bento* is that anything goes. It is not uncommon to open a *bento* and find a small octopus or a tiny whole fish gazing up at you, or even something that completely defies identification.

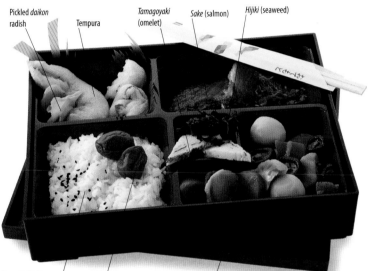

Slivers of pickled ginger

Pickled *daikon* radish

Tempura

Tamagoyaki (omelet)

Sake (salmon)

Hijiki (seaweed)

Rice with black sesame

Umeboshi (pickled plums)

Nishime (simmered vegetables)

Typical selection of food to be found in a *bento* box

IN THE BENTO BOX

Agedofu Fried tofu.

Chikuwa Tubular steamed fishcakes.

Furikake Variety of condiments to add extra flavor, including *nori* (seaweed) flakes and toasted sesame seeds.

Jako Miniature whole dried fish.

Kabocha Squash, often served simmered.

Konnyaku Gelatinous paste made from Devil's Tongue (similar to sweet potato).

Korokke Croquettes filled with potato and meat.

Kurage Jellyfish.

Maguro sashimi Tuna sashimi.

Negi Salad onion, used for flavoring and garnish.

Onigiri Triangles of rice with various fillings.

Saba sashimi Mackerel sashimi.

Takenoko Bamboo shoots.

Tonkatsu Deep-fried breaded pork.

Tsukemono Pickled vegetables.

Umeboshi Pickled apricot.

Unagi Grilled eel in black bean sauce.

Yakiniku Miniature meatballs.

Japanese student eating lunch from a *bento* box

Sushi and Sashimi

Newcomers to Japan are most often both fascinated and intimidated by these native dishes. The term "sushi" applies to a variety of dishes (usually written with the suffix "-zushi") in which cold, lightly sweetened, and vinegared sushi rice is topped or wrapped up with raw fish or other items such as pickles, cooked fish, and meat. Sliced fillets of raw fish served without rice are called sashimi. Even those visitors used to Japanese restaurants abroad may be surprised at how ubiquitous such foods are in Japan. Fresh fish is always used, and the vinegar in sushi rice is a preservative.

Sushi bar counter and sushi chefs with years of training

Shredded daikon radish

Hirame (halibut)

Ebi (shrimp)

Hotate (scallop)

Wasabi (Japanese horseradish)

Gari (ginger), eaten separately

Hokkigai (type of clam)

Suzuki (sea bass)

Kazunoko (salted herring roe)

Nigiri-zushi

Here, thin slices of raw fish are laid over molded fingers of sushi rice with a thin layer of wasabi (green horseradish) in between. Using chopsticks or fingers, pick up a piece, dip the fish lightly in soy sauce, and consume in one mouthful.

Toro (belly flesh of a tuna)

Aji (horse mackerel)

Maguro (tuna)

Shimesaba (salted, vinegared mackerel)

Ika (squid)

Tamagoyaki (sweetened egg omelet), a popular non-fish item often accompanying sushi and sashimi

Denbu, flakes of shrimp and whitefish that have been boiled, then dried and seasoned

Kazunoko (salted herring roe)

Ebi (shrimp)

Aji (horse mackerel)

Uni (the ovaries of a sea urchin), a highly prized delicacy in Japan

Ikura (salmon roe)

Gari (ginger)

Slice of kamaboko, a type of steamed fish-paste roll with pink-dyed rim

Thin slice of ika (squid)

Chirashi-zushi

The "scattered" style of sushi involves a colorful combination of toppings arranged artfully with a deep bed of cold sushi rice. Slices of raw fish, fish roe, chunks of omelet, and other raw or cooked vegetables are placed on top of the rice (as shown).

Maki-zushi

"Rolled" sushi is becoming increasingly familiar outside Japan – the California roll, for instance, is a version using avocado and other non-Japanese ingredients. For *maki-zushi* the sushi rice is combined with slivers of fish, pickles, or other morsels, and rolled up in a sheet of toasted seaweed (*nori*).

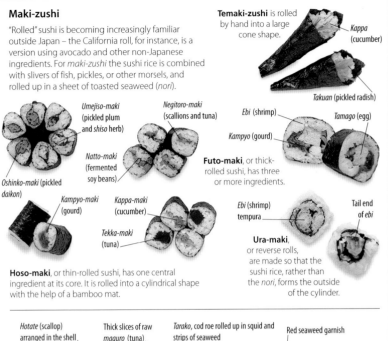

Temaki-zushi is rolled by hand into a large cone shape.

Kappa (cucumber)

Takuan (pickled radish)

Umejiso-maki (pickled plum and *shiso* herb)

Negitoro-maki (scallions and tuna)

Ebi (shrimp)

Kampyo (gourd)

Tamago (egg)

Natto-maki (fermented soy beans)

Futo-maki, or thick-rolled sushi, has three or more ingredients.

Oshinko-maki (pickled daikon)

Kampyo-maki (gourd)

Kappa-maki (cucumber)

Ebi (shrimp) tempura

Tail end of ebi

Tekka-maki (tuna)

Ura-maki, or reverse rolls, are made so that the sushi rice, rather than the *nori*, forms the outside of the cylinder.

Hoso-maki, or thin-rolled sushi, has one central ingredient at its core. It is rolled into a cylindrical shape with the help of a bamboo mat.

Hotate (scallop) arranged in the shell

Thick slices of raw *maguro* (tuna)

Tarako, cod roe rolled up in squid and strips of seaweed

Red seaweed garnish

Hotate (scallop) arranged with thin strips of *nori* (seaweed)

Hokkigai, out of its shell

Sashimi
Sliced fillets of the freshest uncooked fish may be served as a single course. Sashimi is delicate and creamy, and the only accompaniments should be soy sauce, wasabi, daikon, and maybe a *shiso* leaf.

Tako (octopus)

Aji (horse mackerel), topped with finely sliced scallions

Wasabi (green horseradish) molded into the shape of a *shiso* leaf

Fish display at Kochi street market

Popular Fish in Japan

Of the 3,000 or so varieties of fish eaten in Japan, the most common, available year-round, are *maguro* (tuna), *tai* (sea bream), *haze* (gobies), *buri* (yellowtail), *saba* (mackerel), crustaceans such as *ebi* (shrimp) and *kani* (crab), and fish that are usually salted such as *sake* (salmon) and *tara* (cod). Spring is the start of the season for the river fish *ayu* (sweetfish), traditionally caught by trained cormorants. *Katsuo* (skipjack tuna) is available in spring and summer, *unagi* (eel) in midsummer, *sanma* (saury) in the fall. Winter is the time for *dojo* (loach), *anko* (angler fish), and *fugu* (globefish), prized for its delicate flavor but also feared for deadly toxins in its liver and ovaries.

What to Drink in Tokyo

Green tea and sake (rice wine) are the traditional drinks of Japan. Both have ancient histories, with sake being mentioned in the *Kojiki (see p23)*, the first written historical account of Japan. The appreciation of each has been elevated to connoisseurship. The tea ceremony is the ultimate expression of tea appreciation, a social ritual imbued with Buddhist ideals. Sake has long associations with Shinto – the fox god Inari presides over sake – and many Shinto festivals still involve the drink as a central theme. Other Japanese drinks include *shochu* spirit and "health" drinks.

Picking green tea in May, when leaves are at their most tender

Types of Tea

Green tea leaves are divided into three main grades – *gyokuro*, which are the most tender, protected leaves that come out in May; *sencha*, which are tender leaves picked in May or June; and *bancha*, which are large leaves left until August. Leaves are sterilized with steam and then dried. *Bancha* is often roasted or mixed with other ingredients such as brown rice to form robust teas. Other teas are available; of foreign ones the Japanese especially enjoy imported fine English teas.

Basic green tea is sold loose or in tea bags.

Mugicha is a tea brewed from roasted barley.

Hojicha is roasted bancha, a coarse tea.

Genmaicha is brown rice (genmai) and bancha.

Sencha is a popular medium- to high-grade tea.

Gyokuro is a delicate high-grade tea.

Powdered matcha is used in tea ceremonies.

Soft Drinks

With names that conjure up disturbing images for English-speaking foreigners, Calpis and Pocari Sweat are among the most popular Japanese brands of canned soft drinks. Some are marketed as energy and vitamin boosters. Vending machines *(see p139)* stock them alongside canned green tea and coffee, and a wide range of fruit juices.

Chawan, a wide-brimmed cup without handles

Kyusu (teapot)

Wagashi (sweets)

Tea leaves, usually loose, are placed in a teapot. Bancha is brewed with boiling water, but sencha and gyokuro should be brewed with boiled water that has been allowed to cool slightly first. The brewing tea should then stand for about a minute.

Sake (Rice Liquor)

Sake is made from rice and water, which are fermented together then pasteurized to create a superb alcoholic wine-like beverage. Many connoisseurs judge sake on the five qualities of sweetness, sourness, pungency, bitterness, and astringency. Sake may be drunk warm, but the finer types should be lightly chilled to retain the subtle flavors. Unlike wine, sake is rarely expected to improve in the bottle. Store it in a cool, dry place for no more than a few months.

Everyday *hon-jozo* type by Gekkeikan

Fine *ginjo* type by Nihonsakari

Finer *dai-ginjo* by Tsukasa Botan

Taruzake (cask sake) is matured in wooden casks made of cypress. Casks are often presented to Shinto shrines as offerings. The brewer's logo is displayed prominently.

The finest grade of sake, *dai-ginjo*, is made from the hardest core of the rice – more than 50 percent of each grain is shaved away. For the *ginjo* type about 40 percent is shaved; for *hon-jozo*, the average sake, about 30 percent. Some are brewed with added alcohol; those without are called *junmai*, "pure rice."

A classic serving set consists of a ceramic bottle *(tokkuri)* and matching cups *(sakazuki)*. The bottle can be placed in hot water to warm the sake to about 122°F (50°C).

Sake breweries traditionally hang a ball of cedar leaves *(sakabayashi)* and sometimes a sacred rope *(shimenawa)* over their entrance.

Other Alcoholic Drinks

Japan has several beers that have become well known around the world. Suntory whiskey is also sold abroad, popular with those who prefer a milder whiskey. Less well known abroad, *shochu* is a name for a group of Japanese spirits made from barley or other grains, or potatoes. The alcohol content of *shochu* varies from 40 to 90 proof. The distilled spirit is often mixed with hot water or used as a base for cocktails, but it is also drunk neat, either heated or on the rocks. In addition, it is used to make bottled fruit liqueurs such as *umeshu*, which is made with whole Japanese apricots.

Suntory whiskey

Sapporo beer

Asahi beer

Barley *shochu*

Rice *shochu*

Where to Eat and Drink

Central Tokyo

Nakaei ¥
Japanese curry **Map** 5 C4
5-2-1 Tshukiji, Chuo-ku
Tel *(03) 3541-8749* **Closed** *Sun*
This shop, which has been going strong for 100 years, is where the locals go for good, cheap, Japanese-style curry.

Yoshinoya ¥
Noodle **Map** 5 C3
Tsukiji Market Building 1, 5-2-1 Tsukiji, Chuo-ku
Tel *(03) 5550-8504* **Closed** *Sun*
This was the very first branch of this well-established *gyudon* (literally "beef bowl") chain.

Birdland ¥¥
Yakitori **Map** 5 B2
Tsukamoto Sozan Building, B1F, 4-2-15 Ginza, Chuo-ku
Tel*(03) 5250-1081* **Closed** *Sun, Mon*
A high-end restaurant specializing in *yakitori* (grilled chicken skewers). Birdland has a pleasant atmosphere.

DK Choice

Coca ¥¥
Thai **Map** 5 B2
Bic Camera Yurakucho, 6F, 1-11-1 Yurakucho, Chiyoda-ku
Tel *(03) 3201-5489*
A popular Thai restaurant with a difference: the specialty is *Thai suki*, a spicy Thai take on the classic Japanese hotpot dish *sukiyaki*, which has been re-imported to Japan. The Issan-style spicy BBQ chicken is also delicious, and they only use Hakata Hanamidori chickens from Japan's Kyushu region.

Kushiro ¥¥
Traditional Japanese **Map** 5 B1
JP Tower Kitte, 6F, Marunouchi 2-7-2, Chuo-ku
Tel *(03) 6256-0817*
An attractive *izakaya* (bar) that serves charcoal-grilled seafood and vegetable dishes, Kushiro also offers other specialties from the Hokkaido region.

Monja Oedosakai ¥¥
Monjayaki **Map** 6 D3
Eye Mark Tower 102, 1-8-1, Tsukishima, Chuo-ku
Tel *(03) 3531-0521*
Located on Monja Street, this place puts you right at the heart of Tokyo's ever-popular *monjayaki* (pancake) boom.

Nagamine ¥¥
Vegetarian **Map** 5 B3
Ginsho Building B1F, Ginza 4-9-5, Chuo-ku
Tel *(03) 3547-8083* **Closed** *Sun*
Run by a vegetable wholesaler based in nearby Tsukiji, this place serves *kaiseki* cuisine (that is, featuring multiple courses) at its best. Delectable dishes are prepared with no meat or fish.

Sato Yosuke ¥¥
Noodle **Map** 5 B2
Idei Honkan, 6-4-17 Ginza, Chuo-ku
Tel *(03) 6215-6211*
This restaurant specializes in *inaniwa udon* dishes. Hailing from Akita Prefecture, this type of thin noodle is among the best-loved varieties in Japan.

Sushi Iwa ¥¥
Sushi **Map** 5 C3
2-15-10 Tsukiji, Chuo-ku
Tel *(03) 3541-5951*
Boasting a 50-year history, Sushi Iwa knows how to make the perfect sushi. Diners can enjoy it in the restaurant's classy, minimalist surroundings.

Sushi Maru ¥¥
Sushi **Map** 5 C3
Tsukiji Fish Market Area 10, Tsukiji 5-2-1, Chuo-ku
Tel *(03) 3541-8414* **Closed** *Sun*
A popular, counter-style sushi restaurant in Tsukiji Market. Try the *omakase* set, which is huge.

Tenfusa ¥¥
Tempura **Map** 5 C3
Tsukiji Fish Market Building 6, 5-2-1 Tsukiji, Chuo-ku
Tel *(03) 3547-6766*
This is the only place in Tsukiji Fish Market that sells crispy and piping-hot tempura.

> **Price Guide**
> Prices are based on an average dinner for one. Lunchtime menus are often cheaper.
>
> ¥ under ¥1,000
> ¥¥ ¥1,000–¥8,000
> ¥¥¥ over ¥8,000

Warashibe (Tsushima) ¥¥
Monjayaki **Map** 6 D3
1-20-3, Tsukishima, Chuo-ku
Tel *(03) 3534-2929*
An attractive setting in which to savor *monjayaki* (pan-fried batter with various toppings), the Tokyo version of *okonomiyaki* (Japanese pancake).

Akasaka Kikunoi ¥¥¥
Seafood **Map** 2 E4
6-13-8 Akasaka, Minato-ku
Tel *(03) 3568-6055* **Closed** *Sun*
The Tokyo outpost of Japan's top chef Yoshihiro Murata serves up exquisite *kaiscki ryori* in beautiful surroundings. For a glimpse into Japan's culinary art at a fraction of the price, opt for the lunchtime *kodaiji bento* box.

Ginza Okamoto ¥¥¥
Kaiseki **Map** 5 B3
5F, 8-3-12 Ginza
Tel *(03) 3571-5110*
Before opening this excellent *kaiseki* restaurant, owner and head chef Hidetsugu Okamoto trained at the legendary Wakuden in Kyoto. He brings that experience to his kitchen.

Nobu Tokyo ¥¥¥
Seafood **Map** 5 A3
Toranomon Tower Office, 1F, 4-1-28 Toranomon, Minato-ku
Tel *(03) 5733-0070*
Nobu Matsuhisa is probably the best-known Japanese chef in the world. Diners flock to his Tokyo

The minamilist interior of Birdland, one of Tokyo's many *yakitori* restaurants

restaurant for impressive seafood cuisine with strong American influences. Good sake selection.

Les Saisons ¥¥¥
European **Map** 5 B2
Imperial Hotel Tokyo (Main Building), 1-1-1 Uchisaiwaicho, Chiyoda-ku
Tel *(03) 3539-8087*
The place for French dining at its best. Expect delicious and well-presented dishes, with exquisite service.

Sushi Jiro ¥¥¥
Seafood **Map** 5 B3
Tsukamoto Building B1F, 4-2-15 Ginza, Chuo-ku
Tel *(03) 3535-3600*
Home to the star of the film *Jiro Dreams of Sushi*, this place is a must for sushi connoisseurs. Jiro is the oldest chef in the world to hold three Michelin stars, and dining here is a once-in-a-lifetime experience. Advance reservations are essential.

Sushi Sora ¥¥¥
Seafood **Map** 5 C1
2-1-1 Nihonbashimuromachi, Chuo-ku
Tel *(03) 3270-8188*
The austere interior of Sushi Sora focuses the diners' attention on the real stars: the exquisite fish and the stunning views across Tokyo. Unusually for a top-class sushi restaurant, the chefs here all speak English.

Vin Picoeur ¥¥¥
European **Map** 5 B2
4-3-4 Ginza, Chuo-ku
Tel *(03) 3567-4122*
Located on the second floor of a building that also houses a wine merchant (hence the fine wine list), this place serves French-style charcoal-grilled meats and fish with a Japanese twist.

Northern Tokyo

Izakaya Koji ¥
European **Map** 4 E2
2-3-19 Asakusa, Taito-ku,
Tel *(03) 3844-0612*
This restaurant serving hearty beef stew is on Denbouin-dori, an Asakusa back alley filled with eateries offering a similar menu.

Oedo Kaiten Sushi ¥
Sushi **Map** 3 C3
6-2-1 Ueno, Taito-ku
Tel *(03) 5812-2097*
Items on the conveyor belt here start at ¥136. The most popular sushi, *chutoro* (medium fat tuna), is an affordable ¥315.

A low table with sunken leg room at Asakusa Imahan, Northern Tokyo

Park Side Café Ueno ¥
Café **Map** 3-C3
8-4 Ueno Park, Taito-ku,
Tel *(03) 5815-8251*
Gorgeous modern café serving beautifully made cakes, as well as more filling fare.

Ringer Hut Ueno ¥
Noodle **Map** 3 C3
6-8-5 Ueno, Taito-ku,
Tel *(03) 5807-1045*
Ringer Hut is a fast-food chain famous mainly for a Nagasaki-style noodle dish known as *champon*, which is a healthier, seafood-based version of *ramen*.

Shoryu Gyoza ¥
Gyoza (Dim Sum) **Map** 3 C3
6-10-14 Ueno, Taito-ku
Tel *(03) 3831-1579*
Watch the staff as they make large and delicious *gyoza* (dim sum) from scratch in this legendary restaurant tucked away in Ameyoko Market.

Asakusa Imahan ¥¥
Shabu-shabu **Map** 4 E2
3-1-12 Nishi-Asakusa, Taito-ku
Tel *(03) 3841-1114*
Founded in 1895, this *shabu-shabu* and *sukiyaki* chain offers high-grade *wagyu* beef boiled in a tasty broth.

Daikokuya ¥¥
Tempura **Map** 4 E3
1-38-10 Asakusa, Taito-ku
Tel *(03) 3844-1111*
Close to Senso-ji Temple, this long-running restaurant is famous for its *ebi-tendon* – prawn tempura laid on a bowl of rice.

Daitoryo ¥¥
Traditional Japanese **Map** 4 D2
6-10-14 Ueno, Taito-ku
Tel *(03) 3832-5622*
A popular *izakaya* in Ameyoko Market, Daitoryo is a great place to eat, drink, and socialize.

Iidaya ¥¥
Seafood **Map** 4 F2
3-3-2 Asakusa, Taito-ku
Tel *(03) 3843-0881* **Closed** *Wed*
This family restaurant has been serving *dojo* (a freshwater fish) to locals since the Edo period.

Maguro Bito ¥¥
Sushi **Map** 4 E3
1-21-8 Asakusa, Taito-ku
Tel *(03) 5828-5838*
Maguro Bito is said to be the best conveyor-belt sushi restaurant in Asakusa. Try the *otoro* tuna sushi, which is buttery and delicious.

Nezu Café ¥¥
Café **Map** 1 C5
Nezu Museum, Minami-Aoyama 6-5-1, Minato-ku
Tel *(03) 3400-2536*
The café at the Nezu Museum is a destination in itself. Watch as kimono-clad patrons jockey for the best seats overlooking the gardens.

Ocomo ¥¥
Okonomiyaki **Map** 4 E3
1-10-5 Asakusa, Taito-ku
Tel *(03) 6802-7743*
Enjoy *okonomiyaki* (Japanese pancake) on a hot plate at your table in a stylish setting.

Otafuku ¥¥
Oden **Map** 4 E2
1-6-2 Senzoku, Taito-ku
Tel *(03) 3871-2521* **Closed** *Mon*
This place has been serving up *oden* (boiled egg, *daikon*, and processed fish cake) since the Meiji period.

Sasanoyuki ¥¥
Tofu **Map** 4 D1
5-15-10 Negishi, Taito-ku
Tel *(03) 3873-1145* **Closed** *Mon*
The official supplier of tofu to the Imperial family, Sasanoyuki serves a wide range of dishes made from the best tofu in Japan.

For more information on types of restaurants *see page 117*

Sometaro   ¥¥
Okonomiyaki   **Map** 4 E3
2-2-2 Nishi-Asakusa, Taito-ku
Tel *(03) 3844-9502*
Enjoy *okonomiyaki* (Japanese
pancake) made with fresh
seafood in a rustic setting.

Takokyu   ¥¥
Oden   **Map** 3 C3
2-11-8 Ueno, Taito-ku
Tel *(03) 3837-1617*   **Closed** *Sun*
Somewhat of a mecca for *oden*
fans, this legendary restaurant
in downtown Ueno serves its
hotpot with a dark, heavy soup.

Yakiton   ¥¥
Yakitori   **Map** 4 D4
4-10-2 Asakusabashi, Taito-ku,
Tel *(03) 3864-4869* **Closed** *holidays*
This hole-in-the-wall place offers
pretty much any meat you can
think of – including pig heart
and tongue – on a skewer.

Yokichi   ¥¥
Noodle   **Map** 4 E2
*Amano Building 1F, 2-29-6, Asakusa,
Taitou-ku*
Tel *(03) 6231-7273*
Udon is normally a dish eaten
on the run, but this *izakaya* has
made it into a relaxing affair to
be enjoyed with friends over
a few drinks.

DK Choice

Hantei   ¥¥¥
Kushiage   **Map** 3 B2
2-12-15 Nezu, Bunkyo
Tel *(03) 3828-1440*
This gorgeous traditional
restaurant serving *kushiage*
(delicacies coated in panko
breadcrumbs, then fried) is
said to date back to the Meiji
era. It has survived both the
Great Kanto Earthquake and
World War II.

Varied and colorful sushi dishes at Sushi
Gotoku *(see p134)*

Kameya Issuitei   ¥¥¥
Kappo   **Map** 3 C3
2-13-2, Ueno, Taitou-ku
Tel *(03) 3831-0912*
Perfectly located by the edge of
Shinobazu Pond, in Ueno Park,
this restaurant specializes in
grilled eel. The *kappo* method
of cooking involves cutting,
boiling, stewing, and frying.

Kanda Yabu Soba   ¥¥¥
Noodle   **Map** 3 C4
2-10 Kanda-Awajicho, Chiyoda-ku
Tel *(03) 3251-0287*
Diners enjoy handmade soba
noodles while sitting on *tatami*
mats. Housed in a traditional,
wooden, Edo-style building.

Western Tokyo

Fuunji Ramen   ¥
Noodle   **Map** 1 A2
*Hokuto 1st Building, 2-14-3 Yoyogi,
Shibuya-ku*
Tel *(03) 6413-8480*   **Closed** *Sun*
Famed for its *tsukemen ramen*,
this place is extremely popular,
so expect to wait in line to taste
its legendary fish-flavored soup.

Gindaco   ¥
Takoyaki   **Map** 1 B1
1-18-6 Kabukicho, Shinjuku-ku
Tel *(03) 5155-2227*
A cross between a bar and a
stand. Enjoy piping-hot *takoyaki*
(diced octopus rolled into balls
with flour, then deep fried) while
watching the Kabukicho crowds.

Go Go Curry   ¥
Japanese curry   **Map** 1 A2
*YU-WA Building, B1, 2-13-6 Yoyogi,
Shibuya-ku*
Tel *(03) 3320-3855*
Gaudy pop culture meets tasty
curry here. A menu highlight is
the deep-fried pork cutlet, served
over rice, with a rich curry sauce
and shredded cabbage.

Kanetanaka-so   ¥
Kaiseki   **Map** 1 C5
*Cerulean Tower Tokyu Hotel, 2F,
26-1 Sakuragaoka-cho, Shibuya-ku*
Tel *(03) 3476-3420*
This exclusive *kaiseki* restaurant
offers picture-perfect dishes in
a modern setting.

Mos Burger   ¥
American   **Map** 1 B1
7-1-8 Nishishinjuku, Shinjuku-ku
Tel *(03) 3362-0093*
Find out why Japan's favorite
home-grown burger chain has
the edge over its international
rivals. Try one of the rice burgers,
with rice cakes instead of a bun.

Myeongdong Norimaki   ¥
Korean   **Map** 1 B1
1-15-5 Okubo, Shinjuku-ku
Tel *(03) 3232-7887*
If you have had your fill of
Japanese-style sushi, you
might want to try the Korean
version, which is equally tasty,
but has a spicy twist.

Nagai Ramen   ¥
Noodle   **Map** 1 B1
*Shinjuku Golden Gai (G2 Street), 2F,
1-1-10 Kabukicho, Shinjuku-ku*
Tel *(03) 3365-0296*   **Closed** *3rd Sun
of month*
In the heart of the Golden Gai,
Tokyo's historical bar district, this
place is famous for its *niboshi*
soup made from dried sardines.

Shinjuku Asia Yokocho   ¥
Asian   **Map** 1 B1
*Dai 2 Towa Kaikan (roof), 1-21-1
Kabukicho, Shinjuku-ku, Tokyo*
Tel *(03) 3352-2370*   **Closed** *Mon*
This rowdy rooftop food court
in the heart of Kabukicho offers
a range of different cuisines from
across Asia, including Korean
and Indonesian dishes.

Suzuran   ¥
Noodle   **Map** 1 B5
3-7-5 Shibuya, Shibuya-ku
Tel *(03) 3499-0434*   **Closed** *Sun
& hols*
Famous for its very thick and
chewy noodles, this legendary
tsukemen shop was one of the
first restaurants in Tokyo to start
the noodle-dipping craze.

DK Choice

Tenkkaippin Ramen   ¥
Noodle   **Map** 1 B2
*Atlas Nishi-Shinjuku Building, 1F,
1-15-8 Nishi-Shinjuku,
Shinjuku-ku*
Tel *(03) 3342-2427*
This small but lively restaurant
is popular with hardcore
ramen fans, who come flocking
for the heavy, high-fat *kotteri*
broth, which is so thick it is
more like a gravy than
a soup. Ask for an *ajitama*, or
soy sauce-flavored boiled egg,
as a topping. The service is
good and fast.

Azabu Shokudo   ¥¥
Yoshoku   **Map** 2 D5
*Suzuki Building, 1F, 4-2-9 Nishi-
Azabu, Minato-ku*
Tel *(03) 3409-4767*   **Closed** *Sun
& hols*
A slightly upmarket Western-
style restaurant famed for its
delicious *omuraisu* – flavored
rice wrapped in an omelet.

Blackhole ¥¥
Japanese　　　　Map 1 C1
1-2-5 Kabukicho, Shinjuku,
Tel *(03) 6457-6089*
This reliable *yaki-niku* bar is a hit with the locals. Depending on your luck, you may receive Kobe, Saitama, or Kyushu *wagyu* beef.

Chinese Café Eight ¥¥
Chinese　　　　Map 2 E5
Court Annex Roppongi, 2F,
3-2-13 Nishi-Azabu, Minato-ku
Tel *(03) 5414-5708*
Relaxed and popular, this Chinese restaurant is open 24 hours a day and is famed for its Peking duck.

Curry Udon Senkichi ¥¥
Noodle　　　　Map 1 A2
2-13-6 Yoyogi, Shibuya-ku
Tel *(03) 5358-7054*
Slurp down Japanese *udon* noodles from a steaming hot bowl of Thai-style curry soup, which comes in three flavors.

Deniz Roppongi ¥¥
Turkish　　　　Map 2 E5
Kita-Azabu Building, 1F-2F,
3-13-10 Roppongi, Minato-ku
Tel *(03) 6804-2941*
This is the place to visit for a late-night kabob and beer. Enjoy them while indulging in a spot of people-watching in Roppongi. Vegetarian options also available.

Espanya ¥¥
European　　　　Map 1 B2
Tokyo Plaza Building, 3F, 2-10-10,
Yoyogi, Shibuya-ku
Tel *(03) 3379-1159*　　**Closed** *Mon*
Authentic Spanish cuisine and wines in classy surroundings. The seafood paella is especially good.

Fonda de la Madrugada ¥¥
Mexican　　　　Map 1 C4
Villa Bianca, B1, 2-33-12 Jingumae,
Shibuya-ku
Tel *(03) 5410-6288*
There are not many Mexican restaurants in Tokyo, but this is the one to visit if you have a craving. Fantastic guacamole.

Gempin Fugu ¥¥
Fugu　　　　Map 1 B1
2F, 3-8-2 Shinjuku, Shinjuku-ku
Tel *(03) 3341-9529*
This is the place to try *fugu*, the infamous poisonous blowfish. Enjoy it with a bottle of sake.

Ghungroo ¥¥
Indian　　　　Map 1 C4
Seinan Building, 5-9-6 Minami-Aoyama, Minato-ku
Tel *(03) 3406-9144*
A cut above the rest, this fine-dining Indian restaurant serves a range of spicy and tasty curries.

The traditional and airy interior of Maisen, a famous *tonkatsu* chain

Hamaguri ¥¥
Seafood　　　　Map 1 B1
3-8-4 Shinjuku, Shinjuku-ku
Tel *(03) 3354-9018*　　**Closed** *Sun & hols*
This old-school restaurant specializes in shellfish and has a good range of sakes to match.

Hobgoblin Shibuya ¥¥
European　　　　Map 1 B5
Ichiban Building, 3F, 1-3-11,
Dogenzaka, Shibuya-ku
Tel *(03) 6415-4244*
Popular with expats, this British pub serves English ale and comfort food such as bangers and mash and shepherd's pie.

DK Choice

Kabuto ¥¥
Yakitori　　　　Map 1 B1
1-2-11 Nishi-Shinjuku, Shinjuku-ku
Tel *(03) 3342-7671*　　**Closed** *Sun & hols*
Join the local business crowd in this popular *yakitori* restaurant in the former black-market quarter of Omoide Yokocho ("Memory Lane"). The origins of this smoky alley near Shinjuku Station lie in the immediate aftermath of World War II, when dozens of drinking shacks were built here.

Maisen ¥¥
Tonkatsu　　　　Map 1 C5
4-8-5 Jingumae, Shibuya-ku
Tel *(03) 3470-0071*
This well-known *tonkatsu* chain sells the popular breaded and deep-fried pork cutlet.

Masudaya ¥¥
Noodle　　　　Map 1 B1
2-38-3 Kabukicho, Shinjuku-ku
Tel *(03) 3204-4147*
Classy *soba* restaurant with wood decor, a serene ambience, and delicious handmade noodles.

Mr. Chicken ¥¥
Singaporean　　　　Map 1 B4
1-15-4 Jingumae, Shibuya-ku
Tel *(03) 5772-1931*
This stylish restaurant takes a Singaporean street-food staple – chicken on rice – and turns it into a veritable art form. Also on the menu are pork spare ribs in soup.

Nabe-zo ¥¥
Nabe　　　　Map 1 B1
Shinjuku Takano Building No. 2, 8F,
3-30-1 Shinjuku, Shinjuku-ku
Tel *(03) 5363-4629*
A modern Japanese restaurant specializing in a varied range of hotpot dishes, namely *nabe* (hotpot), *sukiyaki* (stew), and *shabu-shabu* (thinly sliced beef boiled in water).

Nagi Shokudo ¥¥
Vegetarian　　　　Map 1 A5
15-10 Uguisudanicho, Shibuya-ku
Tel *(050) 1043-7751*
In the Shibuya area, this innovative vegetarian café/restaurant offers a range of tasty dishes, many of which are vegan. The lunchtime set-menu deal is particularly popular.

Nataraj ¥¥
Vegetarian/Indian　　　　Map 1 C5
Sanwa-Aoyama Building, B1, 2-22-19 Mimami-aoyama, Minato-ku
Tel *(03) 5474-0510*
Enjoy tasty and spicy hot Indian curries in a stylish environment. The food here is prepared with organic ingredients that are 100 percent vegetarian.

Restaurant-I ¥¥
European　　　　Map 1 B4
1F Park Court Jingumae 1-4-20 Jingumae, Shibuya-ku,
Tel *(03) 5772-2091*
Michelin-starred chef Keisuke Matsushima takes the delicate cuisine of the south of France and gives it a Japanese twist.

For more information on types of restaurants *see page 117*

Sasashige Teppan-Yaki
Cuisine ¥¥
Teppanyaki **Map** 2 D5
*Oyama Building, 2F, 2-13-15
Nishiazabu, Minato-ku*
Tel *(03) 5774-4439*
Wagyu beef steaks and fresh
seafood are grilled to perfection
at this high-class restaurant.

Seiko-en ¥¥
Yakiniku **Map** 1 B4
6-4-1 Jingumae, Shibuya-ku
Tel *(050) 5831-1324*
Top-quality *yakiniku*, or Korean-
style BBQ, in a stylish restaurant
with a Hawaiian theme.

Senkoen Kabukicho ¥¥
Chinese **Map** 1-B1
2F, 1-16-12 Kabukicho, Shinjuku-ku
Tel *(03) 5272-2118* **Closed** *Tue*
Laid-back and friendly Chinese
restaurant specializing in spicy
Shichuan dishes. Wash them
down with *shaoxingjiu* rice wine.

The Soul of Seoul ¥¥
Yakiniku **Map** 1 B5
*ARA Eve Beauty Bamboo Building,
B1, 1-2-5, Shibuya, Shibuya-ku*
Tel *(03) 5778-3896*
High-class Korean BBQ restaurant
in the Omotesando area. The fruit
makgeolli is an excellent drink to
match the tender meat.

Sushi Gotoku ¥¥
Sushi **Map** 1 A5
8-2 Kamiyamacho, Shibuya-ku
Tel *(03) 5454-5595*
Sushi with a touch of Western
influence is served at this place
in Shibuya. Opt for the multi-
course menu: chef Ueno will
prepare your dishes according to
the best ingredients available.

Teddy's Bigger Burgers ¥¥
American **Map** 1 B4
6-28-5 Jingu-mae, Shibuya-ku
Tel *(03) 5774-2288*
The Tokyo branch of this popular
Hawaiian chain delivers big, tasty
burgers with lots of flavor.

TGI Fridays ¥¥
American **Map** 2 E5
*Roppongi Plaza Building,
3-12-6 Roppongi, Minato-ku*
Tel *(03) 5412-7555*
This well-known restaurant chain
serves classic American fare, such
as hamburgers, ribs, and shakes.

Tonchang ¥¥
Yakiniku **Map** 1 B1
*Lisbon Building, 1F, 2-32-3 Okubo,
Shinjuku-ku*
Tel *(03) 5155-7433*
In the heart of Korea Town, this
is the place to sample authentic
Korean-style barbecued meats.

Toriyoshi ¥¥
Yakitori **Map** 1 B1
*Kurihashi Building, B1 & B2, 3-13-5,
Shinjuku, Shinjuku-ku*
Tel *(03) 3353-3357*
This well-established restaurant
does pretty much everything
with chicken that you can think
of, including excellent *yakitori*
(grilled skewers). The hotpot also
comes highly recommended.

Ushigoro ¥¥
Yakiniku **Map** 2 D5
2-24-14 Nishi Azabu, Minato-ku
Tel *(03) 3406-4129*
Stylish restaurant serving great
cuts of grilled meat – the beef
tenderloin filet is especially
juicy and delicious. There is
also a surprisingly big wine list.
Reservations recommended.

Yamaga Honten ¥¥
Traditional Japanese **Map** 1 B5
1-5-9 Dogenzaka, Shibuya-ku
Tel *(03) 3461-3010*
A short walk from Shibuya
Station, this old-school Japanese-
style *izakaya* (bar) has a wide-
ranging menu, with a particularly
strong focus on *yakitori*.

Le Bourguignon ¥¥¥
European **Map** 2 D5
3-3-1 Nishi-Azabu, Minato-ku
Tel *(03) 5772-6244* **Closed** *Wed*
A popular restaurant where the
food leans toward the heavier
end of French cuisine. Limited
seating, so book in advance.

L'Estasi ¥¥¥
European **Map** 2 E5
*Gate Tower, 3F, Roppongi Hills,
6-11-1 Roppongi, Minato-ku*
Tel *(03) 5770-4565*
Come here for high-quality
Italian food with a Japanese
twist and a strong focus on
fresh, organic ingredients and
presentation. In addition to pasta
dishes, meats, and fish, there is
also pizza. Good wine list, too.

Inakaya ¥¥¥
Robatayaki **Map** 2 E5
*Renu Building, 1F, 5-3-4 Roppongi,
Minato-ku*
Tel *(03) 3408-5040*
This upmarket *robatayaki*
(Japanese barbecue) restaurant
serves fire-grilled meats, fish,
and vegetables. Enjoy your
dinner with a sake from the
extensive range available.

DK Choice

Ryugin ¥¥¥
Kaiseki **Map** 2 E5
*Side Roppongi Building,
7-17-24 Roppongi, Minato-ku*
Tel *(03) 3423-8006* **Closed** *Sun*
Voted second-best restaurant
in Asia at the influential 50
Best Restaurant Awards, this
three Michelin-starred eatery
effortlessly combines traditional
kaiseki ryori with molecular
gastronomy that focuses on the
four seasonal flavors of Japan.
Reserve a table in advance.

Farther Afield

Grill Bon ¥
Sandwich
7-14-1 Ginza, Chuo-ku
Tel *(03) 5565-3386* **Closed** *Sun*
This tiny restaurant has made
just one type of sandwich
since 1944: the exquisite beef
hirekatsu, a cutlet that is deep
fried and perfectly cooked to
medium-rare, served with
soft white bread.

Ramen Jiro ¥
Noodle
2-16-4 Mita, Minato-ku
Tel *(03) 3455-5551* **Closed** *Sun*
Ramen Jiro has long been a
mecca for *ramen* lovers, who
come here to taste the delicious
soy sauce-based broth.

The chic yet homely interior of Sarabeth's Daikanyama *(see p135)*

Tableaux ¥
European
B1F, Sunroser Daikanyama, 11-6, Sarugaku-cho, Shibuya-ku
Tel *(03) 5489-2201*
Enjoy French- and Italian-inspired cooking with a strong Japanese touch in a refined enviroment.

Tonsui Teishokuya ¥
Traditional Japanese
2-39-13 Kitazawa, Setagaya
Tel *(03) 3468-1315*
This traditional *teishoku-ya* run by an elderly couple serves totally authentic and delicious fare.

Butagumi ¥¥
Tonkatsu
2-24-9 Nishi Azabu, Minato-ku
Tel *(03) 5466-6775*   **Closed** *Mon*
Unlike most *tonkatsu* places, this restaurant serves 50 varieties of pork – everything from *kurobuta* (crispy fried black pork) to Spanish Iberico ham.

Celeb de Tomato ¥¥
Vegetarian
3-15-5 Kita Aoyama, Minato-ku
Tel *(03) 6427-9922*
A restaurant that worships the humble tomato to the exclusion of everything else. A fantastically blinkered Japanese original.

Chabuzen ¥¥
Vegetarian
6-16-20 Daita, Setagaya-ku
Tel *(080) 6603-8587*   **Closed** *Mon*
This restaurant in trendy Shimokitazawa specializes in *yakuzen* cuisine, or food believed to have medicinal properties.

Iseya ¥¥
Yakitori
1-15-8 Kichijoji-Minami-cho, Musashino-shi
Tel *(0422) 43-2806*   **Closed** *Mon*
Iseya is located right on the edge of Inokashira Park, so diners can enjoy an old-school *yakitori* while gazing upon one of Tokyo's most pleasant green spaces.

King Falafel ¥¥
Vegetarian
2-7-31 Minami Azabu, Minato-ku
Tel *(03) 5441 4770*   **Closed** *Sat*
This Israeli-owned stand offers falafel sandwiches or falafel lunch boxes, with rice and side salads. The pitta bread is imported from Jerusalem. Excellent hummus.

Kuro Hitsuji ¥¥
Izakaya
1-11-6, Kamimeguro, Meguro-ku
Tel *(070) 6483-2255*
Serves a good example of the popular Mongolian-style grilled lamb known as Genghis Khan.

Yoshiba, a restaurant renowned for its links to sumo wrestling

Meu Nota ¥¥
Vegetarian
2F, 3-45-11 Koenji-Minami, Suginami-ku
Tel *(03) 5929 9422*
Classy but friendly café in trendy Koenji. On the menu are tasty meat-free soups, pasta dishes, salads, and tapas-style bites.

Momonjiya ¥¥
Nabe
1-10-2, Ryogoku, Sumida-ku
Tel *(03) 3631-5596*   **Closed** *Sun*
The menu here will satisfy the most committed of carnivores, with dishes featuring venison, wild boar, and even badger, plus a great *nabe* hotpot.

NorthField ¥¥
European
Shimokitazawa Coo B1, 2-26-14, Kitazawa, Setagaya-ku
Tel *(03) 6416-8248*
An interesting blend of European dishes is served at this classy eatery in trendy Shimokitazawa.

Pizzeria La Befana ¥¥
Pizzeria
5-31-3, Daita, Setagaya-ku
Tel *(03) 3411-9500*
Proper wood-fired-oven pizza in classy surroundings. Good prices.

Queen's Bath Resort ¥¥
Hawaiian
Aqua City Odaiba 6F, 1-7-1, Daiba, Minato-ku
Tel *(03) 3599-2601*
Enjoy fine Hawaiian fare with a touch of French, accompanied by great views of Tokyo Bay.

Sabaran ¥¥
Turkish
Jiyugaoka Department Store 2F 14, 1-28-8, Jiyuugaoka, Meguro-ku
Tel *(03) 5701-0012*   **Closed** *Wed*
Great Turkish cuisine, including divine desserts, served in a stylish environment. Good service.

Sanzan'uindou ¥¥
Traditional Japanese
1F, 5-29-16, Daizawa, Setagaya-ku
Tel *(03) 3412-8200*
One of Tokyo's best Okinawan restaurants, this place is renowned for the delectable *agu* braised pork belly. The menu also features many other Okinawan treats.

Sarabeth's Daikanyama ¥¥
American
T-SITE Station, 2F, 1-35-17 Ebisu-Nishi, Shibuya-ku, Tokyo
Tel *(03) 5428-6358*
A popular New York-based restaurant chain, Sarabeth's offers delicious breakfast classics, such as eggs Benedict, pancakes, and fluffy French toast.

Sembre Pizza ¥¥
European
3-25-25 Koenji-Kita, Suginami-ku
Tel *(03) 3330-9201*
A back-to-basics shop that serves good pizza at a reasonable price. Try the sausage and broccoli pizza, or opt for a margherita (tomato and mozzarella).

Tonki ¥¥
Tonkatsu
1-1-2 Shimo-Meguro, Meguro-ku
Tel *(03) 3491-9928*   **Closed** *Tue*
Tonki has been serving *tonkatsu* – breaded, deep-fried pork cutlets – to Tokyoites since the 1940s. Diners eat at a counter running along the edge of a spotless and spartan room.

DK Choice

Yoshiba ¥¥
Nabe
2-14-5, Yokoami, Sumida-ku
Tel *(03) 3623-4480*   **Closed** *Sun*
Located in the famous sumo-wrestling district of Ryogoku, this restaurant specializes in hotpot dishes, including *chanko-nabe*, the dish responsible for making the wrestlers put on all those pounds. If that is not authentic enough, the restaurant was formerly a sumo stables, and there is a preserved ring at the center of the dining area.

Shirube ¥¥¥
Izakaya
2-18-2 Shimokitazawa, Setagaya
Tel *(03) 3413-3785*
This classy place in Shimokitazawa manages to retain the typical buzz of an *izakaya* while offering the ambience and food of a proper restaurant.

For more information on types of restaurants *see page 117*

Beyond Tokyo

Hippari Dako
¥
Noodle
1011 Kamihatsuishimachi, Nikko, Tochigi-ken
Tel *(0288) 53-2933*
At this family-run restaurant you will find Japanese comfort food: *ramen* soup, *yakisoba*, plus a *yakitori* menu. The walls are covered with quirky notes left by visitors from all over the world.

Miyadai
¥
Japanese
1-14-19 Hase, Kamakura
Tel *(03) 210-0858*   **Closed** *Tue*
Tucked away in an unassuming back alley near the meat market in Hasedera, this no-frills shop sells some of the best croquettes in the whole of Japan.

Shin-Yokohama
Ramen Museum
¥
Noodle
2-14-21 Shinyokohama, Kohoku-ku, Yokohama City
Tel *(045) 471-0503*
Try all the types of *ramen* Japan has to offer at this museum dedicated to the humble noodle soup. Choose from the nine *ramen* shops set within the replica 1958 Japanese cityscape.

Akai
¥¥
Traditional Japanese
1322-7 Funatsu, Fujikawaguchiko, Minami-Tsuru-gun
Tel *(0555) 72-5259*   **Closed** *Thu*
This *izakaya* serves excellent grilled fish and is a popular drinking spot with the locals.

Bonzo Kamakura
¥¥
Noodle
3-17-33 Zaimokuza, Kamakura-shi, Kanagawa-ken
Tel *(0467) 7373-15*
A Michelin-starred restaurant famous for its handmade *soba* noodles. Excellent tempura, too.

Chaya-kado
¥¥
Noodle
1518 Yamanouchi, Kamakura, Kanagawa Prefecture
Tel *(0467) 23-1673*
Nagashisomen noodles are usually served only at festivals, but at Chaya-kado you can try your hand at catching them with chopsticks as they slide down a cold-water stream in the restaurant's garden.

Gyoshintei
¥¥
Vegetarian
2339-1 Sannai, Nikko, Tochigi Prefecture
Tel *(0288) 53-3751*   **Closed** *Thu*
Try *shojin ryori*, or Buddhist temple cuisine, in this serene location close to many of Nikko's attractive temples and shrines.

Hachinoki Honten
¥¥
Shojin Ryori
7 Yamanouchi, Kita-Kamakura
Tel *(0467) 22-8719*
Enjoy elegant *shojin ryori* vegan cuisine in the peaceful surrounds of Hachinoki Honten, located close to the main entrance of Kencho-ji Temple.

Hakone Atsukian
¥¥
Noodle
184 Yumotochaya, Hakone-machi, Ashigarashimo-gun, Kanagawa-ken
Tel *(0460) 85-6763*
Aficionados swear by the *zaru soba* (cold noodles in a broth) served here. The dish is made with top-quality buckwheat flour and some of the best spring water in Japan.

Hakone Curry Cocoro
¥¥
Japanese Curry
HOT Ogawa Bldg., 1F, 206 Yumoto, Hakone-machi, Ashigarashimo-gun, Kanagawa Prefecture
Tel *(0460) 85-8556*   **Closed** *Mon*
Japanese soup curry is served in a hotpot with lots of hearty meat and vegetables. A glowing robot statue greets you at the door.

Hananomai Izukyu
¥¥
Seafood
1-6-1, Higashihongo, Shimoda-shi, Shizuoka,
Tel *(0558) 25-1330*
Popular and attractive *izakaya* with floor seating. Order from the excellent seafood-heavy menu (the sashimi is particularly good) and wash your food down with the high-grade sake.

Hoto Fudo
¥¥
Nabe
707 Kitamoto, Fujikawaguchiko, Minamitsuru-gun
Tel *(0558) 76-7800*
Hoto noodles, which are similar to *udon*, are a specialty of the Fuji Lakes Area, and you can eat them here, piping hot and served with lots of local vegetables.

Imozen
¥¥
Kaiseki
15-1 Komuro, Kawagoe City, Saitama Prefecture
Tel *(049) 243-8551*   **Closed** *Tue*
Featuring an attractive Japanese garden, this affordable *kaiseki* restaurant specializes in dishes made with sweet potatoes.

Kabuki
¥¥
Izakaya
2F, 814-5, Hanazakicho, Narita-shi, Chiba Prefecture
Tel *(0476) 22-1366*
Conveniently located near Narita Station, this classy *izakaya* offers everything from sashimi and *okonomiyaki* to *wagyu* steaks.

Kawagoe Ichinoya
¥¥
Japanese
1-18-10 Matsue-cho, Kawagoe City, Saitama Prefecture
Tel *(049) 222-0354*
This long-standing Kawagoe institution serves the regional specialty: *unagi-don*, or grilled eel on a bowl of rice.

Magakoro
¥¥
Vegetarian
Hase 2-8-11, 2F, Kamakura, Kanagawa Prefecture
Tel *(0467) 25-1414*   **Closed** *Sun*
This hip organic and vegetarian café looks out onto sunny Kamakura Beach. A highlight is the tofu avocado salad.

Masudaya
¥¥
Kaiseki
439–2 Ishiya-machi, Nikko, Tochigi-ken   **Closed** *Thu*
Locally produced *yuba* (tofu skin) is the base ingredient for the delicious *kaiseki* cuisine at this reasonably priced restaurant. Seating also available in the pleasant garden.

Enjoy a bowl of *hoto* noodles in the modern surroundings of Hoto Fudo

Key to Price Guide *see page 130*

Morisaki ¥¥
Kappo
2-10-18 Komachi, Kamakura, Kanagawa Prefecture,
Tel *(0467) 23-8393*
In the tradition of *kappo* dining, chef Morisaki carefully prepares a range of delicious dishes before your eyes at the counter.

Sakanadon-ya ¥¥
Sushi
Bay Stage Shimoda, 2F, 1-1 Sotogaoka, Shimoda-shi, Shizuoka Prefecture
Tel *(0558) 25-5151*
This reasonably priced restaurant offers *kaiten-zushi*, or conveyor-belt sushi. Its location near the port ensures decent-sized and good-quality cuts of fish.

DK Choice

Sanrokuen ¥¥
Robatayaki
3370-1 Funatsu, Fujikawaguchiko-machi, Minamitsuru-gun
Tel *(0555) 73-1000* **Closed** *Thu*
At this traditional yet fun fireside-cooking restaurant, diners can sit at a traditional *irori*, or sunken fire pit, and roast their own skewers of food. There is a wide range of meat, seafood, and vegetable dishes to choose from, and at the end of the meal you can enjoy a hearty bowl of *hoto* noodles, a local specialty.

Shikajaya ¥¥
Tofu
640 Yumoto, Hakone-machi, Kanagawa-ken
Tel *(0460) 85-5751* **Closed** *Thu*
This vegetarian-friendly restaurant in Hakone specializes in dishes made from tofu and *yamaimo*, a yam-like potato that can be eaten raw.

Shinshin ¥¥
Kaiseki
549-1, Kamicho, Narita-shi, Chiba, 286-0032
Tel *(0476) 22-4252*
Cheap for a *kaiseki*, this place offers a full range of seafood, plus meat dishes such as *shabu-shabu*. If you are feeling brave, try the *fugu* (blowfish).

Shokudo Suzuki ¥¥
European
581-2 Goko-machi, Nikko
Tel *(0288) 54-0662*
Featuring a somewhat cluttered yet intimate feel, this pasta shop also serves great *yuba* dishes, made from tofu skin.

The reconstructed 1958 cityscape at Shin-Yokohama Ramen Museum *(see p136)*

Ton Ebi ¥¥
Traditional Japanese
2-1-7, Higashihongo, Shimoda-shi, Shizuoka
Tel *(0558) 23-0168*
This *tonkatsu* restaurant is famous for its *ebi-furai*, or deep-fried crumbed prawns, which are crunchy and delicious. Cheap lunch sets are available.

Torattoria Rakkio ¥¥
European
Celebrity Narita 103, 1-2-1 Hiyoshidai, Tomisato-shi, Chiba Prefecture
Tel *(0476) 29-5538* **Closed** *Tue*
An authentic Italian restaurant in Narita serving a variety of delectable pasta dishes for a reasonable price. Good wine list.

Tung Fat/Dohatsu Honkan (Yokohama) ¥¥
Chinese
148 Yamashita-cho, Naka-ku, Yokohama
Tel *(045) 681 7273* **Closed** *1st and 3rd Tue of month*
Located on the main drag of Yokohama's China Town, this reliable restaurant specializes in Cantonese food.

Uotami Imaichiten ¥¥
Traditional Japanese
1F, 1385-1 Imaichi, Nikko-shi, Tochigi Prefecture
Tel *(0288) 22-5088*
This attractive Japanese-style *izakaya* with polished wooden floors places a strong focus on fish and seafood.

Yama Soba ¥¥
Noodle
704 Yumoto, Hakone-machi, Ashigarashimo-gun, Kanagawa
Tel *(0460) 85-7889* **Closed** *Thu*
Enjoy delicious *soba* noodles and tempura set meals while sitting on *tatami* mats in a traditional setting.

DK Choice

Heichinrou ¥¥¥
Chinese
149 China Town Main Street, Yamashita-cho, Naka-Ward, Yokohama City
Tel *(045) 681-3001*
Boasting a 120-year history, this high-class restaurant with a focus on Cantonese food is one of the oldest Chinese restaurants in Japan. Take advantage of the reasonably priced set menus to try traditional delicacies such as sea cucumber and abalone, famous for their unusual texture.

Hermitage ¥¥¥
European
22-5 Wakitahoncho, Kawagoe, Saitama Prefecture
Tel *049-243-6607*
Come to this authentic Italian restaurant for the excellent service, the classy setting, and the sublime cuisine. The scallops and sea urchin pasta is especially recommended.

Tonkatsu (deep fried pork cutlets), a traditional favorite

For more information on types of restaurants *see page 117*

SHOPPING IN TOKYO

Tokyo is often described as the "warehouse of the world," and it is possible to procure anything under the sun here, from handcrafted boxwood combs to robot pets. The constant innovation and commercial ingenuity that characterize the city have resulted in a rash of mini shopping cities such as Tokyo Midtown and Omotesando Hills; high-tech convenience stores and high-end fashion towns such as Harajuku and Ginza; and Akihabara, an almost exotic electronic market. The world's highest concentration of vending machines per capita is also visible at every turn. And, compared with other global cities, the prices are not as outrageous as presumed.

Prices and Sales Tax

The Japanese yen continues to be seen as a stable currency. Cash is by far the easiest method to pay for most goods. International credit cards are still unpopular in smaller shops. VISA, American Express, Diners Club, and MasterCard are the most widely accepted.

In department stores and boutiques, and in inner-city areas, prices are usually marked in Arabic numerals. In local shops and supermarkets, and in areas where non-Japanese are few and far between, prices may be written only in kanji characters.

All items and services are subject to a consumption tax of eight percent. The price displayed should by law include the tax, although in practice this may not be the case.

Tax-Free Shopping

Tokyo's tax-free shops offer a good range of domestic and imported brand items without the five percent sales tax added elsewhere. The best authorized outlets are the **Tokyo International Arcade**, near the Imperial Hotel *(see p112)* and **Laox** *(see p47)* for electronic goods.

In some shops, particularly department stores *(depatos)*, you may have to pay the full price for an item, then obtain a refund and customs document from a tax-exemption counter. This document is retained by customs when you leave Tokyo. Most major department stores offer tax exemption, but usually on goods over the value of ¥10,000. One advantage of shopping at department stores is that they usually have

Youth entertainment area in Shibuya

tax-exemption counters with English-speaking staff. The counters will issue a customs document, which they will attach to your passport for presentation when you depart. Large electronic stores in Akihabara *(see p47)*, such as **Yodobashi Camera** and Laox provide this service.

Shopping Zones

Tokyo has many shopping zones identified by the popular goods they display. **Akihabara** *(see p47)* is the world's largest and most up- to-date electronic and camera center. **Aoyama/ Omotesando** *(see p67 & p70)* is known for its high fashion in the city. Visit **Asakusa** for traditional Japanese souvenirs, foods, toys, and pop culture trinkets. **Daikanyama Address Dixsept** *(see pp142–3)* has several reputed boutiques, catering to the young and trend conscious. High-end department stores and art galleries make their home in **Ginza** *(see pp40–41)*. **Harajuku** *(see p67)*, a fun street-oriented clothing, accessories, and cuddly toy district, caters to

high-teens shoppers on small budgets. **Jimbocho** *(see p46)* is Tokyo's oldest book center. **Shibuya** *(see pp68–9)* with its department stores and fashion buildings, is one of the city's most diverse shopping zones. **Shinjuku**, to the west side of the station, is all electronics and software; the east side has department stores and multi-purpose shopping complexes.

Department Stores

Many stores are owned by railroad companies, so that passengers coming off from their platforms are fed through passages bulging with advertising and display goods. Apart from selling a vast variety of top-range items, department stores, like convenience stores, also sell tickets for concerts and exhibitions. Roofs are often set aside as children's attraction parks, mini-golf ranges, and beer gardens. One early innovator was **Mitsukoshi**, perhaps Tokyo's most famous store. The great flagship stores such as **Takashimaya** and **Isetan** follow a similar layout,

with delectable foods in the basement, a wide range of Western and Japanese restaurants on the top floor, and every conceivable type of goods between. Some stores are known for certain commodities – **Matsuya** for top fashion brands and for Japanese crafts, quality souvenirs, and furnishings; **Tokyu Hands** for household goods, and **Wako** for watches and jewelry. The **Marui 0101** department store is the place to check out the edgier side of Japanese fashion.

Multi-Purpose Complexes

Roppongi Hills (see p71), with its high-end shopping options, a prestigious art gallery, observation lounge, cinemas, and live events, was the first of several multipurpose complexes. The **Marunouchi Building** in the Tokyo Station area has turned into a skyscraper shopping, restaurant, and office space. Shiodome, another shopping, office, and residential nexus, seems to grow exponentially with each visit. The shopping centerpiece of this millennium complex, **Caretta Shiodome**, attracts a young office crowd intent on keeping up with the latest in clothing. **Omotesando Hills** (see p67) features many Japanese and overseas designer stores. **Tokyo Midtown** houses several fashion and lifestyle outlets.

Automatic vending machine

Markets

Food markets provide an insight into the Japanese enthusiasm for food and cooking. The basement food floor of a major department store is a good place to start.

A whole street of highly visible plastic food and kitchenware suppliers along **Kappabashi-dori** (see p56) creates the mood of a lively market place along this well patronized street. The ultimate market experience is **Tsukiji Fish Market** (see p42); the area to the east is full of small restaurants and shops with pungent crates of wasabi (horseradish) and dried fish hanging from storefronts.

Convenience Stores and Vending Machines

Convenience stores (konbini) are easy to spot. They have catchy names such as 7-Eleven and AM-PM. Many people depend on these stores for more than just foods, toiletries, and magazines: they also book concert tickets and use ATMs and photocopiers. The quality of konbini food is surprisingly high and fresh. Among the popular take-out food items are boxed lunches, steamed buns, and cup noodles. Beverages include soft drinks, hot coffee, beer, and sake. Stores are often open 24/7. A Tokyo fixture since 1926, besides drinks and snacks, vending machines dispense batteries, flowers, eggs, underwear, disposable cameras, and even oxygen.

Arcades and Malls

Many arcades and malls date from the postwar period and, being generally located in downtown areas, are old-fashioned in style and appearance. Along the approach to Senso-ji temple (see pp58–9) is an arcade of shops selling a mixture of tourist souvenirs, traditional crafts, snacks, and kitsch pop culture items.

Fuji-Torii antique shop displaying pottery

Antique Stores and Flea Markets

Flea markets, a Sunday-only institution, are often held in the grounds of old shrines, adding extra interest. The antique market in the basement of the **International Antique House** along Ometesando-dori may be a little gloomy, but the glassware, swords, and antique jewelry brighten up the setting. Five minutes' walk along the same side of the road in the direction of Harajuku, the **Oriental Bazaar** has genuine and replica antique furniture, pottery, and a good deal more. Nearby **Fuji-Torii** is known for the quality of its antiques, wood-block prints, tansu chests, scrolls, and lacquerware craft.

The market at **Tomioka-Hachimangu shrine**, held on the first two Sundays of the month, is a lively event. With over 250 stalls, **Oedo Market** is the largest outdoor antique market in Japan, specializing in items from the Edo era. The market takes place every first and third Sunday of the month. Closer to the center, the market at **Hanazono Shrine**, near Shinjuku's legendary watering hole Golden Gai (see p63), is open every Sunday.

Beautiful glass building of Prada store, Aoyama

An elegant display of jewelry in Omotesando

Cosmetics, Jewelry, and Accessories

Mikimoto sells its pearls and jewelry in opulent surroundings. For a selection of silver and jewelry, visit Mori Silver in the **Oriental Bazaar** and **Takane Jewelry**. Nakamise-dori at Senso-ji temple *(see pp58–9)* is the place to find Japan's traditional jewelry. **Ginkado** sells *kanzashi* (hairpins), costume swords, and fans. Next door is **Bunsendo**, also selling fans. The last maker of handmade wooden combs is **Jusanya** in Ueno. The red, stucco facade of the **Shiseido Building** in Ginza is complemented by the Shiseido Cosmetics Garden in Omotesando. For "cute" culture accessories, **Takeshita-dori** *(see p67)* is hard to beat.

Traditonal Arts and Crafts

Maruzen in Nihonbashi is an excellent source of traditional arts and crafts including ceramics, woodcraft, and lacquerware, as is **Takumi** in Ginza. **Itoya**, also in Ginza, is packed with crafts, especially fine *washi* (Japanese paper). **Kuroeya**, at Senso-ji temple, has been selling *washi* since the mid-19th century and stocks everything from modern stationery to traditional kites. The **Japan Folk Crafts Museum** *(see p79)* has a small, high-quality selection. The **Japan Traditional Craft Center**

in Ikebukuro is an excellent place for purchasing affordable traditional crafts.

Contemporary Art and Design

The Spiral Garden in Minami-Aoyama's Spiral Building *(see p70)* usually has something interesting by Japanese artists.

In Ginza, you can find works by Japanese artists at **Galleria Grafica**, **Plus Minus Gallery**, and **Yoseido Gallery**. **Ginza Graphic Gallery** exhibits both Japanese and foreign works. The **Karakuri Museum** in Shibuya displays and sells artworks based on optical illusions. Located in the Tokyo Opera City building *(see p179)* in Shinjuku, the **NTT InterCommunication Center** features exhibits and installations using the latest technology. In the same building is the **Tokyo Opera City Gallery**, which displays Japanese painting, and graphic art. Contemporary prints can be found at the **Tolman Collection** near Tokyo Tower. For ceramics, try **Koransha** in Ginza. Good sources of modern houseware are the department stores **Tokyu Hands** and **Matsuya**. For cutting-edge interior design, head to **Axis** in Roppongi, a complex of galleries selling kitchenware, ceramics, furniture, and more. Shibuya's **Loft** has several floors of contemporary novelty housewares, jewelry, accessories, and toys.

Ironware kettle, Japan Traditional Craft Center

Books, Music, and Manga

Isseido, an Art Deco Jimbocho institution, keeps used and rare books. The biggest stock of secondhand English titles though, can be found at **Good Day Books** in Ebisu. Another specialty store, **Crayon House** in Omotesando, caters exclusively to children. The younger of the two Shinjuku **Kinokuniya** stores has the best selections of titles in Tokyo. **Maruzen** has a good choice of titles in its Marunouchi shop. **Tower Records** boasts an up-to-date collection of books. **JET SET Records** travels round the world to source rare secondhand LPs, as well as producing its own records. A keystone of the Japanese indie world, the Shinjuku branch of the **Disk Union** chain has the best stock. Manga fans will love **Mandarake** in the Shibuya Beam building for its second-hand magazines and related products. **Sekaido** in Shinjuku has a good range of manga.

Boxed sweets decorated with characters in a Kabuki play

Specialty Shops

Head to **Sanbido** for religious statues and beautiful dolls; **Nishijima Umbrellas** has traditional umbrellas, while **Tokiwado** has *kaminari okoshi* crackers. **Nakatsuka** sells candies and sweet crackers, and **Kappabashi-dori** *(see p56)* is the place for kitchenware and plastic food. **Puppet House** is a shop, gallery, and workshop. **Isetatsu** specializes in *chiyogami* designs taken from textiles worn by samurai; and **Sagemonoya** sells antique *netsuke*, small, ornate accessories designed to hang from kimono belts.

DIRECTORY

Department Stores

Isetan
3-14-1 Shinjuku. **Map** 1 B1. **Tel** (03) 3352-1111.

Marui 0101
3-30-13 Shinjuku. **Map** 1 A1. **Tel** (03) 3354-0101.

Matsuya
3-6-1 Ginza. **Map** 5 C2. **Tel** (03) 3567-1211.

Mitsukoshi
1-4-1 Nihonbashi Muro-machi. **Map** 5 C1. **Tel** (03) 3241-3311.

Takashimaya
5-24-2 Sendagaya. **Map** 1 B2. **Tel** (03) 5361-1111.

Tokyu Hands
12-18 Udagawacho, Shibuya. **Map** 1 B5. **Tel** (03) 5489-5111.

Wako
4-5-11 Ginza. **Tel** (03) 3562-2111.

Multi-Purpose Complexes

Caretta Shiodome
1-8-2 Higashi-Shimbashi. **Map** 5 B3. **Tel** (03) 6218-2100.

Marunouchi Building
2-4-1 Marunouchi. **Map** 5 B1. **Tel** (03) 5218-5100.

Omotesando Hills
4-12-10 Jingumae, Omotesando. **Map** 1 C4. **Tel** (03) 3497-0310.

Tokyo Midtown
9-7-1 Akasaka. **Map** 2 E3. **Tel** (03) 3475-3100.

Antique Stores and Flea Markets

Fuji-Torii
6-1-10 Jingumae. **Map** 1 C4. **Tel** (03) 3400-2777.

International Antique House
Hanae Mori Bldg B1, 6-10-3 Kita Aoyama. **Map** 1 C4. **Tel** (03) 3407-2675.

Oedo Market
Tokyo Int. Forum, 3-5-1 Marunouchi. **Map** 5 B2. **Tel** (03) 6407-6011.

Oriental Bazaar
5-9-13 Jingumae. **Map** 1 B4. **Tel** (03) 3400-3933.

Tomioka-Hachimangu Shrine Market
1-20-3 Tomioka. **Map** 6 E2. **Tel** (03) 3642-1345.

Cosmetics, Jewelry, and Accessories

Bunsendo
1-30-1 Asakusa. **Map** 4 F3. **Tel** (03) 3841-0088.

Ginkado
1-30-1 Asakusa. **Map** 4 F3. **Tel** (03) 3841-8540.

Jusanya
2-12-21 Ueno. **Tel** (03) 3831-3238.

Mikimoto
4-5-5 Ginza. **Map** 5 B3. **Tel** (03) 3535-4611.

Oriental Bazaar
See Antique Stores and Flea Markets.

Shiseido Building
7-8-10 Ginza. **Map** 5 B3. **Tel** (03) 3571-7731.

Takane Jewelry
1-7-23 Uchisaiwaicho. **Map** 5 A3. **Tel** (03) 3591-2764.

Traditional Arts and Crafts

Itoya
3-7-1 Ginza. **Map** 5 C2. **Tel** (03) 3561-8311.

Japan Folk Crafts Museum
4-3-33 Komaba. **Tel** (03) 3467-4527.

Japan Traditional Craft Center
Metropolitan Plaza Bldg 1- 2F, 1-11-1 Nishi-Ikebukuro. **Tel** (03) 5954-6066.

Kuroeya
1-2-6 Nihonbashi. **Tel** (03) 3272-0948.

Maruzen
Oazo Bldg, 1-6-4 Marunouchi. **Map** 5 C1. **Tel** (03) 5288-8881.

Takumi
8-4-2 Ginza. **Map** 5 B3. **Tel** (03) 3571-2017.

Contemporary Art and Design

Axis
5-17-1 Roppongi. **Map** 2 E5. **Tel** (03) 3587-2781.

Galleria Grafica
Ginza S2 Bldg, 6-13-4 Ginza. **Map** 5 B3. **Tel** (03) 5550-1335.

Ginza Graphic Gallery
DNP Ginza Bldg, 7-7-2 Ginza. **Map** 5 B3. **Tel** (03) 3571-5206.

Karakuri Museum
King Bldg 2F, Shibuya 2-9-10. **Map** 1 C5. **Tel** (03) 3599-3313.

Koransha
6-14-20 Ginza. **Map** 5 B3. **Tel** (03) 3543-0951.

Loft
21-1 Udagawacho, Shibuya. **Map** 1 B5. **Tel** (03) 3462-3807.

Matsuya
See Department Stores.

NTT InterCommunication Center
Tel (0120) 144-199.

Plus Minus Gallery
2F, TEPCO Ginza-kan, 6-11-1 Ginza. **Tel** (03) 3575-0456.

Tokyo Opera City Gallery
Tel (03) 5353-0770.

Tokyu Hands
See Department Stores.

Tolman Collection
2-2-18 Shiba Daimon. **Map** 5 A4. **Tel** (03) 3434-1300.

Yoseido Gallery
5-5-15 Ginza. **Map** 5 B2. **Tel** (03) 3571-1312.

Books, Music, and Manga

Crayon House
3-8-15 Kita-Aoyama. **Map** 1 C5. **Tel** (03) 3406-6409.

Disk Union
3-31-4 Shinjuku. **Map** 1 B5. **Tel** (03) 3352-2691.

Good Day Books
1-11-2 Ebisu. **Map** 4 F3. **Tel** (03) 5421-0957.

Isseido
1-7 Kanda Jimbocho. **Map** 3 B5. **Tel** (03) 3292-0071.

JET SET Records
2-33-12-201 Kitazawa, Setagaya-ku. **Tel** (03) 5452-2262.

Kinokuniya
5-24-2 Sendagaya. **Map** 1 B1. **Tel** (03) 5361-3301.

Mandarake
Shibuya Beams B2, 31-2 Udagawacho, Shibuya. **Map** 1 A5. **Tel** (03) 3477-0777.

Maruzen
See Traditional Arts and Crafts.

Sekaido
3-1-1 Shinjuku. **Map** 1 B1. **Tel** (03) 5379-1111.

Tower Records
1-22-14 Jinnan, Shibuya. **Map** 1 B5. **Tel** (03) 3496-3661.

Specialty Shops

Isetatsu
2-18-9 Yanaka. **Map** 3 B1. **Tel** (03) 3823-1453.

Nakatsuka
1-37-1 Asakusa. **Map** 4 F3. **Tel** (03) 3843-4455.

Nishijima Umbrellas
1-30-1 Asakusa. **Map** 4 F3. **Tel** (03) 3841-8560.

Puppet House
1-8 Shimomiyabi-cho, Shinjuku. **Tel** (03) 5229-6477.

Sagemonoya
Yabane KK, 4-28-20-704 Yotsuya. **Tel** (03) 3352-6286.

Sanbido
1-33-3 Asakusa. **Map** 4 F3. **Tel** (03) 5827-0070.

Tokiwado
1-3-2 Asakusa. **Map** 4 E3. **Tel** (03) 3841-5656.

Clothing

The pace of change in a city where everything seems temporary is perfectly suited to Tokyo's fast-moving fashion world. Extensive media coverage of the fashion industry, relatively high disposable incomes among the young, and an active nightlife have made Tokyo one of the trendiest, most visible fashion centers on the globe. Snapping at the heels of the fashion establishment with their Paris and New York outlets are brat packs of emerging, young Japanese designers creating a host of trendy labels. Some of the leading fashion houses in the world now call Tokyo their home.

Young shoppers browsing through the latest Western wear, Shibuya 109

Fashion Buildings

Fashion buildings house exclusive boutiques, often with a collective theme, target age group, or approach to design. The modern, innovative architecture of the buildings themselves adds much interest to the entire shopping experience.

Shibuya 109 is a silver, circular tower housing several boutiques renowned for teen fashions. It also stages fashion promotion events in front of the building. **Mark City**, a towering modern building connected by passageways to Shibuya Station, is a more ambitious project. Labyrinthine floors of boutiques and accessory stores aimed at the 20s and 30s age group, provide a social setting with restaurants, bakeries, and trendy cafés. The **LaForet Building**, a Harajuku landmark, is strictly for teen shoppers. **Venus Fort** (see p84), a retail outlet targeted at women in Odaiba, looks more like an Italian film set than a fashion store. Food courts, cafés, trinket stalls, and trendy shops create a faux Italian street scene.

Women's Fashions

Ginza has always been synonymous with high chic and prices to match. Large department stores such as **Mitsukoshi** (see p141) have always been the arbiters of taste here, offering classic design cuts, which appeal to women in their 30s and upwards. Luxury foreign brands such as Gucci and Chanel have opened super-modern outlets, providing designer shoes, handbags, cosmetics, and other chic accessories.

Trendy women's wear, Dolce and Gabbana showroom, Omotesando

Aoyama's **Comme des Garçons** store, the brainchild of radical designer Rei Kawakubo, is well worth a look for the building alone. Also in the contiguous Aoyama/Omotesando/Jingumae districts, **Prada Aoyama**, the latest addition to Minami-Aoyama's high-end fashion scene, is another shopping-plus-architecture experience.

The flowing fabrics and colorful embroidery that characterize **Tsumori Chisato** designs, on show in her Shibuya store, enjoy an almost cult following among women. The more radical but fun **Hysteric Glamour** has had a similar effect on the tastes of punk-inclined customers not afraid to wear T-shirts with provocative messages. For a good mix of women's fashions, accessories, and cosmetics, **Daikanyama Address Dixsept**, a retail complex with an open-air plaza and interesting interior consisting of suspension bridges, makes for a great half-day fashion shopping trip. The complex is a little to the northwest of Daikanyama Station.

Menswear

Young Japanese males are almost as fashion conscious as women, though there are not as many exclusive menswear shops in Tokyo. The following recommendations also feature women's fashions. **Muji** design aesthetics – cool, simple, understated – are well known the world over. Besides clothes and accessories, its Roppongi store has a good line in simple homeware designs.

The singular and arresting designs of **Yohji Yamamoto**, another household name in the Japanese fashion cosmos, seem to go from strength to strength. The interior of the bronze-faced store in Omotesando is well worth a look. The name **Issey Miyake** needs no introduction. The anarchist designer burst onto the scene in the 1980s with his innovative use of fabrics, design

A variety of basics for men and women, Uniqlo store, Aoyama

forms, and shapes to create expensive but highly regarded work. The window displays are a joy. Nearby **Undercover** is the brainchild of Jun Takahashi, a punk musician whose designs are inspired by the music his band plays.

The menswear at **Uniqlo**, a popular clothing chain with branches overseas, is simple, contemporary, and bottom-line for many shoppers at this store along Jingumae's Meiji-dori. The fashions here target all age groups.

Kimono with an *obi* sash

Textiles and Kimonos

Silk, cotton, linen, and hemp all feature in Japan's long and rich textile history. While some traditional techniques are fading, most are alive and well. Department stores are often the best places to find a varied range of textiles, from bolts of kimono cloth made in Kyoto to textured *furoshiki* (square wrapping cloths). The shop at the **Tokyo National Museum** *(see pp52–5)* has a good selection of *furoshiki* and scarves made using traditional techniques. Also good is **Bengara**. **Miyashita Obi** on Nakamise-dori at Senso-ji temple *(see pp58–9)* has wonderful *obi* sashes, used to wrap a

kimono at the waist. **Hayashi Kimono** in Yurakucho, sells classic outfits but also a light cotton summer version called *yukata*, which can be comfortable house wear.

The **Oriental Bazaar** *(see p139)* and **Uniqlo** offer a good range of *yukata*. Asakusa's **Nakamise-dori** *(see p58)* has a lot of less expensive fabric kimonos in bright colors, the assumption being that foreigners like brilliant, gaudy designs. There are some terrific traditional and modern kimonos and textile bargains to be found at the eclectic Sunday flea markets *(see p139)*.

A colorful *kimono* with traditional floral motifs

DIRECTORY

Fashion Buildings

LaForet Building
1-11-6 Jingumae. **Map** 1 C5.
Tel (03) 3475-0411.

Mark City
1-12-1, Dogenzaka. **Map** 1 B5.
Tel (03) 3780-6503.

Shibuya 109
2-29-1 Dogenzaka. **Map** 1 B5.
Tel (03) 3477-5111.

Venus Fort
1-3-15 Aomi Odaiba.
Tel (03) 3599-1735.

Women's Fashions

Comme des Garçons
5-22-1 Minami-Aoyama.
Map 1 C5. **Tel** (03) 3406-3951.

Daikanyama Address Dixsept
17-6 Daikanyama-cho Shibuya.
Tel (03) 3461-5586.

Hysteric Glamour
6-23-2 Jingumae.
Tel (03) 3409-7227.

Prada Aoyama
5-2-6 Minami-Aoyama.
Map 1 C5. **Tel** (03) 6418-0400.

Tsumori Chisato
11-1 Sarugaku-cho Shibuya.
Tel (03) 5728-3225.

Menswear

Issey Miyake
3-18-11 Minami-Aoyama
Map 1 C5. **Tel** (03) 3423-1407.

Muji
3-8-3 Marunouchi. **Map** 3 A5.
Tel (03) 5208-8241.

Undercover
5-3-22 Minami-Aoyama.
Map 1 C5. **Tel** (03) 3407-1232.

Uniqlo
6-10-8 Jingumae. **Map** 1 B4.

Yohji Yamamoto
5-3-6 Minami-Aoyama. **Map** 1 C5.
Tel (03) 3409-6006.

Textiles and Kimonos

Bengara
1-35-6 Asakusa. **Map** 4 F2.
Tel (03) 3841-6613.

Hayashi Kimono
2-1-1 Yurakucho. **Map** 5 B2.
Tel (03) 3501-4012.

Gifts, Gizmos, and Toys

In the first months after World War II, de-mobbed men and displaced persons would spread a towel or newspaper on the incinerated wasteland around main stations, and display a saucepan or worn kimono in the hope of finding a customer. These were the tentative beginnings of the black markets. Since then, consumers have long moved from desiring just basic necessities to acquiring gifts, gizmos, and the novelties that flood Tokyo's markets.

Gift Shops

The Japanese are not only avid buyers of souvenirs when they venture overseas, but excellent customers for the interesting products of their own country. The result is countless gift shops.

The traditional and modern stationery, origami paper, and calligraphy tools sold at **Itoya** in Ginza, make light, affordable, and portable gifts. The articles at **Japan Sword**, the oldest dealer in authentic Japanese blades, are a little heavier and more expensive, not to mention dangerous. Replicas of the swords are also sold. The shop and exhibition space are located in the business district of Toranomon.

Right in the heart of Shibuya, **Do** is the stylish Claska Hotel's gift shop. The hotel is known for its design, and the gift shop follows the same model. Occasionally, it also shows works by local artists.

Craft and gift sections of reputed department stores (see p139) are logical places

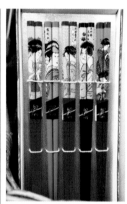
An eye-catching chopsticks box, a traditional souvenir

to do one-stop shopping. Large railroad terminuses, especially Tokyo Station, are crammed with souvenir and gift shops.

Food and Drink

Department store basements have the largest and most interesting single selections of ready-to-go Japanese foods of the kind that make interesting

gifts. Markets (see p139) and even supermarkets have interesting and unfamiliar food items as well, from *sembei* (rice crackers) to traditional Japanese confections. The main ingredient of Japanese sweets is *anko*, red bean paste, which may be an acquired taste for some Westerners. These beautifully made confections are called *wagashi* in Japanese, and are often taken with green tea. **Toraya** is famous – it supplies the imperial family. This Akasaka institution changes its sweet motifs to reflect the seasons. Branches of **Akebono** selling exquisite sweets can be found in the food basements of some of the best Tokyo department stores. The origins of **Iidabashi Mannendo** in Iidabashi, date back to the 17th century, when it began making sweets based on recipes from the old imperial city of Kyoto.

Alcohol is freely available in Tokyo. Individual **sake** shops and, once again, department store basements have shelves full of *nihonshu* (the word "sake" can actually refer to all alcoholic drinks). The choice, though, can be quite bewildering, involving some knowledge of grades and provenance. For an initiation into the mysteries of the drink, **Sake Plaza** in Shimbashi has excellent displays. Entrance to the plaza is free, and for a small fee visitors can enjoy a five-cup sampling.

Gadgets and Gizmos

Tokyu Hands, a treasure trove of inventive and original household goods, is a good place to start for general items from fancy dress costumes to trick store treats evoking a sense of fun. The **Don Quixote** stores, such as the popular one in Shinjuku, are stuffed to the ceilings with novelty, "character" goods, costume wear, mixed in with snacks, camping gear, and ironing boards. For a combination of electronics and eccentricities, **Akihabara** (see p47) is hard to beat. **Ishimaru** and **Sofmap** are two huge electronic department stores

Bewildering variety of sweets in a store on Nakamise-dori, Akihabara

Electronics store stacked with low-priced gadgets, Akihabara

here. **Akky** and **Takarada Musen** are also duty-free stores. **Sato Musen** and **Onoden** are other names to look out for in this "Electric Town." Young women dressed as anime characters from classic series such as *Sailor Moon* and *Neon Genesis Evangelion* greet customers outside **AsoBitCity**, which, in addition to software games and peripherals, sells "character" goods and large model train sets. More Akihabara wonders await at **Tsukumo Robocon Magazine Kan**, where the specialty are cute, owner-friendly robots – mechanized turtles, cats, dogs, insects, and fictitious creatures.

Toys

One of the nice things about Tokyo toy stores is that nobody seems to mind if you pick things up and play with them, even if you are a lone adult. Customers are treated with a measure of tolerance and indulgence in Tokyo. And

surprising numbers of adults shop for themselves in the toy stores, a reminder that a sense of playfulness is alive and well among the hard-working Tokyoites. These places are among the best in the world to pick up souvenirs and the latest craze among children before it hits the international market.

Hakuhinkan Toy Park in Ginza has always been a Mecca for toys and still is, with several crowded floors to prove it; try not to go on a weekend. The six floors of toys, games, and novelties at **Kiddyland** in Jingumae are a wonder to behold. Besides conventional toys, kits, and games, all the popular anime characters are here too, from Pokemon to Hello Kitty. For a slightly more personal experience, **Astro Mike** in Harajuku has many loyal followers. The store traces the history of toy making, both Japanese and Western, from the action figures and models of the 1960s, up to the present day.

Stuffed toys in all sizes at Kiddyland, a major kids' toy store in Jingumae

ENTERTAINMENT IN TOKYO

Entertainment in Tokyo is a wonderful mix of the old world and the cutting edge. Traditional performing arts span the vibrancy of Kabuki theater to the haunting tones of a *shakuhachi* recital. Tokyo is the best place to catch the latest in movies and music from around the world. The abundance of live music on offer ranges from jazz and blues to pop and techno, and even Western classical music. Tokyo enjoys a pulsating and truly international club culture; at many places, you can dance till dawn. Sports fans have a choice between baseball and soccer, or the more traditional forms of martial arts, as well as sumo. At night, the city puts on a different face, and the brightly lit leisure districts show how serious Tokyo is about fun.

Kabuki performance in Kabuki-za Theater

Information Sources

Metropolis, a free weekly magazine and website is a good source of information on leisure activities in the city. **Japanzine**, another free magazine, also covers other cities in Japan if you plan to travel out of the city. The **Japan Times**, *Asahi Shimbun*, *Daily Yomiuri*, and **Japan Today** also have comprehensive listings. All of these publications are in English and available at station kiosks and major stores including **Kinokuniya** *(see p62)*, **Tower Records** *(see p69)*, and **Maruzen** *(see p141)*. Information on current events in and around Tokyo is also given on the **JNTO** *(see p159)* website. Other useful online resources include **Japan Visitor**, **Realtokyo**, and **Tokyo Food Page**.

Booking Tickets

Popular traditional Japanese entertainment, such as Kabuki and sumo, are best reserved ahead of time through a travel agent or hotel travel desk.

For concerts and sporting events, the two major ticket agencies are **Ticket PIA** and **CN Playguide**. They can be hard to reach by phone. It is easier to book in person; a convenient office is Ticket PIA at Ginza's Sony Building *(see p40)*. Department and convenience stores also have ticket desks, sometimes with English-speaking assistants. Alternatively, book directly by phoning the venue; payment is made when the tickets are picked up. Most agencies speak only Japanese, so having a Japanese-speaker at hand will help. Reservations can also be made online, at convenience stores such as **Lawson**, or through the *Metropolis* website.

Cinema

There are several specialist cinemas that screen movies from Asia, as well as Europe and the US. However, most non-Japanese films are shown in the original language with Japanese subtitles. The **Tokyo International Film Festival** *(see p32)* is becoming increasingly high profile. There are also several other interesting film festivals, showcasing both domestic and international movies.

Cinema prices are not cheap, averaging around ¥1,800. On Cinema Day, usually the first of each month, tickets are reduced. In Shibuya, **Bunkamura** *(see p68)* sometimes shows Japanese films with English subtitles and is known for screening independent and European films. Also in Shibuya, **Theater Image Forum** uses the most

Movie poster in Shinjuku, one of Tokyo's centers for cinema

Ebisu Garden Cinema, a popular cinema hall for foreign films

advanced digital technology. The more centrally located **Toho Cinemas Chanter** shows arthouse and independent films. **Marunouchi Piccadilly**, in the Mullion Building in Yurakucho (see p40), has five screens, while **Ebisu Garden Cinema** (see p78) has two. Currently, the most comfortable cinema in the city is at the nine-screen complex in Roppongi Hills (see p71), part of the **Toho Cinema** group, with an in-house bar and late-night screenings.

Anyone with an interest in classic Japanese cinema should visit the superb **National Film Center** (see p44). Fans of animation should visit **Ghibli Museum**; it displays the work of pioneering anime director Hayao Miyazaki, whose films include Spirited Away (2001) and Howl's Moving Castle (2004).

International Theater

The international theater scene in Tokyo encompasses everything from Shakespeare and Broadway musicals to comedy, classical ballet, and modern dance. The main venues are in Shinjuku, Shibuya, and Marunouchi. Although some foreign touring companies come through Tokyo, most shows are in Japanese, with local actors of a consistently high standard. The **Tokyo Comedy Store** offers non-Japanese and Japanese the chance to exhibit their comedy skills in English on the fourth Friday of the month at the Crocodile club in Harajuku.

Live Music

The finest venues for orchestral concerts are the **New National Theater**, **Suntory Hall**, **NHK Hall**, **Orchard Hall** in Bunkamura (see p68), **Sumida Triphony Hall**, and the two halls of the **Tokyo International Forum** (see p45). The New National Theater and Orchard Hall also stage opera and ballet performances.

Tokyo has a vibrant jazz scene too, reflected in the large number of clubs and the quality of the visiting artists. **Blue Note Tokyo** is the best-known club (although prices are high and sets are short). Other places that attract world-class performers include **B Flat**, **Shinjuku Pit Inn**, and the **Cotton Club**. **STB139** offers an eclectic mix of music, with mostly Japanese artists. **Blues Alley Japan** is a small club featuring blues and jazz artists.

Ever since the Beatles played at **Nippon Budokan** in 1966, Tokyo has been an essential stop on the world itinerary of pop and rock bands. Both the aging Budokan and the cavernous Tokyo Dome stadium have poor acoustics. Smaller and far better venues include the inconveniently located **Zepp Tokyo**, **Nakano Sun Plaza**, and **Liquid Room**. **Womb** hosts international superstars such as the Chemical Brothers and Paul Oakenfold. As with jazz, though, it is the more intimate venues where gigs

Street musician giving a live performance

come alive. **Club Quattro** can be claustrophobic but gets top international acts; **Duo Music Exchange** and **O-West** often specialize in techno and J-pop. **Eggman** and the ever-eclectic **SuperDeluxe** showcase experimental, fringe, and upcoming talent. Live bands also play at many of the Irish pubs as well as the **Pink Cow**, a casual, artsy hangout, popular with expats.

Karaoke

The boom for belting out popular hits to backing music tracks dates from the 1960s but remains as popular as ever today in Japan, the birthplace of karaoke. Translated as "empty orchestra," karaoke is enjoyed in traditional bars, lively pubs, at home, and in major entertainment districts, at karaoke "boxes." These complexes range from small, cozy rooms for couples to much larger spaces for groups of friends or office parties. Food and drinks can be ordered. The most performed numbers are local pop songs, current and classic; enka, the Japanese equivalent of French chanson; and some Western pop hits. **Karaoke-kan** in Shibuya (see pp68–9) is the famed location used in the movie Lost in Translation. For the best selection of songs in English follow the expats to **Smash Hits**.

An extravagant opera performance in New National Theater

Sumo wrestlers compete at Tokyo's National Sumo Stadium

Sumo

Three sumo tournaments (*basho*) are held in Tokyo each year, in January, May, and September, all at the impressive 10,000-seat **National Sumo Stadium** in Ryogoku (*see p76*). The 15-day tournaments begin on a Sunday, with each wrestler fighting one bout a day. The action starts at 2:30pm with the lowest-ranking wrestlers; the top ranked appear from 5 to 6pm. The highest-ranking wrestler, usually a *yokozuna* (grand champion) will compete in the last bout.

The best views are on the north side of the stadium. Seating in the main auditorium is Japanese-style, in individual boxes. These are cramped and more expensive than the seats upstairs, but much closer to the action. Tickets should be booked in advance. Easiest to get are midweek tickets in the first week of a tournament. If you cannot buy tickets via an agency, try asking your hotel to check for returns, or just line up at the stadium itself.

It is possible to watch practice sessions at sumo stables, or *beya*. They are open to anyone who wants to watch, with a few basic rules – do not eat or use a camera flash, and be silent. Most of the *beya* are situated near Ryogoku station. Visitors can make a trip to the **Kasugano Beya**, a tall building with a green copper gable over the entrance, the **Izutsu Beya**, or the **Dewanoumi Beya**.

Other Martial Arts

The center for martial arts in Japan is the **Nippon Budokan**, and this is where the top tournaments in judo, karate, and kendo (wooden sword fighting) are held. There are *dojo* (practice halls) for the various martial arts throughout Tokyo. Not all are open to non-Japanese as observers or participants. Contact **Tokyo TIC** (*see p159*) for a list of *dojos* that allow spectators. To participate in martial arts training, contact one of the national regulatory bodies.

Nippon Budokan, an important center for all martial arts

Baseball and Soccer

Baseball is regarded as Japan's de facto national sport. Professional baseball teams are split between the Central League and the Pacific League. The Tokyo-based Yomiuri Giants (Central League) are Japan's most popular team. Their engaging games in the soaring **Tokyo Dome** are always sold out. The Yakult Swallows (also Central League) play at the beautiful **Jingu Stadium**. Book tickets ahead of time.

Soccer fans may want to visit the **Nissan Stadium**, Japan's largest stadium and host to the 2002 World Cup final. It is the home of the J-League's Yokohama F. Marinos. The **Ajinomoto Stadium** is home to FC Tokyo and Tokyo Verdy 1969, both J-League teams. Tickets are available at the stadium on the day of the match.

Other Spectator Sports

Other sports with a significant presence include rugby, tennis, volleyball, swimming, athletics, basketball, cycling, and motor sports. Racing (horses, speed-boats, or cycling) generates fervent interest, especially since gambling is allowed through official channels. Details of competitions are given in the sports pages of *Metropolis*.

Pachinko

Pachinko (*see p69*) is like an electronic vertical pinball and its practitioners appear hypnotized by the bright lights and trance-inducing electronic music. Not just a pastime, it is a form of gambling. Winnings are exchanged for goods, which are then bought back (off the premises, to remain within the law). To experience pachinko firsthand, try the **Maruhan Pachinko Tower** in Shibuya. Here, each floor has a different theme and there are love seats for couples.

Sportsgear on display at the Baseball Hall of Fame, Tokyo Dome

DIRECTORY

Information Sources

Japanzine
w japanzine.jp

Japan Times
w japantimes.co.jp/
culture

Japan Today
w japantoday.com

Japan Visitor
w japanvisitor.com

Metropolis
w metropolis.co.jp

Realtokyo
w realtokyo.co.jp/
english

Tokyo Food Page
w bento.com/tokyofood.
html

Booking Tickets

CN Playguide
w cnplayguide.com

Lawson
w i-tike.com

Ticket PIA
Tel (0570) 02-9999.
w t.pia.jp

Cinema

Bunkamura
2-24-1 Dogenzaka,
Shibuya-ku. **Map** 1 A5.
Tel (03) 3477-9111.

Ghibli Museum
1-1-83 Shimorenjaku,
Mitaka-shi.
Tel (0570) 055-777.

Theater Image Forum
2-10-2 Shibuya,
Shibuya-ku. **Map** 1 C5.
Tel (03) 5766-0114.

Toho Cinema
Keyakizaka Complex,
6-10-2 Roppongi, Minato-
ku. **Tel** (0506) 868-5024
(press 9 for English).

Toho Cinemas Chanter
1-2-2 Yurakucho, Chiyoda-
ku. **Tel** (0506) 868-5024.

International Theater

Tokyo Comedy Store
w tokyocomedy.com

Live Music

B Flat
6-6-4, Akasaka,
Minato-ku. **Map** 2 F4.
Tel (03) 5563-2563.

Blue Note Tokyo
Raika Building,
6-3-16 Minami-Aoyama,
Minato-ku. **Map** 2 D5.
Tel (03) 5485-0088.

Blues Alley Japan
Hotel Wing International
Meguro, 1-3-14 Meguro,
Meguro-ku. **Map** 1 B1.
Tel (03) 5496-4381.

Club Quattro
Parco Quattro 4F,
32-13 Udagawa-cho,
Shibuya-ku. **Map** 1 A5.
Tel (03) 3477-8750.

Cotton Club
2 F Tokia Tokyo Building,
2-7-3 Marunouchi,
Chiyoda-ku. **Map** 5 B2.
Tel (03) 3215-1555.

Duo Music Exchange
2-14-8 Dogenzaka,
Shibuya-ku. **Map** 1 A5.
Tel (03) 5459-8716.

Eggman
1-6-8 Jinnan, Shibuya-ku.
Map 1 B5.
Tel (03) 3496-1785.

Liquid Room
3-16-6 Higashi,
Shibuya-ku.
Tel (03) 5464-0800.

Nakano Sun Plaza
4-1-1 Nakano,
Nakano-ku.
Tel (03) 3388-1151.

New National Theater
1-1-1 Honmachi,
Shibuya-ku. **Map** 1 A2.
Tel (03) 5351-3011.

NHK Hall
2-2-1 Jinnan, Shibuya-ku.
Map 1 B4.
Tel (03) 3465-1751.

Nippon Budokan
2-3 Kitanomaru-Koen,
Chiyoda-ku. **Map** 3 A5.
Tel (03) 3216-5100.

Orchard Hall
Bunkamura, 2-24-1
Dogenzaka, Shibuya-ku.
Map 1 A6.
Tel (03) 3477-9111.

O-West
2-3 Maruyama-cho,
Shibuya-ku. **Map** 1 A5.
Tel (03) 5784-7088.

Pink Cow
5-5-1 Roppongi, Roi
Building, B1F, Minato-ku.
Map 2 E5.
Tel (03) 6434-5773.

Shinjuku Pit Inn
B1 Accord Building, 2-12-
4 Shinjuku, Shinjuku-ku.
Map 1 B1.
Tel (03) 3354-2024.

STB139
6-7-11 Roppongi,
Minato-ku. **Map** 2 E5.
Tel (03) 5474-0139.

Sumida Triphony Hall
1-2-3 Kinshi, Sumida-ku.
Tel (03) 5608-1212.

Suntory Hall
1-13-1 Akasaka,
Minato-ku. **Map** 2 F4.
Tel (03) 3505-1001.

SuperDeluxe
B1F 3-1-25 Nishi-Azabu,
Minato-ku. **Map** 2 E5.
Tel (03) 5412-0515.

Womb
2-16 Maruyamacho,
Shibuya-ku. **Map** 1 B5.
Tel (03) 5459-0039.

Zepp Tokyo
Palette Town, 1-3-11
Aomi, Koto-ku. **Map** 2 E5.
Tel (03) 3599-0710.

Karaoke

Karaoke-kan
K&F Building,
30-8 Udagawa-cho,
Shibuya-ku.
Map 1 B5.
Tel (03) 3462-0785.

Smash Hits
M2 Building B1F, 5-2-26
Hiroo, Shibuya-ku.
Tel (03) 3444-0432.

Sumo and Other Martial Arts

Dewanoumi Beya
2-3-15 Ryogoku,
Shibuya-ku. **Map** 4 E5.

Izutsu Beya
2-2-7 Ryogoku,
Sumida-ku. **Map** 4 E5.

Kasugano Beya
1-7-11 Ryogoku,
Sumida-ku. **Map** 4 E5.

National Sumo Stadium
1-3-28 Yokoami,
Sumida-ku. **Map** 4 E4.
Tel (03) 3623-5111.

Nippon Budokan
See Live Music.

Baseball and Soccer

Ajinomoto Stadium
376-3 Nishimachi, Chofu
City. **Tel** (0424) 40-0555.

Jingu Stadium
3-1 Kasumigaoka,
Shinjuku-ku. **Map** 2 D4.
Tel (03) 3404-8999.

Nissan Stadium
3300 Kozukue-cho,
Kohoku-ku, Yokohama
City 222-0036.
Tel (045) 477-5000.
w nissan-stadium.jp/
english

Tokyo Dome
1-3-61 Koraku, Bunkyo-ku.
Map 3 A3.
Tel (03) 5800-9999.

Pachinko

Maruhan Pachinko Tower
28-6 Udagawa-cho,
Shibuya.
Tel (03) 5221-7777.

Traditional Performing Arts

Despite Tokyo's ultra-modern exterior, its heart still moves to a traditional beat. The rarified, otherworldly court music known as *gagaku* dates back much further than the city itself, as does the Noh Theater *(see p18)*. It is, however, the performing arts of the Edo period *(see p27)*, especially Kabuki and the Bunraku puppet theater *(see p19)*, that capture the rich, vibrant cultural life of premodern Japan. Such displays are not hard to find – at the Kabuki-za Theater, for example, just walk in off the street, buy a one-act ticket, and travel back in time.

An elegant cypress performance stage, Noh National Theater

Traditional Theater

Kabuki and Noh, the two best-known forms of traditional theater *(see pp18–19)*, are well represented in Tokyo. Of the two traditions, Kabuki provides a much more flamboyant spectacle, with rousing stories, elaborate sets, and amazing costumes. However, dramatic action sequences can often be interspersed with extended soliloquies. The **Kabuki-za Theater** *(see p42)* is the main venue for Kabuki, with almost daily performances starting mid-morning and lasting three or more hours. It is also possible to buy a ticket to see just one act if you are short of time. Prices range from around ¥2,500 to as much as ¥16,000; one-act tickets are around ¥700. Earphone guides giving explanations and commentary in English are available to hire. The **National Theater** also stages Kabuki performances in January, March, October, November, and December. A number of unorthodox versions of Kabuki have been developed to make it more contemporary. Super Kabuki, introduced in 1985 and staged at the **Shinbashi Enbujo**, adds high-tech special effects (such as actors flying through the air) to the traditional plots. Cocoon Kabuki, a project launched in 1994, brings the traditional plays and costumes each summer to the **Theater Cocoon** in Shibuya, which is also known for visiting foreign theatrical productions.

In contrast, a Noh performance can be heavy going for those unprepared for its slow pace. As a theatrical experience, however, it can be exceptionally powerful. The **Noh National Theater** near Sendagaya JR station usually has weekend performances. Tickets vary from ¥2,300 to ¥4,300. It is also possible to see plays at a Noh school, for instance **Kanze Nohgakudo**. Outdoor Noh performed by torchlight (*Takigi Noh*) can be wonderfully atmospheric, especially when staged in front of an ancient shrine or temple, such as with the annual fall performances at the Kamakura-gu shrine, in the hills of Kamakura. More information is readily available from **JNTO** *(see p159)* or the **Kamakura Tourist Association**.

The puppet theater, Bunraku, predates Kabuki, and many of its plays were later adapted to the stage. The black-robed puppeteers are so skillful, you soon ignore their presence and just watch the lifelike movements of the puppets themselves. Performances can be seen at the National Theater's Small Hall.

Kyogen (short comic farces) is one of Japan's oldest forms of drama, and includes acrobatics and juggling. Now played to comic effect, Kyogen is often performed as part of Noh, or as individual plays between Noh plays. Another lighthearted theatrical tradition is Rakugo. Dressed in a kimono and sitting on a *zabuton* (cushion), the storytellers act out comic situations, often retelling old and well-loved stories. Held at intimate theaters such as **Suzumoto** in Ueno or **Suehirotei** in bustling Shinjuku, they give great insight into characteristic Japanese traditional humor, even without understanding the language. A few Rakugo artists have also started doing occasional shows in English.

A giant Bunraku puppet

A Kabuki performance at the Kabuki-za Theater, Ginza

Takarazuka Theater, a venue for dance and theater performances

Traditional and Contemporary Dance

Performances of traditional dance are staged regularly by the **Nihon Buyo Kyokai**. The Azuma Odori, an annual production of dance and drama usually held at the end of May, brings Tokyo's geisha community on stage at **Shinbashi Enbujo**.

A unique theater experience is Takarazuka, a company divided into five troupes and composed entirely of women. With their own state-of-the-art **Takarazuka Theater** in Yurakucho, they perform traditional adaptations in Japanese of Western musicals and historical love stories, and are famed for their extravagant productions.

Butoh is a distinct and compelling form of contemporary dance developed in the 1960s that draws on elements of mime and traditional ascetic practice.

Often shaven-headed and almost naked with body makeup, the dancers follow a slow choreography that seeks to create beauty out of self-imposed grotesqueness. Look out for performances by established troupes such as Dairakudakan or Buto-sha Tenkei, staged at **Setagaya Public Theater** but more often at small fringe theaters in outlying areas.

Traditional Music

The oldest Japanese musical traditions are those of the *matsuri* or festivals (*see pp30–33*), featuring instruments such as drums and flutes. Performances of captivating ancient court music, known as *gagaku*, are given occasionally at the **National Theater** or at major temples in the city. The **Ono Gagaku Kai** holds major concerts featuring other regional instruments such as the stringed *koto* and *shamisen*, and the *shakuhachi* (flute). Do not miss a chance to catch a concert by one of the troupes of Japanese drummers, performing on *taiko* drums ranging from the size of small snares to huge barrels 6ft (2 meters) or more in diameter. The most dynamic of the performing groups is Kodo, which plays an annual series of concerts at venues such as the popular Bunkamura (*see p68*) in Shibuya each December.

A woman playing a *shamisen* instrument

DIRECTORY

Traditional Theater

Kabuki-za Theater
4-12-5 Ginza, Chuo-ku.
Map 5 C3.
Tel (03) 3545-3131.

Kamakura Tourist Association
Tel (0467) 23-3050.

Kanze Nohgakudo
1-16-4 Shoto, Shibuya-ku.
Map 1 A5.
Tel (03) 3469-5241.

National Theater
4-1 Hayabusa-cho, Chiyoda-ku.
Map 2 F3.
Tel (03) 3265-7411.

Noh National Theater
4-18-1 Sendagaya, Shibuya-ku. **Map** 1 C3.
Tel (03) 3423-1331.

Shinbashi Enbujo
6-18-2 Ginza, Chuo-ku.
Map 5 C3.
Tel (03) 3541-2600.

Suehirotei
3-6-12 Shinjuku, Shinjuku-ku.
Map 1 B1.
Tel (03) 3351-2974.

Suzumoto
2-7-12 Ueno, Taito-ku.
Map 3 C3.
Tel (03) 3834-5906.

Theater Cocoon
Bunkamura, 2-24-1 Dogenzaka, Shibuya-ku.
Map 1 A5.
Tel (03) 3477-9999.

Traditional and Contemporary Dance

Nihon Buyo Kyokai
2-18-1 Kachidoki, Chuo-ku.
Map 5 D4.
Tel (03) 3533-6455.

Setagaya Public Theater
4-1-1 Taishido, Setagaya-ku.
Tel (03) 5432-1526.
w setagaya-pt.jp/en

Takarazuka Theater
1-1-3 Yurakucho, Chiyoda-ku.
Map 5 B2.
Tel (03) 5251-2001.

Traditional Music

Ono Gagaku Kai
2-13-14 Shitaya, Taito-ku.
Tel (03) 3873-2780.

Japanese women performing traditional opera dance

Nightlife

Evening does not signal any let-up in the pace of life in Tokyo. If anything, it seems to intensify, especially in areas where the neon burns brightest. Fashionable Ginza, the cosmopolitan party district of Roppongi, sophisticated Nishi-Azabu, youthful Shibuya, or vibrant Shinjuku – there are plenty of choices. Tokyo is rapidly becoming an all-night city, and it is one of the most exciting places in the world to party. It is not just the clubs and cabarets, many restaurants, bars, and traditional *izakaya (see p118)* now stay open until 2am or later.

A DJ performing at La Fabrique, Shibuya

High-Rise Bars

The best place to get into the mood for an evening out is at one of the city's high-rise hotel bars. The Conrad's **TwentyEight Bar** has a brilliant view over the Rainbow Bridge and the Odaiba waterfront. In Shibuya, there is the Cerulean Tower Hotel, with its 40th-floor **Bello Visto Bar**. Best of all is the Park Hyatt Hotel's *(see p112)* luxurious 52nd-floor **New York Bar**, as seen in the movie *Lost in Translation*. Cradle a cocktail, watch the dusk fall and the

New York Bar offers superb views of the city below

lights come on, then descend to street level and plunge into the neon night.

Clubs and Bars

Ginza remains one of Tokyo's most exclusive and priciest nightlife districts. But alongside the costly hostess bars, there are also more affordable spots, such as the standing-only **300 Bar**, where the food or drink all cost around ¥300. The Ginza Corridor, a row of bars and restaurants built right under the expressway between Ginza and Shinbashi, also offers good options.

Central to the city's night-life since postwar occupation, Roppongi stays lively through the night. A popular place to start the evening is **Hobgoblin**, Tokyo's largest British pub. For more recreation, catch one of the retro-themed shows at **Kaguwa** *(see p177)*, a unique dinner theater (entrance ¥3,500). Dance the night away at **El Café Latino**, which offers

Logo of British pub, Hobgoblin

salsa evenings and classes. Smoke a Havana cigar and sip premium aged tequila at **Agave** or rub shoulders with celebrities at **NewLex Edo**.

The scene is more relaxed in nearby Nishi-Azabu. **The Baron** offers tapas and weekend DJ events. **SuperDeluxe** is an eclectic bar-cum-event space with performance art and live music. The enduringly lively bar **Acaraje Tropicana** swings to a Brazilian rhythm.

Shibuya is the center of Tokyo youth culture and the Center-Gai pedestrian alley is its promenade and fast-food kitchen. Good watering holes in the area include **Tasu-Ichi**, a standing bar with very reasonable prices; and **The Aldgate**, an Anglophile pub with an extensive selection of ales on draught.

Chic, upscale Akasaka also has a good range of clubs and bars. Shinjuku's Kabukicho, with its maze of streets and future-world feel, boasts numerous restaurants and clubs. It is also the city's most notorious red-light district. It is safe to explore, but beware of pickpockets and venues that do not post their prices. A more restful neighborhood is Shinjuku Sanchome, close to Isetan Department Store. Recommended watering holes include the **Marugo** wine bar.

If sightseeing in Asakusa leaves you thirsty, cross the Sumida River to the **Flamme D'Or** bar in the premises of the Asahi Breweries headquarters. Close to Kaminarimon gate is the **Kamiya Bar**, the oldest bar in Tokyo. Near the sumo stadium, look for **Beer Station Ryogoku**, a German-style bierkeller.

DJ and Dance Clubs

Tokyo's clubbing scene has exploded in the last decade, attracting top DJs from around the world. Roppongi, Shinjuku, and Shibuya offer a wealth of options. In terms of scale, the

A row of clubs and bars, Shinjuku Sanchome

stylish bar playing house and techno.

The leading online magazine **Cyberjapan** carries up-to-date listings. Dance clubs warm up around 11pm and keep going all night. Expect a cover charge of between ¥2,000 and ¥4,000.

Gay and Lesbian

The undisputed center of Tokyo's gay world is the concentration of bars, clubs, and saunas in the small area of Shinjuku called Ni-Chome ("2nd Block"). Many of the venues here cater exclusively to the local gay community, but

there are still a good number of bars that are open to non-Japanese speakers. The most popular places to meet are **GB** and **Advocates Café**, a tiny, lively venue where the action spills out onto the street. The second-floor **Kinsmen** bar is more sedate, attracting a mix of all persuasions. Its lesbian counterpart, the women-only **Kinswomyn**, is equally relaxed and welcoming. Ni-Chome is also the location for the mega-scale **24 Kaikan** bathhouse complex which also has branches in Asakusa, Ueno, and Shinjuku. A good source of online information is the **Utopia Asia** website.

top spot is **AgeHa**, in Shin-Kiba, on the other side of Odaiba. Other substantial venues include favorite **Feria**; hip **Air**; cavernous **Womb**; longtime stalwart **Club Asia**; and **Club Harlem**. On a more manageable scale, **Loop** is a

DIRECTORY

High-Rise Bars

Bello Visto Bar
26-1, Sakuragaoka-cho,
Shibuya-ku.
Tel (03) 3476-3000.

TwentyEight Bar
1-9-1 Higashi-Shinbashi,
Minato-ku.
Map 5 B4.
Tel (03) 6388-8000.

Clubs and Bars

300 Bar
5-9-11 Ginza, Chuo-ku.
Map 5 B3.
Tel (03) 3572-6300.

Acaraje Tropicana
1-1-25 Nishi-Azabu,
Minato-ku.
Map 2 E5.
Tel (03) 3479-4690.

Agave
7-15-10 Roppongi,
Minato-ku.
Map 2 E5.
Tel (03) 3497-0229.

Beer Station Ryogoku
1-3-20 Yokoami,
Sumida-ku. **Map** 4 E5.
Tel (03) 3623-5252.

El Café Latino
3-15-24 Roppongi,
Minato-ku. **Map** 2 E5.
Tel (03) 3402-8989.

Flamme D'or
1-23-1 Azumabashi,
Sumida-ku.
Map 4 F3.
Tel (03) 5608-5381.

Hobgoblin
3-16-33 Roppongi,
Minato-ku.
Map 2 E5.
Tel (03) 3568-1280.

Kamiya Bar
1-1-1 Asakusa,
Taito-ku. **Map** 4 F3.
Tel (03) 3841-5400.

Marugo
3-7-5, Shinjuku,
Shinjuku-ku.
Map 1 B1.
Tel (03) 3350-4605.

NewLex Edo
3-13-14 Roppongi,
Minato-ku.
Map 2 E5.
Tel (03) 3479-7477.

SuperDeluxe
B1, 3-1-25 Nishi-Azabu,
Minato-ku.
Map 2 E5.
Tel (03) 5412-0515.

Tasu-Ichi
33-14 Udagawa-cho,
Shibuya-ku.
Map 1 B5.
Tel (03) 3463-0077.

The Aldgate
30-4 Udagawa-cho,
Shibuya-ku. **Map** 1 B5.
Tel (03) 3462-2983.

The Baron
2-25-18 Nishi-Azabu,
Minato-ku. **Map** 2 D5.
Tel (03) 6427-1619.

DJ and Dance Clubs

AgeHa
2-2-10 Shin-Kiba,
Koto-ku.
Tel (03) 5534-1515.

Air
Hikawa Bldg, B1,
2-11 Sarugaku-cho,
Shibuya-ku.
Tel (03) 5784-3386.

Club Asia
1-8 Maruyamacho,
Shibuya-ku.
Tel (03) 5458-2551.

Club Harlem
Dr. Jeekahn's Bldg 2-3F,
2-4 Maruyamacho,
Shibuya-ku.
Tel (03) 3461-8806.

Cyberjapan
🅦 cyberjapan.tv

Feria
7-13-7 Roppongi,
Minato-ku. **Map** 2 E5.
Tel (03) 5785-0656.

Loop
2-1-13 Shibuya,
Shibuya-ku. **Map** 1 B5.
Tel (03) 3797-9933.

Womb
2-16 Maruyama-cho,
Shibuya-ku.
Map 1 A5.
Tel (03) 5459-0039.

Gay and Lesbian

24 Kaikan
2-13-1 Shinjuku,
Shinjuku-ku. **Map** 1 C1.
Tel (03) 3354-2424.

Advocates Café
2-18-1 Shinjuku,
Shinjuku-ku. **Map** 1 C1.
Tel (03) 3358-3988.

GB
2-12-16 Shinjuku,
Shinjuku-ku.
Map 1 C2.
Tel (03) 3352-8972.

Kinsmen
2-18-5 Shinjuku,
Shinjuku-ku. **Map** 1 C1.
Tel (03) 3354-4949.

Kinswomyn
Dai-ichi Tenka Bldg 3F,
2-15-10 Shinjuku,
Shinjuku-ku.
Map 1 B1.
Tel (03) 3354-8720.

Utopia Asia
🅦 utopia-asia.com

SURVIVAL GUIDE

PRACTICAL INFORMATION

Tokyo is much easier for foreign visitors to negotiate than is generally believed. Being unable to speak or read Japanese is rarely a serious problem in the city, since many everyday signs at tourist attractions and in major suburbs are displayed in Roman script as well as in Japanese characters. English-speaking locals are generally quick to offer assistance, and the infrastructure for tourism (public transportation, accommodations, sightseeing) is highly developed. Where problems can arise for visitors is in the surprising clashes in Tokyo's unique East–West culture – for instance, the contrast between the ease with which even tourists can get around on the efficient rail network compared with the difficulty everyone, including the Japanese, has with locating an address in the city *(see p171).*

When to Go

The best times to visit Tokyo are spring (April–May) and fall (October–November). July and August tend to be hot and humid. The rainy season runs from early June to mid-July, while typhoon season, which may bring heavy rainfall and strong winds, peaks in August and September.

Tokyo hosts many festivals throughout the year *(see pp30–33).* Cherry-blossom season (usually late March to early April) draws large crowds to the parks. Peak vacation periods for the Japanese are New Year (December 29–January 3/4), Golden Week (April 29–May 5), the period around Obon (the Buddhist Festival of the Dead; mid-August), and Silver Week (mid-September, approximately every six years). At these times, flights and accommodations fill up fast. However, the only big shutdown of tourist attractions occurs at New Year.

What to Bring

Keep luggage to a minimum, with items that are easy to carry. Train stations often have many steps and no porters.

Modern buildings tend to be overheated in winter and overcooled in summer, so take clothes that you can layer. Casual clothing is acceptable everywhere, even in smart restaurants. Footwear often has to be removed when entering tourist attractions, so wear shoes that can be easily slipped on and off, and perhaps check that there are no holes in your socks.

Picnics in Tokyo's Ueno Park at cherry-blossom time

During rainy and typhoon seasons an umbrella is a must; cheap ones are available from convenience stores *(konbini).* Almost anything you need can be bought in Tokyo. Items may be expensive, but ¥100 stores, found in the larger neighborhoods, sell a vast range of goods, mostly costing just ¥100. Note that clothes and shoes may be available only in smaller sizes.

A colorful display of practical and souvenir fans for sale

Visas and Passports

Citizens of most Western countries may enter Tokyo for short visits (up to 90 days) as Temporary Visitors with only a valid passport; no visa is needed. US journalists are an exception and must always obtain a visa before traveling to Tokyo on business. Temporary Visitors are not allowed to undertake paid employment.

Citizens of some countries, including the UK, may extend their Temporary Visitor by up to a further 90 days at the **Tokyo Regional Immigration Bureau** at least 10 days before the original expiration date.

If you wish to undertake paid or voluntary work or long-term study in Tokyo, you must obtain a visa from a Japanese embassy before traveling. Foreigners who stay in Tokyo for more than 90 days must also apply for a Certificate of Alien Registration from the Ward Office of the area in which they live within 90 days

◀ A bullet train speeding past Mt. Fuji

of arrival in Japan. This certificate, or your passport, must be carried at all times – not doing so can occasionally lead to arrest. Visa holders who want to leave the country and return within the duration of their visa need a re-entry permit from the Tokyo Regional Immigration Bureau. For up-to-date information, contact the nearest Japanese embassy or consulate ahead of travel.

On the plane, you will be given a landing card. Fill in the first part; the second part will be attached to your passport to be completed upon departure. All foreigners are required to be fingerprinted and photographed upon arrival in Japan. A refusal to cooperate may result in being denied entry into the country.

Customs Information

For non-residents, duty-free allowances are 400 cigarettes or 18 oz of tobacco or 100 cigars; three 0.76-liter bottles of alcohol; 2 oz (57 g) of perfume; and gifts and souvenirs of a total value up to ¥200,000 (excluding items less than ¥10,000). Prohibited articles include narcotic drugs or stimulants (including Vicks inhalers, some medicines for allergies and sinus problems, and painkillers containing codeine); counterfeit money; articles that infringe on patents or copyrights; pornography; and firearms and ammunition. Animals and plants are subject to quarantine inspection.

For guidelines on tax-free shopping in Tokyo, see page 138. Guns, swords, and some personal computers require an export license from the **Ministry of Economy, Trade, and Industry**. Art objects may be subject to restrictions.

Tourist Information

Before traveling, request leaflets and brochures from the **Japan National Tourism Organization** (JNTO) in your own country. The JNTO does not make recommendations or reservations, nor does it sell Japan Rail Pass Exchange

An "i" tourist information office, with multilingual staff

Orders *(see p175)*, but it can suggest travel agents that do.

Tokyo's **Tourist Information Center** (TIC) offers literature and advice on tour itineraries in and outside the city; it does not make transport bookings. The TIC also has a counter for the Welcome Inn Reservation Center www.itcj.or.jp, where staff will arrange hotel reservations at locations beyond Tokyo for free.

Most towns outside Tokyo have a tourist information office, usually in or near the main train station. Nearly 100 of these are designated "i" tourist information offices, which have multilingual staff and carry pamphlets in English.

Details of attractions and events in Tokyo can be found in such free local publications as *Metropolis* (also online at http://metropolis.co.jp) and *Japanzine*. Free listings brochures are also available at the TIC, most bookstores, and hotels. Hotel staff will usually help reserve

tickets for local events and shows. Ticket-agency booths, located near train stations and inside department and convenience stores, also book seats in advance and sell tickets up to the last minute. CN Playguide, Ticket PIA *(see p149)*, and **Ticket Saison** are the main agencies.

Admission Prices

Admission to Tokyo temples and shrines is free, however, in historical towns and cities, such as Kamakura, a fee (¥200–500) is often charged. Some attractions may cost over ¥1,000.

For discounts on tourist facilities and services, invest in a **Welcome Card**. There are several types to choose from, offering different benefits and discounts at museums, sights, hotels, and restaurants, for example. Visit the website for further details *(see Directory on p159)*.

Opening Hours

Buddhist temples are typically open 8 or 9am–4pm (until 5pm in summer), but times may vary. Shinto shrines are often open 24 hours. Museums, art galleries, and many tourist attractions are usually open 10am–4 or 5pm daily except Monday (Tuesday if Monday is a public holiday). Most attractions close for the New Year holiday period.

Shopping hours are mostly 10am–8pm, though many supermarkets stay open until midnight. For banking hours, see page 164; for post offices, see page 167.

Kencho Temple in Kamakura, where an admission fee is charged

Public Conveniences

Toilets in Japan range from basic to highly sophisticated. Japanese-style toilets are simple troughs over which one squats, facing the end with the hood. Many public places, including trains, have both traditional and western-style facilities. Toilet paper and hand towels may not be provided, so it is wise to carry some tissues with you.

Modern toilets may have a panel that, when pressed, plays a tune or produces a flushing sound to discreetly mask natural noises. They may also have heated seats, automatic seat covers, bidets, and hot-air-drying facilities. For protocol on toilet slippers, see page 161.

At many train stations, it is not possible to use the toilets unless you have first paid for your ticket and passed through the ticket barrier. For those in need, public toilet facilities can usually be found in major stores, fast-food outlets, and in quieter neighborhoods' convenience stores.

Travelers with Special Needs

Facilities for the disabled in Tokyo are of mixed quality: the visually impaired are well provided for, but people in wheelchairs may face problems with subway and train stations and pedestrian overpasses, which often have no escalators or elevators. However, barrier-free access and universal design are slowly becoming implemented, so the situation is improving. Most modern buildings have excellent toilet facilities. For detailed information on disabled facilities, contact **Accessible Tokyo**.

Travelers with Children

Children are welcome in most places, including restaurants, and parents need have few worries about their offspring's safety. Discreet breastfeeding in public is accepted, and baby food, formula, and disposable diapers are easily obtainable. Top hotels usually offer babysitting

Japanese children playing on the sidewalk

services and nurseries, while at traditional inns, a maid may be willing to babysit.

Many theme parks and museums are great fun for kids, but some temples and galleries may have age restrictions. At most attractions, children get reduced rates, which are typically half the adult price. Children under 6 can ride for free on buses and trains; those aged 6 to 11, pay half-fare. It is unwise to travel on rush-hour trains with small children. Care should be taken with little ones in hot *onsen* pools.

If your children are curious about their forthcoming trip to Japan, **Kids Web Japan** is full of child-friendly information about the country.

Student and Senior Travelers

Upon presentation of an International Student Identity Card or ISIC (www.isic.org), students can enjoy reductions of up to 50 percent at a number of locations in Tokyo, including major museums, a couple of hotels and ferries, and some eateries, such as the Hard Rock Café. At several other places that do not formally recognize the ISIC, students may receive

International Student Identity Card (ISIC), great for discounts

a discount with their regular student identity cards, or simply with a verbal claim to being a student.

The general safety of the country makes Japan a popular choice among senior travelers. People aged 60 and above often receive discounts on admission fees. However, not many facilities are adapted to support the needs of those with mobility issues (*see also Travelers with Special Needs*).

Gay and Lesbian Travelers

Same-sex couples traveling around Japan are unlikely to encounter many problems. Open displays of affection may be frowned upon by some Japanese, but attitudes are broader in Tokyo, which has an active gay scene and a small but lively gay quarter (*see p153*). However, even this only really comes out at night. **Magnet Tours** is a gay-owned tour operator specializing in gay vacations. For more information on the local gay and lesbian scene, visit the **Utopia Asia** website.

Time and the Calendar

Tokyo is 9 hours ahead of Greenwich Mean Time and 14 hours ahead of US Eastern Standard Time. There is no daylight-saving time: when countries that use daylight-saving time switch to summer time, the time difference is an hour less.

Years are numbered both by the Western system and the reign of the current emperor. The present era, Heisei (meaning "achieving peace"), began when Emperor Akihito came to the throne in 1989, which became Heisei 1; 2013 is Heisei 25. The Japanese system of years is generally used within the country, especially on official documents; the Western system is often used in international contexts.

Electricity

The electric current in Tokyo is 100 volts, AC, 50 cycles – a system similar to that in the US. The country has two different cycles: 50 cycles in eastern Japan (including Tokyo) and 60 cycles in western Japan. Plugs with two flat pins are standard, so US appliances can be used, but sometimes at reduced efficiency.

European appliances can be used only with transformers suitable for US voltage. If in doubt, consult the appliance instructions. Some international hotels have two outlets – 110 and 220 volts – although these accept only two-pin plugs. Adapters are available from electrical stores.

Conversions

Metric to US/UK Standard
1 millimeter = 0.04 inch
1 centimeter = 0.4 inch
1 meter = 3 feet 3 inches
1 kilometer = 0.6 mile
1 gram = 0.04 ounce
1 kilogram = 2.2 pounds
1 liter = 2.1 US/1.8 UK pints

Responsible Tourism

As might be expected from the country that produces the world's best-selling hybrid car, environmental consciousness is quite strong in Japan. For decades, the Japanese have been separating their garbage into burnable and non-burnable types. Containers for recycling Styrofoam food trays, PET bottles, and paper drink cartons in addition to other categories stand outside most supermarkets. This kind of eco-thinking does not, however, extend to the use of disposable wooden chopsticks (waribashi), which are the most common implements in eateries serving Japanese food. Tourists can do their bit to avoid this waste of wood by taking their own reusable chopsticks to restaurants. Organic food has not really taken off in Japan as it has in the West. However, there are certainly some decent organic restaurants in Tokyo.

Separate recycling bins can be found outside most supermarkets

DIRECTORY

Visas and Passports

Tokyo Regional Immigration Bureau
W moj.go.jp

UK Embassy
W ukinjapan.fco.gov.uk/eng

US Embassy
W japan.usembassy.gov

Customs Information

Ministry of Economy, Trade, and Industry
W meti.go.jp

Tourist Information

Japan National Tourism Organization (JNTO)
10F Tokyo Kotsu Kaikan Bldg, 2-10-1 Yurakucho, Chiyoda-ku, Tokyo.
Tel (03) 3201-3331.
W jnto.go.jp

Australia: **Tel** (02) 9279-2177. W jnto.org.au

Canada: **Tel** (416) 366-7140. W ilovejapan.ca

UK: **Tel** (020) 7398-5670.
W seejapan.co.uk

US: **Tel** (212) 757-5640 (New York) or (213) 623-1952 (Los Angeles).
W japantravelinfo.com

Ticket Saison
Tel (03) 3341-1824.

Tourist Information Center (TIC)

Marunouchi Trust Tower North 1F, 1-8-1 Marunouchi, Chiyoda-ku, Tokyo. **Tel** (03) 5220-7055.
W tictokyo.jp/en/

Welcome Card
W jnto.go.jp/eng/arrange/essential/welcome.html

Travelers with Special Needs

Accessible Tokyo
W accessible.jp.org/tokyo/en

Travelers with Children

Kids Web Japan
W web-japan.org/kidsweb

Gay and Lesbian Travelers

Magnet Tours
2F Sereno Nishishinbashi Bldg, 2-11-14 Nishishinbashi, Minato-ku, Tokyo.
Tel (03) 3500-4819.
W magnettours.jp

Utopia Asia
W utopia-asia.com/tipsjapn.htm

Useful Websites

Eventful
W eventful.com/tokyo/events

Japan Guide
W japan-guide.com/

Seek Japan
W seekjapan.jp/

Etiquette and Language

Etiquette is important in Tokyo – the social lubricant for a crowded community. In recent decades, attitudes have relaxed, yet even the most apparently rebellious Tokyoite will not break certain rules. What constitutes correct behavior often varies according to the situation and status of the individuals involved. Foreigners will be forgiven most gaffes, but good manners will earn them respect. The best approach is to be as sensitive as possible to situations, avoid loud or dogmatic behavior, and follow the lead of those around you.

Taboos

Few allowances are made even for foreigners on certain points, mainly relating to Japanese standards of hygiene. It is considered unforgivable to get soap or shampoo in a bathtub; washing belongs to the shower area (*see p111*).

At one time, eating while walking and on local trains and buses was frowned upon. Such constraints have become more relaxed, though some older people would still never engage in such practices. Eating on longer train trips is fine.

Bodily emissions are considered very rude, though anything drawn inward is acceptable. Thus, sniffing is fine, but blowing your nose in public is reviled. Gauze face masks are worn in public to prevent the spread of colds.

The Japanese wear gauze masks to prevent the spread of colds

The Hierarchy

Respect for seniors is fundamental to Japanese society. Seniors include not only parents, grandparents, company bosses, and teachers, but even those a year or two senior in school or employment. The term *sensei* (teacher) is used as a term of respect for those with high professional status, such as doctors. Many Japanese regard the emperor as being at the pinnacle of the social hierarchy and show him great respect, but stop short of veneration.

Social attitudes are reflected in the Japanese language, which has a special form of honorific speech. This is vitally important in many social situations to indicate the speaker's respect, humility, and politeness.

Smoking

In a number of Tokyo's wards, smoking on the street (except in specially designated areas) is punishable by on-the-spot fines. There is often a small smoking zone outside major stations. Smoking is banned on buses and trains (except for some long-distance trains, such as the *shinkansen*, which has smoking cars), as well as all stations. Lighting up is usually permitted in restaurants and bars, but the number of non-smoking venues is on the rise.

Attitudes to Physical Contact and Sex

Members of the same sex are physically at ease with each other, and the atmosphere in single-sex public baths is relaxed. Between the sexes, however, public contact is more limited than in the West. Couples hold hands in public, but kissing is not so common; even a kiss on the cheek might cause embarrassment. In general, sex is seen as free from shame, but something to be indulged in discreetly. Homosexual activity is less openly accepted than in many Western nations (*see p158*). Sadly, the sleazier side of the sex trade includes schoolgirl prostitution, and pornography is widely sold in convenience stores. Nonetheless, everyday life is relatively sanitized, and it is important to remember that geisha and most bar hostesses are not prostitutes.

Bowing

The formal greeting in Tokyo is a bow, its depth reflecting the relative status of the participants. However, visitors rarely need to bow – a handshake is fine. In department stores, restaurants, and hotels, bows are part of the service, and they can be ignored or met with a brief smile. If you wish to bow, hold your arms and back straight, and bend from the waist, pausing for a moment at the low point.

Bowing between business colleagues who are close in status to each other

Traditional footwear neatly lined up on racks outside a temple

Etiquette at Temples and Shrines

The atmosphere in Buddhist temples and Shinto shrines is casual, and there are no restrictions on clothing. Visitors should show respect and not be noisy, but there are few of the taboos found in some Buddhist nations. If you enter buildings in a shrine or temple, except those with stone floors, leave your shoes at the entrance or carry them with you. Plastic bags may be provided for this, especially if you can use a different exit. Some temples allow photography, some only without flash, and others not at all.

Shoes

It is a serious mistake to wear shoes indoors in all private and many public buildings. The principle is that the clean interior should not be contaminated with dirt from the outside. Always remove your shoes if the area immediately beyond the entrance to a room or building is at a higher level than the entrance itself.

When you enter a Japanese house or traditional restaurant, take off your shoes and put on slippers before stepping onto the raised floor. Other people's shoes will usually be evident, or there will be a rack in which shoes can be stored. If no slippers are provided, go in stockinged feet. In Western-style hotels, the main part of the room is not raised above the entrance, and so shoes can be worn by both guests and staff. Slippers should be removed to walk on *tatami* matting – go in stockinged feet.

Many restrooms, public and private, have special slippers inside the toilet area. Remove your own slippers outside before stepping into the toilet slippers, which are then left behind upon exiting the toilet area.

Taxes and Tipping

A consumption tax of 8 percent (planned to rise over the next few years) is paid by consumers for goods and services. Shops and service providers include the tax in the prices shown.

Other than for exceptional service, there is no tipping in Japan; indeed, an attempt at tipping might even cause offense.

Language

Tokyo is well signposted in English, and it is not hard for visitors to find their way around. Many, especially younger, Japanese do speak at least a little English. It is not uncommon for English-speaking Japanese to offer help to what they perceive as the foreign visitor in distress. However, do not expect too much English to be understood by taxi drivers, policemen, or station clerks.

Japanese Names

Japanese names are given as family name followed by first name. However, many Japanese automatically reverse this order when giving names to Westerners, so you may need to check which is which. The Japanese generally call each other by the family name, even if they are close friends, but they will happily call you by your first name if you prefer.

When speaking to or about an adult, add "-san," which stands for Mr., Mrs., or Ms., to their name – for instance, Smith-san or John-san. For babies and young girls, add "-chan," for young boys "-kun." However, one should never refer to oneself as "-san."

Gift-Giving

Gift-giving is an important aspect of social etiquette in Japan. Any trip means bringing home souvenirs for friends and colleagues, usually something edible. Small gifts may be exchanged at a first business meeting, and if you visit someone's home, you should buy a luxury food item or take a small gift from your home country. Keep gifts small to avoid placing an obligation on the recipient. Gifts are often not opened in front of the giver. Note that it is regarded as unlucky to give four of anything.

Box of cookies elegantly gift-wrapped in paper, then cloth

Lining Up and Jaywalking

When waiting, such as for a train, people line up neatly. To get off a crowded train, gently push your way through. If you are stuck and cannot reach the door in time, call out *"orimass"* ("I'm getting off") as you attempt to push your way toward the exit.

Jaywalking is heavily discouraged. Pedestrians in Tokyo invariably wait for the crossing lights, even when there is no traffic coming.

Personal Security and Health

Medical facilities and general hygiene standards are high and crime rates in Tokyo are low, though pickpockets occasionally operate in crowds. *Koban* (manned police boxes) are found in every neighborhood, usually near the train station; their presence helps to keep crime down. Due to its vulnerable position at the juncture of several tectonic plates, Japan is particularly prone to earthquakes and volcanic eruptions, some of which cause extreme devastation. The country also lies in the path of typhoons, which can wreak enormous damage.

Police

Japanese police are generally helpful. Those at the *koban* are accustomed to dispensing directions, though their English may be limited. The police can legally demand visitors to produce their passport or Certificate of Alien Registration *(see p156)*, so keep yours with you at all times. Failure to do so could result in arrest and 23 days' detention while the case is investigated. Under questioning, which can last many hours, detainees will not have access to a lawyer. Interviews are not recorded.

What to Be Aware Of

Tokyo is regarded as a safe city, though episodes of bag-snatching and pickpocketing sometimes occur in crowded areas, on trains, and at airports. It is generally safe to walk around at night, but take extra care in the Roppongi district. There have been reports of drinks being spiked with drugs that leave the victim unconscious for hours, allowing fraudulent billings to be made to their credit card.

Due to the nuclear accident that occured in 2011, follow government advice by not going within a 49-mile (80-km) radius of the Fukushima Daiichi nuclear facility.

Women should take sensible precautions regarding where they go and with whom. Be wary of men outside train stations who try to start a conversation – it may lead to an unwanted advance. These can usually be shaken off with a simple "no."

A uniformed Tokyo policeman

In an Emergency

Emergency calls are free. The Tokyo **police** operates a help line for foreign visitors; your hotel, embassy, or consulate may also be able to help. The **Tokyo Metropolitan Health and Medical Information Center** offers information in English, Spanish, Chinese, Korean, and Thai. In case of language difficulties regarding medical matters, contact the **Emergency Medical Translation Services**.

The **Japan Helpline** is a great 24-hour resource in English. The **Tokyo English Life Line** offers free counseling, while **Befrienders International** is a suicide prevention hotline.

Natural Disasters

Each year, Japan experiences more than 1,000 earthquakes large enough to be felt; most are nothing to worry about. Tremors are more noticeable in tall buildings, which sway markedly but usually have mechanisms to absorb the motion. In a larger earthquake, especially in an old building, open the doors (to prevent them from buckling and jamming) and turn off any gas. Do not rush outside, where debris may be falling, but shelter under a reinforced doorway or a sturdy table. Don't sleep close to heavy furniture not securely fixed to the wall or under air-conditioning units. The Tokyo Government has issued a useful bilingual **Earthquake Survival Manual**, and the **Japan Meteorological Agency** provides early warnings.

The peak months for typhoons are August and September. Typhoons bring violent winds; the worst may cause flooding or landslides. Active volcanoes are usually fenced off so that no one can get close, but toxic fumes occasionally seep from the crater or its vicinity; look out for warning notices.

In the event of a natural disaster, you can reassure your loved ones that you are safe by calling the **Disaster Emergency Message Dial**.

Lost and Stolen Property

The Japanese are very honest people, and found items are often handed in to the authorities, so it pays to report

Schoolchildren practicing an earthquake drill

the loss of any item at the nearest *koban* or with the transport authorities. For items lost on the JR network, call the number given in the Directory on page 175. Lost or stolen passports should be reported at the local police station, which will provide an official report. This can be presented at the embassy or consulate in order to obtain a replacement or emergency passport.

Hospitals and Pharmacies

Medical facilities in Japan are excellent, but you will be expected to pay the cost of any treatment you receive. If you are sick, go to a hospital; for minor problems, try consulting a pharmacist first.

If you need to find a hospital or another medical institution, contact the Tokyo Metropolitan Health and Medical Information Center, which has multilingual staff. The **AMDA (Asian Medical Doctors Association) International Medical Information Center** offers free medical consultations over the telephone in eight languages and a free telephone interpreter service. The hospitals listed in the Directory

below have English-speaking staff and deal with 24-hour emergencies.

Medicines are dispensed at pharmacies, though there may be problems with fullfilling a prescription from abroad. Western brands are available, if expensive, at international pharmacies, such as Tokyo's **American Pharmacy**. Contact lenses can be obtained with relative ease, and Western-brand lens solutions are reasonably priced. The prevalence of mosquitoes in the warmer months calls for insect repellents and soothing lotions for mosquito bites, sold in pharmacies. Mu-hi is a popular brand. Chinese herbal medicine is widely available.

Illuminated pharmacy sign

Minor Hazards

Despite the nuclear accident in Fukushima in 2011, there should be no danger to food and water in Tokyo and surrounding regions. Tap water is drinkable, and food poisoning is rare thanks to good hygiene standards. An upset stomach is likely to be due only to a change in diet.

Raw seafood in sushi and sashimi is not a risk. Though extremely toxic if inexpertly prepared, *fugu* (blowfish) is safe, since all the fish served in restaurants and on sale in supermarkets is prepared by licensed chefs, who undergo the most rigorous training. Eat raw meat only in good restaurants. Insecticides are widely used, so always wash or peel fruit before eating.

Travel and Health Insurance

It is advisable to take out comprehensive travel insurance in advance of the trip. It is important to confirm that it covers medical costs, since these can be very high in Japan. Insurance should also cover such areas as loss of belongings, theft, cancellation of journey, and repatriation.

DIRECTORY

In an Emergency

Befrienders International
Tel (03) 3207-5040.

Emergency Medical Translation Services
Tel (03) 5285-8185.
Open 5–8pm daily (from 9am Sat, Sun, & pub hols).

Fire/Ambulance
Tel 119 (English rarely spoken).

Japan Helpline
Tel 0570-000-911.

Police
Tel 110 (emergencies; English rarely spoken).
Tel (03) 3501-0110 (English help line).

Tokyo English Life Line
Tel (03) 5774-0992.
Open 9am–11pm.

Tokyo Metropolitan Health and Medical Information Center
Tel (03) 5285-8181.
Open 9am–8pm daily.

Natural Disasters

Earthquake Survival Manual
[w] metro.tokyo.jp/
ENGLISH/POLICY/
security.htm

Disaster Emergency Message Dial
Tel 171 (voice message).
[w] ntt-east.co.jp/
saigai_e/voice171

Japan Meteorological Agency
[w] jma.go.jp/jma/en/
Activities/eew.html

Hospitals and Pharmacies

AMDA International Medical Information Center
Tel (03) 5285-8088.

American Pharmacy
B1 Marunouchi Bldg,
2-4-1 Marunouchi,
Chiyoda-ku, Tokyo.
Tel (03) 5220-7716.

Japanese Red Cross Medical Center
4-1-22 Hiroo, Shibuya-ku,
Tokyo. Tel (03) 3400-1311.

St. Luke's International Hospital
9-1 Akashicho,
Chuo-ku, Tokyo.
Tel (03) 3541-5151.

Seibo International Catholic Hospital
2-5-1 Naka-Ochiai,
Shinjuku-ku,
Tokyo.
Tel (03) 3951-1111.

Tokyo Medical and Surgical Clinic
32 Shiba-koen
Building 2F, 3-4-30
Shiba-koen,
Minato-ku, Tokyo.
Tel (03) 3436-3028.

Banking and Currency

For visitors used to easy and instant cash access 24 hours a day, Japan's banking system can prove frustrating. Credit cards are accepted at a growing number of shops (including convenience stores), restaurants, most hotels, and major railway stations, but Japan is still largely a cash society. Make sure you always have some cash at hand. Payments can be made using debit cards where the appropriate sign (such as VISA or MasterCard) is displayed; however, cash withdrawals using debit cards are possible only at a limited number of ATMs. Personal checks are unknown.

Banks and Bureaux de Change

Buying yen, exchanging traveler's checks, and other regular banking transactions can be easily conducted via major Japanese banks, including **Bank of Tokyo-Mitsubishi UFJ**, **Sumitomo Mitsui**, and **Mizuho Bank**. Some foreign banks, such as **Citibank**, offer a similar range of services.

Most banks open 9am–3pm on weekdays and are closed on weekends and national holidays. The exchange rate is posted at about 10am for US dollars; later, for other currencies. Banks usually exchange currency between 10am and 3pm; some city banks, however, offer this service from as early as 9am.

It is possible to change cash and traveler's checks at banks, major hotels (which offer the same rates as banks), main post offices, *ryokan*, and some city department stores.

Bureaux de change are often near major train stations.

At major international airports, currency exchange counters may keep longer hours than banks; at Tokyo International, for example, the counter is open from 6:30am to 11pm. Rates at airports are not very competitive, though.

Even leading city banks may be unfamiliar with foreign currency other than dollars, so be prepared for bank tellers to check with their superiors if they have not experienced such notes before. In city centers, staff may speak English, and forms are often supplied in English; if not, staff will show you where to write. Transactions are relatively simple but may be time-consuming. Always carry your passport with you.

It is illegal for public transportation, stores, and restaurants to accept payment in foreign currencies, so you will need some Japanese yen

on arrival to cover any immediate needs. It is always wise to obtain cash before traveling anywhere outside of Japan's major cities.

Some banks and post offices also offer money transfer facilities.

ATMs

Automatic Teller Machines (ATMs) are easily available in large urban areas throughout Japan. However, many do not take foreign credit or cash cards – for example, Cirrus, Maestro, Link, and Delta cash cards are not widely accepted. Most Japanese post offices and all 7-Eleven stores (more than 17,000 in the Tokyo area) have ATMs that will accept VISA, MasterCard, American Express, Maestro, Plus, Cirrus, and JCB cards; they also provide an English menu for users. ATMs at 7-Eleven stores are

ATM typically found in a post office

DIRECTORY

Banks

Bank of Tokyo-Mitsubishi UFJ
2-7-1 Marunouchi,
Chiyoda-ku, Tokyo.
Tel (03) 3240-1111.

Citibank
B1-2F Kawase Building,
3-17-5 Shinjuku, Tokyo.
Tel (03) 5462-5000.
Ⓦ citibank.co.jp/en

Mizuho Bank
1-1-5 Uchi-saiwai-cho,
Chiyoda-ku, Tokyo.
Tel (03) 3596-1111.

Sumitomo Mitsui
1-1-2 Yurakucho,
Chiyoda-ku, Tokyo.
Tel (03) 3501-1111.

ATMs

Shibuya Post Office
1-12-3 Shibuya,
Shibuya-ku, Tokyo.
Tel (03) 5469-9823.

Toyko Central Post Office
2-7-2 Marunouchi,
Chiyoda-ku, Tokyo.
Tel (03) 3217-5231.

Credit and Debit Cards

American Express
Lost cards:
Tel 0120-020-120
(toll-free; English language after Japanese).
Ⓦ americanexpress.com

Diners Club
Lost cards:
Tel 0120-074-024
(toll-free nationwide).
Ⓦ dinersclub.com

MasterCard
Tel 00531-11-3886
(free international assistance).
Ⓦ mastercard.com

VISA
Tel 00531-44-0022
(24-hour assistance).
Ⓦ visa.com
Ⓦ visa.com/atmlocator

open 24 hours. The operating hours of post office ATMs vary: those at major post offices are typically open 7am–11pm Monday to Friday, with shorter hours at weekends; those at minor post offices are usually open 9am–4pm during the week and closed at weekends. The ATMs at the main post offices – **Tokyo Central Post Office**, **Shibuya Post Office**, and Shinjuku *(see p167)* – are open around-the-clock (except 8pm–midnight on Sundays and public holidays). Some Citibank ATMs are open 24 hours, though Citibank branches are not so numerous in the Tokyo area. Visit the Citibank website for a list of locations.

Credit and Debit Cards

International credit cards, such as **American Express**, **VISA**, **MasterCard**, and **Diners Club**, are generally accepted by leading banks, hotels, and stores in larger cities in Japan. They can be used to buy train tickets at major JR stations, and they are also accepted by some taxis. Note that there may be a charge to use a credit card.

Obtaining cash with credit or debit cards is not always possible – even if a machine displays the sticker for your card, it may have a problem reading it *(see also ATMs)*.

Traveler's checks are usually accepted only in major city banks and large hotels. Travelex,

American Express, and VISA checks are the most widely recognized.

If your credit or debit card gets stolen or lost, contact your bank to cancel the card.

Currency

The Japanese currency is the yen (¥). Coins come in denominations of ¥1, ¥5, ¥10, ¥50, ¥100, and ¥500. Bank notes are printed in denominations of ¥1,000, ¥2,000 (very rare), ¥5,000, and ¥10,000.

Japanese bank notes (but not coins) can be reconverted to foreign currency at the point of departure; the amount is limited only by the funds carried by the airport exchange center.

Bank Notes

Each of the bank note denominations carries a portrait of a historical figure, such as the novelist Ichiyo Higuchi on the ¥5,000 note.

¥10,000 note

¥5,000 note

¥2,000 note

¥1,000 note

Coins

The denominations of Japan's coins are all marked in Arabic numerals, except for the ¥5. On the reverse side of most of the coins is a design of a flower or plant design; on the ¥10 it is a temple.

¥500 coin

¥100 coin

¥50 coin

¥10 coin

¥5 coin

¥1 coin

Communications and Media

Tokyo basks in the image of being a high-tech megalopolis, and though there is some truth in this – the Japanese were accessing the Internet on their mobile phones long before anyone else – the city is far from being the wired, computer-geek capital one might suppose. Just about everyone has mobile phones, while Internet cafés and free Wi-Fi hotspots are still surprisingly rare. Public phones are easy to find, though not all are suitable for making international calls. English-language newspapers and magazines are readily available, and the postal system is fast and efficient.

A green public telephone, used for making local calls only

International and Local Telephone Calls

Some public phones accept international credit cards as well as phone cards. The call will be routed via **NTT Communications**, unless you purchase a phone card issued by one of the other major telecom companies offering international calls, such as **KDDI** (KDDI Super World Card) and **SoftBank Telecom** (Super Moshi Moshi Card). Each company has a toll-free number for information on charges and services. To make a call, dial the relevant company's access code, then the country code, area code (minus the initial zero), and the desired number.

All major hotels in Tokyo offer international direct dialing, but there may be a surcharge for calls from your room. NTT Communications and KDDI offer international collect calls; simply dial the relevant access code, then ask the operator to place a collect call. The cheapest times for making international calls

are 11pm–8am daily, though the rates between 7 and 11pm are also off-peak.

The charge for a local call is ¥10 per minute. Use small coins or phone cards in a public phone; unused coins will be returned to you. In this guide, the area code is given in parentheses; omit it if calling from within the area.

Mobile Phones

Some foreign mobile phones may work in Japan if the operator is an inbound roaming partner of **SoftBank Mobile** or **NTT DoCoMo**. Check with your service provider before traveling.

As an alternative, visitors can rent a mobile phone from companies like **Rentafone Japan**. Payment is typically made by credit card. Prepaid phones (though not prepaid SIM cards) are also available from such mobile operators as KDDI and SoftBank. The operator's conditions may

differ, but a passport as ID and a hotel address usually suffice.

Public Telephones

Public phones are found in train stations, often outside convenience stores, and on some busy streets. Green public phones, which accept coins and phone cards, are for domestic calls only. For international calls, use the gray public phones, which have a button for English-language information and another for the emergency services. They also have digital jacks for data transmission. Old-style pink phones, occasionally found in restaurants, are for local calls and accept ¥10 coins only.

Useful Dialing Codes And Numbers

- Domestic directory enquiries, **104**
- Domestic operator, **100**
- International directory enquiries, **0051**

Use these codes after the international access codes to dial the following countries: Australia **61**, Brazil **55**, Canada **1**, China **86**, France **33**, Germany **49**, Hong Kong **852**, India **91**, Indonesia **62**, Ireland **353**, Israel **972**, Italy **39**, Republic of Korea **82**, Malaysia **60**, Netherlands **31**, New Zealand **64**, Peru **51**, Philippines **63**, Russia **7**, Singapore **65**, Spain **34**, Sweden **46**, Switzerland **41**, Taiwan **886**, Thailand **66**, United Kingdom **44**, and US **1**.

A phonecard dispenser and a gray public telephone that provides local and international dialing access

Internet and Email

Internet cafés are not as plentiful as might be expected, but access to the Internet is slowly on the rise. **Kinko's** provides Internet access at its branches throughout the city. Some computer stores, including **Apple**, also provide free Internet access.

For a list of Wi-Fi hotspots, check www.hotspot-locations.com and www.freespot.com/users/map-e/map_tokyo.html; however, bear in mind that many of the entries may be out of date. The lobbies of large hotels sometimes have free Wi-Fi access.

Postal Services

Post offices (yubin-kyoku) and mailboxes can be identified by a character looking like the letter "T" with an extra horizontal bar across the top. Main post offices are usually open 9am–5pm on weekdays and 9am–12:30pm on Saturdays. Smaller post offices may open 9am–4:30pm on weekdays, but they are often closed on weekends. Stamps are also sold at convenience stores and larger hotels.

All post offices provide **EMS** express mail services. For urgent mail, the **Tokyo Central Post Office** and **Shinjuku Post Office** both provide all-night counters.

Several door-to-door delivery services (takkyubin), including Yamato and Sagawa-Kyubin, offer prompt and efficient services throughout Japan. Small packages can be sent via these courier services from convenience stores and other shops. International courier services include **FedEx** and **DHL**.

Newspapers and Magazines

Three English-language daily newspapers – The Japan Times, the International Herald Tribune-Asahi Shimbun, and The Daily Yomiuri – are sold at kiosks in train stations, major hotels,

Selection of local newspapers at a Tokyo newsstand

foreign-language bookstores, and in some convenience stores. These newspapers and The Mainichi Daily News are also available online. The best publication for business and technology is the Nikkei Weekly.

Imported magazines can be found at foreign-language bookstores. Free English-language magazines are also easily available. In particular, Metropolis and Japanzine have extensive listings and classified ads. Metropolis is also available online (http://metropolis.co.jp); another useful website is Japan Today (www.japantoday.com).

Television and Radio

The state public broadcaster, NHK, has two terrestrial and two satellite TV channels. Its 7pm and 9pm news bulletins (7pm on weekends) can be heard in English on bilingual TV stations, which are often available in hotels. Other networks include Nippon TV, TBS, Fuji TV, and TV Asahi. Check Metropolis for English-language programs. Overseas networks are widely available via cable or satellite.

NHK Radio airs news and classical music on both AM and FM. There are several commercial radio stations in Tokyo: J-Wave (www.j-wave.co.jp) and Inter FM (www.interfm.co.jp) offer some programs in English.

DIRECTORY

International and Local Telephone Calls

KDDI
Tel 001 (access code).
Tel 0057 (toll-free info).
W kddi.com

NTT Communications
Tel 0033 (access code).
Tel 0120 54-0033 + 8# (toll-free info).
W 506506.ntt.com/english/service/p_card

SoftBank Telecom
Tel 0061 (domestic long-distance access code).

Tel 0041 (international call service access code).
Tel 0066-11 & 0088-41 (toll-free info).
W tm.softbank.jp/english

Mobile Phones

NTT DoCoMo
W nttdocomo.com

Rentafone Japan
W rentafonejapan.com

SoftBank Mobile
W mb.softbank.jp/en

Internet and Email

Kinko's
W kinkos.co.jp

Apple
3-5-12 Ginza, Chuo-ku.
Tel (03) 5159-8200.
W apple.com/jp

Postal Services

DHL
Tel 0120-39-2580, then 0.
W dhl.co.jp/en.html

EMS
W post.japanpost.jp/int/ems/index_en.html

FedEx
Tel 0120-00-3200 (toll-free).
W fedex.com/jp_english

Shinjuku Post Office
1-8-8 Nishi-Shinjuku, Shinjuku-ku, Tokyo.
Tel (03) 3340-9512.

Toyko Central Post Office
2-7-2 Marunouchi, Chiyoda-ku, Tokyo.
Tel (03) 3217-5231 (domestic mail);
(03) 3284-9540 (international mail).

TRAVEL INFORMATION

Tokyo is served by flights from across the world, most of them arriving at Narita Airport. Although Narita is a long way from the city center, this gives visitors their first introduction to the prompt and highly efficient public transportation system that makes traveling so easy in Japan. Tokyo can be used as the hub for travel to other parts of the country, either by air from Haneda Airport or by *shinkansen* bullet train *(see p174)*. There are direct bus and train connections from Narita to Haneda. The Japan National Tourism Organization (JNTO) website *(see p159)* provides useful travel information for visitors, including lists of travel agents that can make reservations and sell travel tickets and Rail Pass vouchers *(see p175)*. In Tokyo, the JNTO has a tourist information center that provides travel information in English *(see p159)*.

Arriving by Air

All major international airlines fly to Tokyo. Most flights land at Narita Airport, formally known as Tokyo New International Airport. Tokyo's other airport, Haneda (also, confusingly, referred to as Tokyo International Airport) is served by a growing number of international flights and is also the major hub for domestic flights. The two airports are linked by an efficient network of train, bus, and helicopter services.

Tickets and Fares

Japan Airlines (JAL) and **All Nippon Airways (ANA)** are Japan's main airlines. They fly nonstop between London and Tokyo, along with **Virgin** and **British Airways**. The flying time is around 12 hours. **Qantas**, **Air New Zealand**, and JAL operate nonstop flights between Tokyo and Australia (flying time: about 10 hours) and New Zealand (12 hours). JAL and **United** are the main carriers between Tokyo and North America, but Northwest, American, Delta, and ANA also link Tokyo with several US cities.

Prices are highest over the major holiday periods of New Year and Golden Week, and in the summer (July and August).

On Arrival

Immigration forms are handed out on the plane in advance of landing. Immigration procedures tend to go more smoothly for the Japanese. All foreigners entering the country are photographed and fingerprinted on arrival. With both immigration and customs, a neat appearance and politeness help. For more details regarding customs, see p157. Both Narita and Haneda airports are well signposted in English.

Getting to and from Narita Airport

Narita Airport, 35 miles (60 km) northeast of the center of Tokyo, has two terminals linked by a free shuttle bus. There is a **Tourist Information Center** in the arrival lobby of each terminal.

Holders of a Japan Rail Pass Exchange Order *(see p175)* should have it validated at the Japan Railways (JR) counter; they can then use it to travel into Tokyo by JR train. Airport **Limousine Buses** are frequent and have drop-offs at most major hotels within Tokyo, Yokohama, and other nearby cities. Traveling to Tokyo by taxi will cost at least ¥22,000.

The most convenient fast link to Tokyo is the **Narita Express (N'EX)** train, which departs from beneath the terminal buildings and travels nonstop to Tokyo Station in 53 minutes, and then on to Shinjuku, Shinagawa, Shibuya, and Ikebukuro in the capital, or to Yokohama and Ofuna. You can use the Japan Rail Pass on the N'EX, but you must reserve a seat (free of charge) at the ticket booth before traveling. All signs and announcements are in Japanese and English.

Travelers without a Japan Rail Pass can take the **Keisei Skyliner** from the station under the terminal buildings. This train takes 36 minutes to get to Nippori Station and 41 minutes to Ueno Station.

Local Keisei trains offer the cheapest but slowest link between Narita and Tokyo.

Check-in area of Tokyo New International Airport, at Narita

Entrance to Terminal 2, Haneda Airport

city and beyond. You can also have your luggage picked up for delivery to the airport, though this has to be ordered two days in advance. Companies offering this service operate counters at Narita and Haneda airports. Among the service providers are **JAL ABC** and **ANA Sky Porter**. The cost is about ¥2,000 for one large bag.

On Departure

It can take up to 90 minutes to reach Narita Airport from central Tokyo, so set out about 4 hours before your departure time. If traveling by the Narita Express, reserve seats well in advance, especially during Golden Week and the New Year holiday. All trains stop at Terminal 2 first, and terminate at Terminal 1. The departure lobbies of both terminals are on the 4th floor. Many flights from Terminal 2 are boarded at the satellite terminal, reached via a shuttle train. Other flights require shuttle bus connections in order to board the plane.

Getting to and from Haneda Airport

Lying just to the south of central Tokyo, Haneda Airport has three terminals, only one of which handles international flights. The terminals are linked by a free shuttle bus and an underground walkway.

Limousine Buses run to several destinations in central Tokyo, including major hotels. The Keikyu private train line (see p175) departs from underneath the airport and connects with the JR network at Shinagawa Station (about 11 minutes). The Tokyo Monorail (see p171) links Haneda with Hamamatsucho Station, on the JR Yamanote Line (about 20 minutes). It is pretty cramped at rush hour, but it gives a fascinating view over parts of Tokyo Bay. A taxi into Tokyo will cost at least ¥5,000.

Domestic Flights

An extensive flight network run by JAL and ANA covers Japan's four main islands and many of the smaller ones, too. For trips up to around 350 miles (600 km), *shinkansen* bullet trains (see p174) may be faster and more convenient than planes; in addition, there is often little difference in price. Domestic flights have both economy seats and, at an extra cost, a "Super Seat" service, which combines first and business class. The domestic low-cost airline **Skymark** connects Haneda and Narita to various cities in Hokkaido and Kyushu, and to Naha in Okinawa.

Luggage Delivery

It is possible to have your luggage delivered from the airports to any address in the

Luxurious N'EX, traveling from Narita Airport to central Tokyo

---

DIRECTORY

Tickets and Fares

Air New Zealand
W airnewzealand.com

All Nippon Airways (ANA)
Tel 0120-029-222 (toll-free).
W ana.co.jp

British Airways
W britishairways.com

Japan Airlines (JAL)
Tel 0120-25-5931 (toll-free; international reservations); or 0120-25-5971 (toll-free; domestic reservations).
W jal.co.jp/en/

UK:
Tel (0845) 7-747-700.
W uk.jal.com/ukl/en/

USA and Canada:
Tel 1-800 525 3663.
W ar.jal.com/arl/en/

Qantas
W qantas.com.au

United
W united.com

Virgin
W virgin-atlantic.com

Narita Airport

Keisei Skyliner
W keisei.co.jp

Limousine Buses
W limousinebus.co.jp/en

Narita Airport
W narita-airport.jp/en/index.html

Narita Express (N'EX)
W jreast.co.jp/e/nex

Tourist Information Center
Terminal 1.
Tel (0476) 30-3383.
Terminal 2.
Tel (0476) 34-6251.

Domestic Flights

Skymark
Tel 050-3116-7370.
W skymark.jp/en

Luggage Delivery

ANA Sky Porter
W ana.co.jp/eng/amc/reference/tameru/other/delivery/skyporter.html

JAL ABC
W jalabc.com/english

Getting Around Tokyo

Equipped to handle a daytime population swelling to well over 10 million every weekday, Tokyo's public transportation system is remarkably diverse. Besides using the very efficient subway system, visitors can explore the city by bus, overground train (notably the Japan Railways Yamanote and Chuo lines, and the private railway lines), tram, monorail, boat, taxi, bicycle, or even rickshaw. Buses are good for areas not reached by subway or train, though the lack of English signage can pose a difficulty. Taxis are numerous and can be easily hired for short trips within the city. Maps are available at the Tourist Information Center *(see p159)*.

"Himiko" water bus speeding along the skyscraper-lined Sumida River

Green Travel

Travel in Tokyo is pretty green. The superb public transportation network means that this is the one metropolis in the world where you would feel least inclined to drive your own car. Very efficient mass transportation – albeit sometimes very crowded – is the rule in this city, and this results in a very small carbon footprint per passenger mile.

As indicated by the huge numbers of bikes parked on city streets, the bicycle is an extremely popular way of getting around parts of Tokyo, even though there are no cycle paths to speak of. In fact, for distances of up to around 6 miles (10 km), the bicycle is the fastest way of getting around. Eco-friendly velotaxis can be seen in the more touristy parts of Tokyo. In such areas, rickshaws are also frequently an option for those who prefer a more leisurely and traditional form of transportation. An increasing number of regular taxis now use hybrid cars.

Buses

Bus companies such as **Keio**, **Toei Bus**, and **Tokyu Bus** connect many parts of Tokyo. Buses are much slower than trains and, with no information in English, difficult to use for people who do not read Japanese. Buses in central Tokyo have a flat-fare system. As you enter, place your fare in the box beside the driver. Suica and Pasmo cards *(see p173)* can be used on most forms of public transportation.

If you travel often by bus, you can buy a prepaid card from the driver or from bus sales offices around Tokyo.

Monorail

The **Tokyo Monorail** starts at Haneda Airport, skirts along Tokyo Bay, and terminates at Hamamatsucho Station (on the JR Yamanote Line). The journey takes 20 minutes.

Though technically not a monorail, the driverless **Yurikamome Line** offers fabulous views as it crosses the Rainbow Bridge over Tokyo Bay. You can buy a one-day Open Pass (¥800) for unlimited travel on this line; a combined ticket with the Water Bus costs ¥900.

Water Bus

The most popular water bus *(suijo basu)* route is the **Tokyo Cruise Ship Company**, running Sumida River Water Bus, between Asakusa and the Hama Detached Palace Garden. Other routes ply to various points along the waterfront. All services depart from Hinode Pier, close to Hinode Station (Yurikamome Line) and a 10-minute walk from Hamamatsucho JR Station (Yamanote Line). Boats run approximately every half-hour.

Trams

Tokyo's two tramlines are somewhat removed from most tourist haunts. The **Arakawa Line** *(see p75)* trundles through the backstreets of

Visitors on a city tour of Tokyo in an open-topped sightseeing bus

northern Tokyo. The stations at either end have subway connections, and the tram can also be boarded at Otsuka, where it crosses the JR Yamanote Line.

In the west of the city, the **Setagaya Line** links Sangenjaya (Denentoshi Line) and Shimotakaido (Keio Line).

Car Rental

Renting a car in Tokyo is not recommended; few roads are signposted in English, and although rental cars usually feature sat nav systems, the on-screen text is in Japanese.

If you wish to explore Japan by car, head out of Tokyo by train and rent a vehicle in a smaller town. The **Japan Automobile Federation (JAF)** offers details about car rental companies such as **Nippon Rent-a-Car**, **Toyota Rent-a-Car**, and **Nissan Rent-a-Car**.

Taxis

Taxis can be hailed on major thoroughfares and found at large hotels and at railway stations. A red light in the front window indicates availability. Few taxi drivers speak English, so have your destination written in Japanese.

Taxi fares start at ¥740 for the first mile (2 km), then cost around ¥100 for each additional 1,640 ft (500 m). Fares increase by about 30 percent between 11pm and 5am. Tipping is not required.

Rickshaws

The rickshaw (*jinriki-sha*) is a popular, if expensive, vehicle for sightseeing. Look for the rickshaw men, in their *happi* coats and shorts, in front of the Kaminarimon Gate in Asakusa. They will pull two slender Japanese people at a time, but they may ask bigger-built foreigners to ride solo.

A ride on an old-fashioned rickshaw

Cycling

Cycling is a popular way of covering short distances around Tokyo. Most streets have no sidewalks, so cars, bikes, and pedestrians essentially share the same space. It is perfectly permissible

to cycle on sidewalks if they are available. The **Muji** store in Yurakucho, close to the Imperial Palace, rents bicycles (¥525/day; ¥1,050 holidays and weekends).

Walking

Walking is an excellent way to explore parts of Tokyo. The **City of Tokyo Walking Tours** (in various languages) are free and depart from Shinjuku. The city also arranges tours that focus on such themes as sumo, traditional gardens, the tea ceremony, and architecture. Each tour lasts about three hours and costs ¥650–3,540.

Finding an Address

Only the main thoroughfares in Tokyo have street names. In an address – for example, 2-3-4 Otemachi – the first number refers to the *chome*, or main block. The second number indicates a smaller block of buildings within the *chome*. The last is the number of a yet smaller block of buildings. There is no logical order to this system. Officers at police boxes are used to helping people find their destinations.

DIRECTORY

Buses

Keio
w keio-bus.com/bus/index.html (Japanese)

Toei Bus
w kotsu.metro.tokyo.jp/eng

Tokyu Bus
w tokyubus.co.jp (Japanese)

Monorail

Tokyo Monorail
w tokyo-monorail.co.jp/english

Yurikamome Line
w yurikamome.co.jp/en/

Water Bus

Tokyo Cruise Ship Company
w suijobus.co.jp

Trams

Arakawa Line
w kotsu.metro.tokyo.jp/eng/services/streetcar.html

Setagaya Line
w setagaya-line.com (Japanese)

Car Rental

Japan Automobile Federation (JAF)
w jaf.or.jp/e

Nippon Rent-a-Car
Tel 0800-500-0919 (toll-free) or (03) 3485-7196.
w nipponrentacar.co.jp/service/general.html

Nissan Rent-a-Car
Tel 0120-00-4123 (toll-free).
w nissan-rentacar.com (Japanese)

Toyota Rent-a-Car
Tel 0070-8000-10000 (toll-free) or (03) 5954-8008.
w rent.toyota.co.jp/en

Cycling

Muji
Yurakucho Building 3-8-3 Marunouchi, Chiyoda-ku, Tokyo.
Tel (03) 5208-8241.
w mujiyurakucho.com/info/index.asp (Japanese)

Walking

City of Tokyo Walking Tours
w gotokyo.org/en/tourists/guideservice/guideservice/index.html

Using Trains in Tokyo

The fastest way of getting around Tokyo is by train. The various systems that make up Tokyo's train network – Toei Subway and Tokyo Metro lines, overground Japan Railways (JR) lines, and a number of private lines – are clean, efficient, and punctual. Some of Tokyo's huge stations can be daunting, but the system is safe and fairly straightforward to negotiate, with color-coded train lines and maps, directional arrows, and bilingual signs. Trains run 5am–midnight daily; on some lines, trains run approximately every 5 minutes at peak times. Avoid rush hour (8–9am and 6–8pm) if possible, especially if you are carrying luggage or traveling with small children.

Well-designed and comfortable interior of a metro car

Uniformed subway staff assisting train commuters

Railway Network

The Japan Railways' (JR) Yamanote Line forms a loop encircling most of central Tokyo. Many of its stations act as hubs, linking with long-distance JR lines, suburban private rail lines, and subway stations. Four other JR lines run through the city. The Sobu Line (yellow) cuts east–west across the center of the loop, from Shinjuku to Akihabara and then farther eastward. Next to it is the express Chuo Line (orange), linking Tokyo JR Station with Shinjuku and the western suburbs. The Keihin Tohoku Line (turquoise) runs north–south along the eastern side of the Yamanote Loop. The Saikyo Line (green) runs parallel with the Yamanote Line between Osaki and Ikebukuro before extending north beyond Tokyo to Saitama Prefecture. These JR lines offer fascinating above-ground glimpses of the metropolis and its suburbs. For more on JR trains beyond Tokyo, see pages 174–5.

The private railway lines generally run from hubs along the Yamanote Line to other points in Tokyo and beyond. The most useful private railway lines for visitors are the Keihin Electric Express Railway (from Shinagawa to Haneda Airport) and the Odakyu Electric Railway (from Shinjuku to Odawara and Hakone). There are also the Rinkai Line and Yurikamome, both of which can be used to reach Odaiba. For more on private railway lines, see page 174.

Subway Network

Tokyo's subway network consists of the **Tokyo Metro** (nine lines) and **Toei Subway** (four lines) systems. Tokyo Metro and Toei Subway have different symbols (a white "M" on a blue background and a green fan-shaped symbol respectively), but they share the same subway sign (a blue train on its track), which is usually prominent at the street-level entrance to the subway. Besides being color-coded, each subway line is designated a letter (G for the Ginza Line, for example), and each station is assigned a number. Hence, Shibuya, the western terminal of the Ginza Line, is G-01 *(see also Back Endpaper)*. Metro maps in English are available at all major train and metro stations, tourist hotels, and the TIC *(see p169)*.

Routes and Fares

For an online route planner, visit the **Jorudan** website.

On both JR and subway lines, directions to various platforms are indicated with appropriate color codes; sometimes the distance is given in meters. Prominent signs in Japanese and English give the name of the station, as well as the next and previous stations on the line. Inside many trains, there are bilingual (or quadrilingual) indicators above the doors

Metro platform with prominent signs displaying station names

showing the name of the next station. On some trains, route maps and the current position are displayed on screens above the exit doors. Announcements may also be made in English before arrival at the next station.

Tickets are dispensed from automatic vending machines, usually located close to the entrance gates at each station. Most accept both bank notes and coins; they also dispense change. Electronic touch-screen vending machines have instructions in English.

To access the platform, feed the ticket into the slot in the automatic ticket gate. Retrieve your ticket and retain it until your final destination, as you will need it when you exit.

Fares are charged according to distance traveled, starting at ¥160 (¥170 on Toei lines), with children aged 6 to 11 charged half-fares; children under 6 ride

for free. Some stations have route maps showing the fares and place names in Roman script. If you are unsure or cannot work out the exact fare to your destination, buy the cheapest ticket available and pay the difference when you arrive. There are fare adjustment machines by the exit gates: you insert your ticket, the amount due is indicated, you pay the difference in fare, and a new ticket is dispensed.

For those who intend to do a lot of travel on the subway, the Toei One-Day Economy Pass *(Toei marguto kippu)* is a good option. It costs ¥700 and offers unlimited use of subways, city buses, and the Arakawa tram. The **Tokyo Tour Ticket** (¥1,580) allows unlimited use for one day on JR trains within the 23 wards of Tokyo, subway lines, city buses, and the Arakawa tram.

Subway turnstile at entry and exit points at a train station

Smart CARD System

Suica and **Pasmo** are inter-operable smart cards that can be used for virtually all forms of public transportation in Tokyo and surrounding areas. They cost ¥2,000, including a ¥500 refundable deposit. Suica cards can be bought at JR stations, and Pasco cards at Tokyo Metro and Toei Subway stations, where they can subsequently be charged in ¥1,000 increments.

The cards can also be used for making purchases at many stores around town, as well as at vending machines and station baggage lockers.

Hold your card over the sensor at the ticket barrier; an acoustic signal will tell you that the card has been registered and the minimum fare deducted; the balance (if any) is deducted on exit at your destination.

Strips of yellow tiles on the floor marking the routes to the ticket barriers

Commuter Culture

Commuters packed into trains are a common sight morning and evening at Tokyo's major train stations. High urban land prices force families to look farther out of the city for affordable housing. A commute of at least an hour each way is practically the standard. The majority of commuters are men, since they still tend to be the prime earners in most families. The commute effectively removes them from family life – they leave before the children get up, come back after they are in bed, and collapse on weekends with fatigue. The other major group on the trains is unmarried younger women (after marriage, women are often expected to stay home and raise the children). An entire industry has grown up around these commuters: dozens of magazines are produced for killing time, and stand-up restaurants offer cheap meals to those with a long ride ahead.

DIRECTORY

Subway Network

Toei Subway
W kotsu.metro.tokyo.jp

Tokyo Metro
W tokyometro.jp

Routes and Fares

Jorudan
W jorudan.co.jp/english

Tokyo Tour Ticket
W jreast.co.jp

Smart CARD System

Pasmo
W pasmo.co.jp/en

Suica
W jreast.co.jp/e/pass/suica.html

Traveling Beyond Tokyo

With roads often clogged with traffic, trains are the best way of exploring Tokyo and the surrounding area. Japan's rail system leads the world in terms of safety, efficiency, and comfort. The city and surrounding area are served by a bewildering complexity of lines. In addition to the Japan Railways (JR) trains, there are many private railway companies serving suburban areas. For many destinations, such as Nikko, travelers have a choice of lines. Fares on private lines tend to be cheaper than on JR trains. Even in the most rural areas, the names of stations are given in Roman script.

People buying tickets at Shinjuku JR Station

The Railway Network

The main operator in the country is the Japan Railways Group (JR), which includes all the *shinkansen* super expresses (bullet trains) and a nationwide network of almost 17,000 miles (27,350 km) of tracks. JR is divided into regional groups, and operations in Tokyo and the surrounding area are run by **JR East**. Many private railway lines link smaller communities in more remote regions.

The Shinkansen: Bullet Train

The first "bullet train," as the *shinkansen* was quickly nicknamed by the media, drew out of Tokyo Station in 1964, the year of the Tokyo Olympics. Symbolic of Japan's economic recovery and future drive, it became, and remains, a source of national pride.

Shinkansen are no longer the world's fastest trains, but their efficiency, as proved by the punctuality of the long-distance journeys (an average of within

six seconds of the scheduled time was recorded in 2003), is legendary. There are five *shinkansen* lines serving Tokyo. The Tokaido Line runs south to Nagoya, Kyoto, and Osaka (continuing as the Sanyo Line to Hiroshima and Fukuoka). The Tohoku Line runs north via Sendai and Morioka to Aomori. The Joetsu Line serves Niigata. In addition, there are *shinkansen* lines to Nagano and Yamagata. All *shinkansen* services start from Tokyo Station. Many Tokaido Line trains can also be boarded at Shinagawa. Trains on the Tohoku, Joetsu, Nagano, and Yamagata *shinkansen* lines stop briefly at Ueno. Announcements in English and clear signs make the *shinkansen* an appealing form of transportation, often more convenient than flying, though there is little room for large suitcases.

It is advisable to reserve a seat, especially during a holiday period, as the non-reserved carriages can get very crowded.

Private Railway Lines

Private train lines, which tend to be cheaper than JR, also operate express trains, some of which try to rival the *shinkansen* for luxury.

The **Odakyu Railway** (from Shinjuku) runs the luxury Romancecar service to the tourist area of Hakone; it also has trains to Enoshima, on the Shonan coast, close to Kamakura. **Tobu Railway** operates the fastest and cheapest route to Nikko from Asakusa. Take the **Tokyu Railway** (from Shibuya) if you are going to Yokohama's port area or the city's Chinatown. Other private lines include **Seibu Railway** (destinations include the mountainous area of Chichibu), **Keisei Railway** (to Narita), and **Keikyu** (Yokohama and Yokosuka).

Station Signs and Facilities

Tokyo's Shinjuku Station *(see p65)* is the world's busiest, and several others – including Tokyo JR Station – are vast warrens built on several levels. Finding a particular line or exit during rush hour can be intimidating for newcomers with heavy baggage. If you can, find out which named or numbered exit is best for your destination before arriving at one of the major stations.

Shinkansen lines are clearly marked, and signs for other lines are color-coded. The yellow bobbled tracks on the floor are intended to help visually impaired people navigate,

Aerodynamic nose of the fabled *shinkansen*, or "bullet train"

Ticket barriers for the Tobu Railway at Tobu Asakusa Station

but the tracks do not make it easy for those pulling suitcases with wheels. Escalators are readily available for commuters.

Note that many trains, especially the *shinkansen*, stop only briefly in order to maintain their timetables. Thus, travelers are encouraged to line up on some platforms. Floor markings on the platform indicate where the train doors will open; however, these are written in Japanese, so they can be difficult for most visitors to decipher.

On trains with reserved seats, such as the *shinkansen* and the N'EX, the car number is the first of the two numbers that appear on the ticket. This is followed by a letter, which indicates the actual seat. Again, this information is in Japanese.

Stations in major tourist areas have baggage lockers and information booths where staff may speak English.

On-Board Facilities

On *shinkansen* and other long-distance routes, trolleys serving snacks, beverages, *bento* lunchboxes, and edible *omiyage* (local specialties) are wheeled up and down the length of the train. There is often a choice of Western- (sit-down) and Japanese-style (squat) toilets. Washrooms and toilets may be electronically operated, requiring a hand to be passed in front of a panel for flushing, or use a lever.

The Japan Rail Pass

In a country with some of the world's highest train fares, the **Japan Rail Pass** is a wonderful deal. Specially devised for tourists, the pass is not for sale inside Japan and must be purchased from an agent abroad before your visit.

The pass gives unlimited travel on all JR lines and affiliated buses, including the N'EX *(see p168)* between Narita Airport and Tokyo, city-center JR trains (including the Yamanote Line), and *shinkansen*, except Nozomi and Mizuho trains. Also included is the ferry to the island of Miyajima, near Hiroshima. Subways and private railways are not included. You may have to reserve a seat on long-distance trains, but the reservation will be free.

The Japan Rail Pass

You can choose a 7-day (¥28,300), 14-day (¥45,100), or 21-day (¥57,700) pass; there are also more expensive passes that allow travel in Green Cars (equivalent to first class). If you intend to do much traveling by train, the pass will save you money. If you want to explore Japan by train for more than 21 days, or prefer to break up your travels by staying in one place for more than a few days, consider buying more than one pass.

JNTO offices *(see p159)* have a full list of rail-pass agents in your country. The agent will issue a Japan Rail Pass Exchange Order, usually at a price based on the day's rate of exchange with the yen. This voucher is exchanged

for the actual Japan Rail Pass at designated JR Travel Service Centers in Japan, including Narita Airport and major train stations. When you get your pass, you must specify the date on which you wish to start using it; the date has to be within three months of the issue of the exchange order. After the start date of the pass, the cost cannot be refunded, neither can the exchange order or pass be replaced if lost or stolen.

Other Passes

There are also other, less expensive regional rail passes. The **JR East Rail Pass**, which can be bought both outside Japan and within the country, covers Honshu, northeast of Tokyo. A 5-day pass costs ¥20,000 (children ¥14,000) and a 10-day pass costs ¥44,800 (children ¥22,400). Tobu Railway issues two-day and four-day passes for Nikko. Odakyu offers various passes to Kamakura and the Hakone area. Seibu issues passes for the popular spots of Chichibu and Kawagoe.

DIRECTORY

The Railway Network/ Private Railway Lines

JR East
Tel (03) 3423-0111 (English info).
W jreast.co.jp/e

Keikyu
W keikyu.co.jp

Keisei Railway
W keisei.co.jp

Odakyu Railway
W odakyu.jp/english/

Seibu Railway
W seibu-group.co.jp/railways/tourist/english/index.html

Tobu Railway
W tobu.co.jp/foreign/tobu.html

Tokyu Railway
W tokyu.co.jp/global/index.html

Rail passes

Japan Rail Pass
W japanrailpass.net

JR East Rail Pass
W jreast.co.jp/e/eastpass/

TOKYO STREET FINDER

Tokyo is notoriously hard for visitors to find their way around, due to the scarcity of street names and the complex numbering system for buildings. The Tokyo sights covered in this guide, plus Tokyo hotels (*see pp112–15*), restaurants (*see pp130–37*), and many of the city's key landmarks are plotted on the maps on the following pages. Transportation points are also marked, and indicated by the symbols listed in the key below. When map references are given, the first number tells you which Street Finder map to turn to, and the letter and number that follow refer to the grid reference. The map below shows the area of Tokyo covered by the six Street Finder maps. The Street Finder index opposite lists street names, buildings, and stations. For a map of the Tokyo subway system, see the inside back cover.

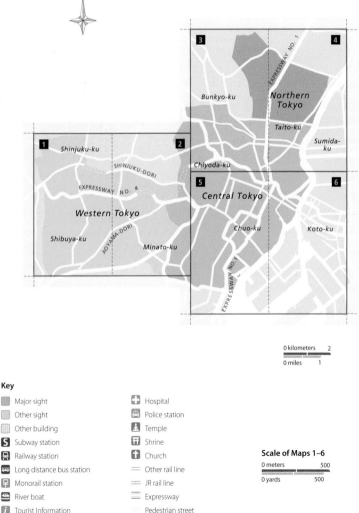

0 kilometers 2

0 miles 1

Key

▨	Major sight	✚	Hospital
▨	Other sight	⊞	Police station
▨	Other building	⚑	Temple
S	Subway station	⊞	Shrine
▣	Railway station	⊡	Church
▥	Long distance bus station	═	Other rail line
▣	Monorail station	═	JR rail line
▩	River boat	═	Expressway
i	Tourist Information		Pedestrian street

Scale of Maps 1–6

0 meters 500

0 yards 500

Street Finder Index

3

A **B** **C**

HONKOMAGOME

NAKASENDO-DORI
HONGO-DORI

SENDAGI

Kyoo-ji Temple

OGUBASHI-DORI

Nippori

Yamanote Line

1

HAKUSAN-DORI

Sendagi

Asakura Choso Museum

Tenno-ji Temple

Honkomagome

Daien-ji Temple

Zensho-en Temple

YANAKA CEMETERY

HAKUSAN

KYU-HAKUSAN-DORI

SHINOBAZU-DORI

Isetatsu

YANAKA

Hakusan

Medical School Hospital

Shitamachi Museum Annex

Daimyo Clock Museum

NICHI-IDAI-TSUTSUJI-DORI

Ryokan Sawanoya

BUNKYO-KU

Nezu Shrine

NEZU

Rinko-ji

HAKUSAN-DORI

KOTOTOI-DORI

Tokyo Metropolitan Art Museum

2

SENKAWA-DORI

Todaimae

NISHIKATA

Hantei

Nezu

Ryokan Katsutaro

UENO ZOO

UENO

HONGO-DORI

Yayoi Art Museum

HONGO

Tosho-Gu Shrine

Park Side Café Ueno

SHINOBAZU-DORI

UENO PARK

Tokyo Metropolitan Festival Hall

Japan Art Academy

University of Tokyo

Benten Hall

Kiyo mizu Hall

Ueno Royo Museum

KASUGA-DORI

Homeikan Honkan

University of Tokyo Hospital

Shinobazu Pond

Keisei-ueno

Kasuga

Shitamachi Museum

Amey Mark

3

Korakuen

Hotel Parkside

Jusanya

Kameya Issuitei

Suzumoto Theater

Takokyu

KOISHIKAWA KORAKUEN GARDEN

Bunkyo Ward Office

KASUGA-DORI

Sauna and Capsule Hotel Dandy

Ueno-okachim

Hongo-sanchome

Yushima

Uenohirokoji

Okachimachi

HONGO

HONGO-DORI

Yushima Tenjin

UENO

Tokyo Dome

Ueno First City Hotel

CHUO-DORI

KORAKU

Iidabashi

SOTOBORI-DORI

Suidobashi

BUNKYO KU

Ochanomizu St. Hills Hotel

YUSHIMA

KARAMAEBASHI-DORI

SHOHEIBASHI-DORI

SOTOKANDA

EXPRESSWAY NO. 5

Suidobashi

Century Tower

Kanda River

Kanda Myojin Shrine

Suehirocho

4

Nihonbashi River

Chuo Line

KAEDE-DORI

Ochanomizu

Yushima Seido Temple

YUSHIMA-ZAKA

Tokyo Anime Center

FUJIMI

MISAKICHO

NISHI-KANDA

Archeological Museum of Meiji University

Ochanomizu

AIOI-ZAKA

AsoBitCity

Tsukumo Robocon Magazine Kan

Senshu University

MEIDAI-DORI

Nikolai Cathedral

Ryokan Ryumeikan Honten

Akihabara

Remm Akihabara

KANDA-JIMBOCHO

Casals Hall

Shin-ochanomizu

Kanda Yabu Soba

Kudanshita

Jimbocho

Isseido

YASUKUNI-DORI

KANDA

2

Tayasumon

Sakura Hotel

Ogawamachi

Awajicho

Nippon Budokan

Chiyoda Ward Office

CHIYODA-KU

Science and Technology Museum

UCHIBORI-DORI

HAKUSAN-DORI

HONGO-DORI

Kanda

Shinkansen Lines

5

KITANOMARU PARK

KANDA-NISHIKICHO

KANDA-DORI

Kanda

CHUO-DORI

SHOWA-DORI

Chidorigafuchi

Science and Technology Museum

UCHI-KANDA

EXPRESSWAY NO.

Crafts Gallery

Takebashi

Ote-bori

SOTOBORI-DORI

Capsule Value Kanda

National Museum of Modern Art

Shin-nihonba

A **5** **B** **C**

General Index

Page numbers in **bold** type refer to main entries.

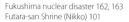

Acknowledgments

Dorling Kindersley would like to thank the many people whose help and assistance contributed to the preparation of this book.

Main Contributors

Jon Burbank is a travel writer and photographer who lives in Chiba prefecture, to the east of Tokyo, with his family.

Emi Kazuko is a writer and broadcaster who moved to London from Japan in the 1980s. She is the author of several books about the cuisine of her home country.

Stephen Mansfield is a British photo-journalist and author based in the Tokyo region. His work has appeared in over 60 magazines, newspapers, and journals world-wide, including *The Geographical*, *South China Morning Post*, *The Traveller*, *Japan Quarterly*, and *Insight Japan*. He is a regular book reviewer for *The Japan Times*. His pieces cover a variety of subjects such as travel, contemporary issues, and cultural and literary themes. His photographs have appeared in several books. He has authored eight books and is currently working on a book on the cultural history of Tokyo. He is also the author of *Japan: Islands of the Floating World*, *Birmanie: Le Temps Suspendu*, and *China: Yunnan Province*.

Robbie Swinnerton moved to Japan in 1980, impelled by his fascination for sake, seaweed, and soba noodles, plus all other aspects of the traditional Japanese diet and culture. For the past 26 years, he has been based in Kamakura, balancing his life by the ocean in the old Japanese capital with writing assignments around Japan and East Asia. While writing extensively on foods of all flavors – his restaurant review column Tokyo Food File has run in the *Japan Times* for over a decade – it is Japanese cuisine in all its intricate simplicity that remains his first and abiding love.

Design and Editorial

Publisher Douglas Amrine
Publishing Manager Jane Ewart
Managing Editor Kathryn Lane
Project Editor Mani Ramaswamy
Project Art Editor Kate Leonard
Senior Cartographic Editor Casper Morris
DTP Designer Natasha Lu
Picture Researcher Ellen Root
Production Controller Shane Higgins
Factchecker Yumi Shigematsu
Proofreader Gowri Mohanakrishnan

Revisions Team

Emma Anacootee-Parmar, Marta Bescos, Imogen Corke, Surya Deogun, Stephen Forster, Emily Grigg-Saito, Katrina Grigg-Saito, Mohammad Hassan, Sumita Khatwani, Priya Kukadia, Rupanki Kaushik, Jason Little, Hayley Maher, Nicola Malone, Sonal Modha, George Nimmo, Scarlett O'Hara, Susie Peachey, Helen Peters, Simon Richmond, Ellen Root, Sands Publishing Solutions, Simon Scott, Susana Smith, Jaynan Spengler, Matthew Wilcox

Additional Photography

Stephen Bere, Demetrio Carrasco, Katrina Grigg-Saito, Martin Hladik, Ian O'Leary, Clive Streeter, Linda Whitwam, Peter Wilson.

Additional Illustrations

Gary Cross, John Fox, Nick Gibbard, David Harris, Kevin Jones Associates, Claire Littlejohn, Mel Pickering, John Woodcock.

Special Assistance

Bunka Gakuen Costume Museum; Dolce & Gabbana Showroom, Omotesando; Drum Museum; Goto Art Museum; Isetan Department Store; Isetatsu; Japan Folk Craft Museum; Mikimoto, Ginza; Mitsu-koshi, Mitsukoshimae; National Museum of Western Art; National Science Museum, Ueno; Noh National Theater; Shibuya 109; Sony Showroom, Ginza; Tosho-gu Museum of Art

Picture Credits

a-above; b-below/bottom; c-centre; f-far; l-left; r-right; t-top.

The publisher would like to thank the following for their kind permission to reproduce their photographs:

(Key: a-above; b-below/bottom; c-centre; f-far; l-left; r-right; t-top)

4Corners: Richard Taylor 38
Alamy Images: Ablestock 144c; AHowden - Japan Stock Photography 48; allOver photography 97tl; AM Corporation 31cl; Jon Arnold Images 17bl, 30cl, 32cra, 43b, 144bl; Peter Arnold, Inc. 18c; Koen Broker 106-107; Jonah Calinawan 143bc; Chromepix.com 16bc; FantasticJapan 159cr; Frederick Fearn 87b; Stéphane Groleau 136bl; Jeremy Sutton-Hibbert 123c, 124cla, 137tr; Peter Horree 164cr; LOOK Die Bildagentur der Fotografen GmbH 139bl, Iain Masterton 89tr, 147c; Megapress 21bc; MIXA 137br, Pacific Press Service 123tl, 128tr; Photo Japan 18clb, 29crb, 124br; rollie rodriguez 4br, 10br; Eitan Simanor 156cra; Chris Willson 125br
Eve Astrid Andersson: 104cl
AWL Images: Gavin Hellier 86; Travel Pix Collection 2-3
Axiom Photographic Agency: Mitchell Coster 20br, 20-21c; Jim Holmes 161tl; Paul Quayle 21cr, 21bl
Dave Bartruff: Dave Bartruff 19bc, 20tr, 21br
The Bridgeman Art Library: Fuji in Clear Weather', from the series '36 Views of Mt. Fuji' ('Fugaku sanjurokkei'), pub. by Nishimura Eijudo, 1831 (hand-colored woodblock print) (see also 77485), Hokusai,

Katsushika (1760-1849) / British Museum, London, UK 27br; Mitsukini Defying the Skeleton Spectre, c.1845 (hand colored woodcut print), Kuniyoshi, Utagawa (1798-1861) / Victoria & Albert Museum, London, UK 57crb; Mountains and coastline, two views from '36 Views of Mount Fuji', pub. by Kosheihei, 1853, (color woodblock print), Hiroshige, Ando or Utagawa (1797-1858) / Private Collection 99crb; P.438-1937 Block Cutting and Printing Surimono, 1825 (woodblock print and embossing), Hokusai, Katsushika (1760-1849) / Fitzwilliam Museum, University of Cambridge, UK. 5cl, 57bc

By permission of The British Library: Early map of Edo / 27clb

Christie's Images Ltd: 25t, 27tc, 57clb

Corbis: 29tl; Asian Art & Archaeology, Inc. 18tr, 57cla; B.S.P.I. 30br, Morton Beebe 126tr, Bettmann 28cb, Burstein Collection 24c, Christie's Images 8-9; Dex Image 151c; Ric Ergenbright 98tr; Eye Ubiquitous / Paul Thompson 88cl; Werner Forman 18bl, 18br, 19tr; Historical Picture Archive 99br; Image Plan 89br; Robbie Jack 18crb; Richard T. Nowitz 84bc; Philadelphia Museum of Art 28tl; Photo & Co. / Stephane Reix 21cb; Jose Fuste Raga 85tr; Ken Straiton 138cra; Liba Taylor 160ca; TWPhoto 148tl; Frank Leather/Eye Ubiquitous 100bl; Michael S. Yamashita 19c, 19clb, 19crb, 20cl, 21tc, 98bc, 111bc, 146cla

Corbis: Jon Arnold 167c, EPA / Akio Suga 32bc; EPA / Franck Robichon 32clb; CHRISTOPHER JUE / epa 40bl; Kimimsa Mayama / Reuters 150bl; Michael S. Yamashita 1c

Aron Danburg: 95cra

Dreamstime.com: Filip Fuxa 13bl; Greir11 67br; Sean Pavone 34-35, 154-155; Radzian 174cla; Siraanamwong 13tr; Torsakarin 12tc; Nonchai Trongsathidkul 90tr

Stephen Forster: 166tr

Fotolia: targezed 163c

Getty Images: Thierry Cazabon / Stone 20clb; Paul Chesley / Getty 162br; Charles Gupton / Stone 117tc, 122cla; Stone / Charles Gupton 160br

Getty Images: AFP / Stringer 29c; Greg Elms 117br; Kiyoshi Ota / Stringer 169crb

Grand Hyatt Tokyo: 108cra

Martin Hladik: Martin hladik 17tl

Hobgoblin Japan Ltd.: Hobgoblin Japan Ltd. 152crb

Homeikan: Honkan 114bl

Image courtesy of Tokyo National Museum: 22, 24tl, 25c, 37cr, 52bl, 53tl, 53ca, 53cr, 53cb, 54tr, 54cra, 54bl, 54br, 55tr, 55cla, 55crb, 55bc; Important Cultural Properties 54cla; Important Cultural Properties / Honkan Museum 52cl; Important Cultural Properties / Horyuji Museum 52bc

Japan National Tourism Organization : Japan Convention Services, 174br; Japan Convention Services, Inc. 175tl

Maisen/Izutsu My Izumi Co., Ltd.: 133tr

Mandarin Oriental Hotel Group: 109bl, 112br

Masterfile: Allen Birnbach 71tl

Narita International Airport Corporation: 168bl

New National Theatre: Chikashi Saegusa 147br

Park Hyatt Tokyo: 152bl

photographersdirect.com: Mantis Metalworks / Jonathan Christopher Roberts 11tr

Photolibrary: Jtb Photo Communications Inc . 151bl

Tokugawa Reimeikai: Tokugawa Reimeikai 26tl

Reuters: Toshiyuki Aizawa 33bl; Issei Kato 31br, 170cla; Yuriko Nakao 33c; Susumu Toshiyuki 145tl

Robert Harding Picture Library: Gavin Hellier / Robert Harding 72

Sarabeth's Daikanyama: WDI Corporation 134br

STA Travel Group: 158bc

SuperStock: age fotostock 69cra; Pixtal / Pixtal 12bl; José Fuste Raga / age fotostock 60

Sushi Gotoku: 132bl

The Tokyo Station Hotel: 113tr

TIC Tokyo: 157tc

Uniqlo Stores: Fast Retailing Co.,Ltd. 2007 143tl

Werner Forman Archive: Victoria & Albert Museum, London. 57cra

Wikipedia: 29br

Front Endpapers: 4Corners: Richard Taylor br (R); **Alamy Images:** AHowden - Japan Stock Photography tr (R); **AWL Images:** Gavin Hellier cra (L); **Robert Harding Picture Library:** Gavin Hellier / Robert Harding cla (L); **SuperStock:** José Fuste Raga / age fotostock bl (L)

Jacket images: Front and Spine – **Getty Images:** John Banagan

Map Cover: Getty Images: John Banagan

All other images © Dorling Kindersley
For further information see: www.dkimages.com

Phrase Book

The Japanese language is related to Okinawan and is similar to Altaic languages such as Mongolian and Turkish. Written Japanese uses a combination of three scripts – Chinese ideograms, known as *kanji*, and two syllable-based alphabet systems known as *hiragana* and *katakana*. These two latter are similar, *katakana* functioning as italics are used in English. Traditionally, Japanese is written in vertical columns from top right to bottom left, though the Western system is increasingly used. There are several romanization systems; the Hepburn system is used in this guide. To simplify romanization, macrons (long marks over vowels to indicate longer pronunciation) have not been used. Japanese pronunciation is fairly straightforward, and many words are "Japanized" versions of Western words. This Phrase Book gives the English word or phrase, followed by the Japanese script, then the romanization, adapted to aid pronunciation.

Guidelines for Pronunciation

When reading the romanization, give the same emphasis to all syllables. The practice in English of giving one syllable greater stress may render a Japanese word incomprehensible.

Pronounce vowels as in these English words:

a	as the "a" in "cat "
e	as in "red"
i	as in "big"
o	as in "solid"
u	as the "oo" in "wood"

When two vowels are used together, give each letter an individual sound:

ai	as in "pine"
ae	as if written "a-eh"
ei	as in "pay"

Consonants are mostly pronounced as in English. The letter *g* is always hard as in "gate," and *j* is always soft as in "joke." *R* is pronounced something between *r* and *l*. *F* is sometimes pronounced as *h*. "*Si*" always becomes "*shi*," but some people pronounce "*shi*" as "*hi*." *V* in Western words (e.g., "video") becomes *b*. If followed by a consonant, *n* may be pronounced as either *n* or *m*.

All consonants except *n* are always followed by a vowel unless they are doubled; however, sometimes an *i* or *u* is barely pronounced. In this Phrase Book, to aid pronunciation, apostrophes are used where an *i* or *u* is barely pronounced within a word, and double consonants where this occurs at the end of a word.

Dialects

Standard Japanese is used and understood throughout Japan by people of all backgrounds. But on a colloquial level, there are significant differences in both pronunciation and vocabulary, even between the Tokyo and Osaka-Kyoto areas, and rural accents are very strong.

Polite Words and Phrases

There are several different levels of politeness in the Japanese language, according to status, age, and situation. In everyday conversation, politeness levels are simply a question of the length of verb endings (longer is more polite), but in formal conversation entirely different words (*keigo*) are used. As a visitor, you may find that people try to speak to you in formal language, but there is no need to use it yourself; the level given in this Phrase Book is neutral yet polite.

In an Emergency

Help!	たすけて！	Tas'kete!
Stop!	とめて！	Tomete!
Call a doctor!	医者をよんでください！	Isha o yonde kudasai!
Call an ambulance!	救急車をよんでください！	Kyukyusha o yonde kudasai!
Call the police!	警察をよんでください！	Keisatsu o yonde kudasai!
Fire!	火事！	Kaji!
Where is the hospital?	病院はどこにありますか？	Byoin wa doko ni arimass-ka?
police box	交番	koban

Communication Essentials

Yes/no.	はい／いいえ	Hai/ie.
… not …	・・・ない／ちがいます。	… nai/ chigaimass.
I don't know.	しりません。	Shirimasen.
Thank you.	ありがとう。	Arigato.
Thank you very much.	ありがとうございます。	Arigato gozaimass.
Thank you very much indeed.	どうもありがとうございます。	Domo arigato gozaimass.
Thanks (casual).	どうも。	Domo.
No, thank you.	結構です。ありがとう。	Kekko dess, arigato.
Please (offering).	どうぞ。	Dozo.
Please (asking).	おねがいします。	Onegai shimass.
Please (give me or do for me).	・・・ください。	… kudasai.
I don't understand.	わかりません。	Wakarimasen.
Do you speak English?	英語を話せますか？	Eigo o hanasemass-ka?
I can't speak Japanese.	日本語は話せません。	Nihongo wa hanasemasen.
Please speak more slowly.	もう少しゆっくり話してください。	Mo s'koshi yukkuri hanash'te kudasai.
Sorry/Excuse me!	すみません。	Sumimasen!
Could you help me please? (not emergency)	ちょっと手伝っていただけませんか？	Chotto tets'datte itadakemasen-ka?

Useful Phrases

My name is ….	わたしの名前は・・・です。	Watashi no namae wa … dess.
How do you do, pleased to meet you.	はじめまして、どうぞよろしく。	Hajime-mash'te, dozo yorosh'ku.
How are you?	お元気ですか？	Ogenki dess-ka?
Good morning.	おはようございます。	Ohayo gozaimass.
Hello/ Good afternoon.	こんにちは。	Konnichiwa.
Good evening.	こんばんは。	Konbanwa.

Good night.	おやすみなさい。	Oyasumi nasai.
Good-bye.	さよなら。	Sayonara.
Take care.	気をつけて。	Ki o ts'kete.
Keep well (casual)	お元気で。	Ogenki de.
The same to you.	そちらも。	Sochira mo.
What is (this)?	(これは）何ですか？	(Kore wa) nan dess-ka?
How do you use this?	これをどうやって使いますか？	Kore o doyatte ts'kaimass-ka?
Could I possibly have …? (very polite)	・・・をいただけますか？	… o itadake-mass-ka?
Is there … here?	ここに・・・がありますか？	Koko ni … ga arimass-ka?
Where can I get …?	・・・はどこにありますか？	… wa doko ni arimass-ka?
How much is it?	いくらですか？	Ikura dess-ka?
What time is …?	・・・何時ですか？	… nan-ji dess-ka?
Cheers! (toast)	乾杯！	Kampai!
Where is the restroom/toilet?	お手洗い／おトイレはどこですか？	Otearai/otoire wa doko dess-ka?
Here's my business card.	名刺をどうぞ。	Meishi o dozo.

Useful Words

I	わたし	Watashi
woman	女性	josei
man	男性	dansei
wife	奥さん	ok'san
husband	主人	shujin
daughter	むすめ	musume
son	むすこ	mus'ko
child	こども	kodomo
children	こどもたち	kodomo-tachi
businessman/ woman	ビジネスマン／ウーマン	bijinessuman/ wuman
student	学生	gakusei
Mr./Mrs./Ms. …	・・・さん	…-san
big/small	大きい／小さい	okii/chiisai
hot/cold	暑い／寒い	atsui/samui
cold (to touch)	冷たい	tsumetai
warm	温かい	atatakai
good/ not good/bad	いい／よくない／悪い	ii/yokunai/warui
enough	じゅうぶん／結構	jubun/kekko
free (no charge)	ただ／無料	tada/muryo
here	ここ	koko
there	あそこ	asoko
this	これ	kore
that (nearby)	それ	sore
that (far away)	あれ	are
what?	何？	nani?
when?	いつ？	itsu?
why?	なぜ？／どうして？	naze?/dosh'te?
where?	どこ？	doko?
who?	誰？	dare?
which way?	どちら？	dochira?

Signs

Open	営業中	eigyo-chu
closed	休日	kyujitsu
entrance	入口	iriguchi
exit	出口	deguchi
danger	危険	kiken
emergency exit	非常口	hijo-guchi
information	案内	annai
restroom, toilet	お手洗い／手洗い／おトイレ／トイレ	otearai/tearai/ otoire/toire
free (vacant)	空き	aki
men	男	otoko
women	女	onna

Money

Could you change this into yen please.	これを円に替えてください。	Kore o en ni kaete kudasai.
I'd like to cash these travelers' checks.	このトラベラーズチェックを現金にしたいです。	Kono toraberazu chekku o genkin ni shitai dess.
Do you take credit cards/ travelers' checks?	クレジットカード／トラベラーズチェックで払えますか？	Kurejitto kado/ toraberazu chekku de haraemass-ka?
bank	銀行	ginko
cash	現金	genkin
credit card	クレジットカード	kurejitto kado
currency exchange office	両替所	ryogaejo
dollars	ドル	doru
pounds	ポンド	pondo
yen	円	en

Keeping in Touch

Where is a telephone?	電話はどこにありますか？	Denwa wa doko ni arimass-ka?
May I use your phone?	電話を使ってもいいですか？	Denwa o ts'katte mo ii dess-ka?
Hello, this is … .	もしもし、・・・です。	Moshi-moshi, …dess.
I'd like to make an international call.	国際電話、お願いします。	Kokusai denwa, onegai shimass.
airmail	航空便	kokubin
e-mail	イーメール	i-meru
fax	ファクス	fak'su
postcard	ハガキ	hagaki
post office	郵便局	yubin-kyoku
stamp	切手	kitte
telephone booth	公衆電話	koshu denwa
telephone card	テレフォンカード	terefon kado

Shopping

Where can I buy …?	・・・はどこで買えますか？	… wa doko de kaemass-ka?
How much does this cost?	いくらですか？	Ikura dess-ka?
I'm just looking.	見ているだけです。	Mite iru dake dess.
Do you have …?	・・・ありますか？	… arimass-ka?
May I try this on?	着てみてもいいですか？	Kite mite mo ii dess-ka?
Please show me that.	それを見せてください。	Sore o misete kudasai.
Does it come in other colors?	他の色もありますか？	Hoka no iro mo arimass-ka?
black	黒	kuro
blue	青	ao
green	緑	midori
red	赤	aka
white	白	shiro
yellow	黄色	kiiro
cheap/expensive	安い／高い	yasui/takai
audio equipment	オーディオ製品	odio seihin
bookstore	本屋	hon-ya
boutique	ブティック	butik
clothes	洋服	yofuku
department store	デパート	depato
electrical store	電気屋	denki-ya
fish market	魚屋	sakana-ya
folk crafts	民芸品	mingei-hin
ladies' wear	婦人服	fujin fuku
local specialty	名物	meibutsu
market	市場	ichiba
menswear	紳士服	shinshi fuku
newsstand	新聞屋	shimbun-ya

pharmacist	薬屋	kusuri-ya
picture postcard	絵葉書	e-hagaki
sale	セール	seru
souvenir shop	お土産屋	omiyage-ya
supermarket	スーパー	supa
travel agent	旅行会社	ryoko-gaisha

Sightseeing

Where is …?	···はどこ ですか？	… wa doko dess-ka?
How do I get to …?	···へは、どうやって いったらいいですか？	… e wa doyatte ittara ii dess-ka?
Is it far?	遠いですか？	Toi dess-ka?
art gallery	美術館	bijutsukan
reservations desk	予約 窓口	yoyaku madoguchi
bridge	橋	hashi/bashi
castle	城	shiro/jo
city	市	shi
city center	街の 中心	machi no chushin
gardens	庭園／庭	tei-en/niwa
hot spring	温泉	onsen
information office	案内所	annaijo
island	島	shima/jima
monastery	修道院	shudo-in
mountain	山	yama/san
museum	博物館	hakubutsukan
palace	宮殿	kyuden
park	公園	koen
port	港	minato/ko
prefecture	県	ken
river	川	kawa/gawa
ruins	遺跡	iseki
shopping area	ショッピング街	shoppingu gai
shrine	神社／神宮／宮	jinja/jingu/gu
street	通り	tori/dori
temple	お寺／寺	otera/tera/dera/ji
tour, travel	旅行	ryoko
town	町	machi/cho
village	村	mura
ward	区	ku
zoo	動物園	dobutsu-en
north	北	kita/hoku
south	南	minami/nan
east	東	higashi/to
west	西	nishi/sei
left/right	左／右	hidari/migi
straight ahead	真っ直ぐ	mass-sugu
between	間に	aida ni
near/far	近い／遠い	chikai/toi
up/down	上／下	ue/sh'ta
new	新しい／新	atarashii/shin
old/former	古い／元	furui/moto
upper/lower	上／下	kami/shimo
middle/inner	中	naka
in	に／中に	ni/naka ni
in front of	前	mae

Getting Around

bicycle	自転車	jitensha
bus	バス	basu
car	車	kuruma
ferry	フェリー	feri
baggage room	手荷物一時 預かり所	tenimotsu ichiji azukarijo
motorcycle	オートバイ	otobai
one-way ticket	片道切符	katamichi kippu
return ticket	往復切符	ofuku kippu
taxi	タクシー	takushi
ticket	切符	kippu
ticket office	切符売場	kippu uriba

Trains

What is the fare to …?	···までいくら ですか？	… made ikura dess-ka?
When does the train for… leave?	···行きの電車 は、何時に 出ますか？	… iki no densha wa nan-ji ni demass-ka?
How long does it take to get to …?	···まで時間は、 どのぐらい かかりますか？	… made jikan wa dono gurai kakarimass-ka?
A ticket to …, please.	···行きの切符 をください。	… yuki no kippu o kudasai.
Do I have to change?	乗り換えが 必要ですか？	Norikae ga hitsuyo dess-ka?
I'd like to reserve a seat, please.	席を予約 したいです。	Seki o yoyaku shitai dess.
Which platform for the train to …?	···行きの 電車は、 何番ホーム から出ますか？	… yuki no densha wa nanban homu kara demass-ka?
Which station is this?	この駅は、 どこですか？	Kono eki wa doko dess-ka?
Is this the right train for …?	···へは、この 電車でいい ですか？	… e wa kono densha de ii dess-ka?
bullet train	新幹線	shinkansen
express trains: "limited express" (fastest)	特急	tokkyu
"express" (second)	急行	kyuko
"rapid" (third)	快速	kaisoku
first-class	一等	itto
line	線	sen
local train	普通／各駅 電車	futsu/kaku-eki-densha
platform	ホーム	homu
train station	駅	eki
reserved seat	指定席	shitei-seki
second-class	二等	nito
subway	地下鉄	chikatetsu
train	電車	densha
unreserved seat	自由席	jiyu-seki

Accommodations

Do you have any vacancies?	部屋があります か？	Heya ga arimass-ka?
I have a reservation.	予約をして あります。	Yoyaku o sh'te arimass.
I'd like a room with a bathroom.	お風呂つきの 部屋、お願い します。	Ofuro-ts'ki no heya, onegai shimass.
What is the charge per night?	一泊いくら ですか？	Ippaku ikura dess-ka?
Is tax included in the price?	税込みですか？	Zeikomi dess-ka?
Can I leave my luggage here for a little while?	荷物を ちょっとここに 預けてもいい ですか？	Nimotsu o chotto koko ni azukete mo ii dess-ka?
air-conditioning	冷房／エアコン	reibo/eakon
bath	お風呂	ofuro
check-out	チェックアウト	chekku-auto
hair drier	ドライヤー	doraiya
hot (boiled) water	お湯	oyu
Japanese-style inn	旅館	ryokan
Japanese-style room	和室	wa-shitsu
key	鍵	kagi
front desk	フロント	furonto
single/twin room	シングル／ツイン	shinguru/tsuin

shower	シャワー	shyawa
Western-style hotel	ホテル	hoteru
Western-style room	洋室	yo-shitsu

Eating Out

A table for one/two/three, please.	一人／二人／三人、お願いします。	Hitori/futari/sannin, onegai shimass.
May I see the menu.	メニュー、お願いします。	Menyu, onegai shimass.
Is there a set menu?	定食がありますか？	Teishoku ga arimass-ka?
I'd like ….	私は・・・がいいです。	Watashi wa … ga ii dess.
May I have one of those?	それをひとつ、お願いします。	Sore o hitotsu, onegai shimass?
I am a vegetarian.	私はベジタリアンです。	Watashi wa bejitarian dess.
Waiter/waitress!	ちょっとすみません。	Chotto sumimasen!
What would you recommend?	おすすめは何ですか？	Osusume wa nan dess-ka?
How do you eat this?	これはどうやって食べますか？	Kore wa doyatte tabemass-ka?
May we have the check please.	お勘定、お願いします。	Okanjo, onegai shimass.
May we have some more …	もっと・・・、お願いします。	Motto …, onegai shimass.
The meal was very good, thank you.	ごちそうさまでした、おいしかったです。	Gochiso-sama desh'ta, oishikatta dess.
assortment	盛りあわせ	moriawase
boxed meal	弁当	bento
breakfast	朝食	cho-shoku
buffet	バイキング	baikingu
delicious	おいしい	oishii
dinner	夕食	yu-shoku
to drink	飲む	nomu
a drink	飲みもの	nomimono
to eat	食べる	taberu
food	食べもの／ごはん	tabemono/gohan
full (stomach)	おなかがいっぱい	onaka ga ippai
hot/cold	熱い／冷たい	atsui/tsumetai
hungry	おなかがすいた	onaka ga suita
Japanese food	和食	wa-shoku
lunch	昼食	chu-shoku
set menu	セット／定食	setto (snack)/teishoku (meal)
spicy	辛い	karai
sweet, mild	甘い	amai
Western food	洋食	yo-shoku

Places to Eat

Cafeteria/canteen	食堂	shokudo
Chinese restaurant	中華料理屋	chuka-ryori-ya
coffee shop	喫茶店	kissaten
local bar	飲み屋／居酒屋	nomiya/izakaya
noodle stall	ラーメン屋	ramen-ya
restaurant	レストラン／料理屋	resutoran/ryori-ya
sushi on a conveyor belt	回転寿司	kaiten-zushi
upscale restaurant	料亭	ryotei
upscale vegetarian restaurant	精進料理屋	shojin-ryori-ya

Foods (see also Reading the Menu pp120–21)

apple	りんご	ringo
bamboo shoots	たけのこ	takenoko
beancurd	とうふ	tofu
bean sprouts	もやし	moyashi
beans	豆	mame
beef	ビーフ／牛肉	bifu/gyuniku
beefburger	ハンバーグ	hanbagu
blowfish	ふぐ	fugu
skipjack tuna/tuna	かつお／ツナ	katsuo/tsuna
bread	パン	pan
butter	バター	bata
cake	ケーキ	keki
chicken	とり／鶏肉	tori/toriniku
confectionery	お菓子	okashi
crab	かに	kani
duck	あひる	ahiru
eel	うなぎ	unagi
egg	たまご	tamago
eggplant/aubergine	なす	nasu
fermented soybean paste	みそ	miso
fermented soybeans	納豆	natto
fish (raw)	さしみ	sashimi
fried tofu	油揚げ	abura-age
fruit	くだもの	kudamono
ginger	しょうが	shoga
hamburger	ハンバーガー	hanbaga
haute cuisine	会席	kaiseki
herring	ニシン	nishin
hors d'oeuvres	オードブル	odoburu
ice cream	アイスクリーム	aisu-kurimu
jam	ジャム	jamu
Japanese mushrooms	まつたけ／しいたけ／しめじ	mats'take/shiitake/shimeji
Japanese pear	なし	nashi
loach	どじょう	dojo
lobster	伊勢えび	ise-ebi
mackerel	さば	saba
mackerel pike	さんま	sanma
mandarin orange	みかん	mikan
meat	肉	niku
melon	メロン	meron
mountain vegetables	山菜	sansai
noodles:		
buckwheat	そば	soba
Chinese	ラーメン	ramen
wheatflour	うどん／そうめん	udon (fat)/somen (thin)
octopus	たこ	tako
omelet	オムレツ	omuretsu
oyster	カキ	kaki
peach	もも	momo
pepper	こしょう	kosho
persimmon	柿	kaki
pickles	つけもの	ts'kemono
pork	豚肉	butaniku
potato	いも	imo
rice:		
cooked	ごはん	gohan
uncooked	米	kome
rice crackers	おせんべい	osenbei
roast beef	ローストビーフ	rosutobifu
salad	サラダ	sarada
salmon	鮭	sake
salt	塩	shio
sandwich	サンドイッチ	sandoichi
sausage	ソーセージ	soseji
savory nibbles	おつまみ	otsumami
seaweed:		
laver	のり	nori
kelp	こんぶ	konbu

shrimp	えび	ebi
soup	汁／スープ	shiru/supu
soy sauce	しょうゆ	shoyu
spaghetti	スパゲティ	supageti
spinach	ほうれんそう	horenso
squid	いか	ika
steak	ステーキ	suteki
sugar	砂糖	sato
sushi (mixed)	五目寿司	gomoku-zushi
sweetfish/smelt	あゆ	ayu
taro (potato)	さといも	sato imo
toast	トースト	tosuto
trout	鱒	masu
sea urchin	ウニ	uni
vegetables	野菜	yasai
watermelon	すいか	suika
wild boar	ぼたん／いのしし	botan/inoshishi

Drinks

beer	ビール	biru
coffee (hot)	ホットコーヒー	hotto-kohi
cola	コーラ	kora
green tea	お茶	ocha
iced coffee:		
black	アイスコーヒー	aisu-kohi
with milk	アイスオーレ	kafe-o-re
lemon tea	レモンティー	remon ti
milk	ミルク／牛乳	miruku/gyunyu
mineral water	ミネラルウォーター	mineraru uota
orange juice	オレンジジュース	orenji jusu
rice liquor	酒	sake
(non-alcoholic)	（甘酒）	(ama-zake)
tea (Western-style)	紅茶	kocha
tea with milk	ミルクティー	miruku ti
water	水	mizu
whiskey	ウイスキー	uis'ki
wine	ワイン／ぶどう酒	wain/budoshu

Health

I don't feel well.	気分が よくないです。	Kibun ga yokunai dess.
I have a pain in …	…が痛いです。	… ga itai dess.
I'm allergic to …	…アレルギーです。	… arerugi dess.
asthma	喘息	zensoku
cough	せき	seki
dentist	歯医者	haisha
diabetes	糖尿病	tonyo-byo
diarrhea	下痢	geri
doctor	医者	isha
fever	熱	netsu
headache	頭痛	zutsuu
hospital	病院	byoin
medicine	薬	kusuri
Oriental medicine	漢方薬	kampo yaku
pharmacy	薬局	yakkyoku
prescription	処方箋	shohosen
stomachache	腹痛	fukutsu
toothache	歯が痛い	ha ga itai

Numbers

0	ゼロ	zero
1	一	ichi
2	二	ni
3	三	san
4	四	yon/shi
5	五	go
6	六	roku
7	七	nana/shichi
8	八	hachi
9	九	kyu

10	十	ju
11	十一	ju-ichi
12	十二	ju-ni
20	二十	ni-ju
21	二十一	ni-ju-ichi
22	二十二	ni-ju-ni
30	三十	san-ju
40	四十	yon-ju
100	百	hyaku
101	百一	hyaku-ichi
200	二百	ni-hyaku
300	三百	san-byaku
400	四百	yon-hyaku
500	五百	go-hyaku
600	六百	ro-ppyaku
700	七百	nana-hyaku
800	八百	ha-ppyaku
900	九百	kyu-hyaku
1,000	千	sen
1,001	千一	sen-ichi
2,000	二千	ni-sen
10,000	一万	ichi-man
20,000	二万	ni-man
100,000	十万	ju-man
1,000,000	百万	hyaku-man
123,456	十二万三千 四百五十六	ju-ni-man-san-zen-yon-hyaku-go-ju-roku

Time

Monday	月曜日	getsu-yobi
Tuesday	火曜日	ka-yobi
Wednesday	水曜日	sui-yobi
Thursday	木曜日	moku-yobi
Friday	金曜日	kin-yobi
Saturday	土曜日	do-yobi
Sunday	日曜日	nichi-yobi
January	一月	ichi-gatsu
February	二月	ni-gatsu
March	三月	san-gatsu
April	四月	shi-gatsu
May	五月	go-gatsu
June	六月	roku-gatsu
July	七月	shichi-gatsu
August	八月	hachi-gatsu
September	九月	ku-gatsu
October	十月	ju-gatsu
November	十一月	ju-ichi-gatsu
December	十二月	ju-ni-gatsu
spring	春	haru
summer	夏	natsu
fall/autumn	秋	aki
winter	冬	fuyu
noon	正午	shogo
midnight	真夜中	mayonaka
today	今日	kyo
yesterday	昨日	kino
tomorrow	明日	ash'ta
this morning	今朝	kesa
this afternoon	今日の午後	kyo no gogo
this evening	今晩	konban
every day	毎日	mainichi
month	月	getsu/ts'ki
hour	時	ji
time/hour (duration)	時間	jikan
minute	分	pun/fun
this year	今年	kotoshi
last year	去年	kyonen
next year	来年	rainen
one year	一年	ichi-nen
late	遅い	osoi
early	早い	hayai
soon	すぐ	sugu

Tokyo Subway Map

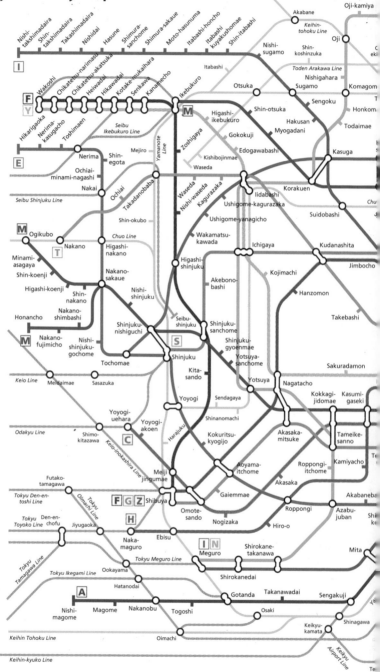